# READING IT WRONG

# Reading It Wrong

## AN ALTERNATIVE HISTORY OF EARLY
## EIGHTEENTH-CENTURY LITERATURE

ABIGAIL WILLIAMS

PRINCETON UNIVERSITY PRESS

PRINCETON & OXFORD

Published by Princeton University Press
41 William Street, Princeton, New Jersey 08540
99 Banbury Road, Oxford OX2 6JX

press.princeton.edu

Library of Congress Cataloging-in-Publication Data

Names: Williams, Abigail, author.
Title: Reading it wrong : an alternative history of early eighteenth-century literature / Abigail Williams.
Description: Princeton : Princeton University Press, 2023. | Includes bibliographical references and index.
Identifiers: LCCN 2022055147 (print) | LCCN 2022055148 (ebook) | ISBN 9780691170688 (hardback ; acid-free paper) | ISBN 9780691252346 (ebook)
Subjects: LCSH: English literature—18th century—History and criticism. | English literature—Appreciation. | Satire, English—History and criticism. | Books and reading—England—History—18th century. | BISAC: LITERARY CRITICISM / Modern / 18th Century | HISTORY / Modern / 18th Century | LCGFT: Literary criticism.
Classification: LCC PR441 .W55 2023 (print) | LCC PR441 (ebook) | DDC 820.9/005—dc23/eng/20230329
LC record available at https://lccn.loc.gov/2022055147
LC ebook record available at https://lccn.loc.gov/2022055148

British Library Cataloging-in-Publication Data is available

Editorial: Ben Tate and Josh Drake
Production Editorial: Natalie Baan
Jacket Design: Chris Ferrante
Production: Danielle Amatucci
Publicity: Carmen Jimenez and Alyssa Sanford
Copyeditor: Jane Simmonds

Jacket image: Jacques-Louis David, *Madame François Buron*, 1769. The Art Institute of Chicago.

This book has been composed in Arno

Printed on acid-free paper. ∞

Printed in the United States of America

10  9  8  7  6  5  4  3  2  1

For my students

# CONTENTS

# ACKNOWLEDGEMENTS

BOOKS TAKE TIME, and I am deeply grateful to the Masters and Fellows of St Peter's College, and to the Faculty of English at Oxford for the research leave that enabled me to write this one. Thank you to Marina Mackay and Francis Leneghan for being the best and most supportive of colleagues. Adam Smyth, Dennis Duncan, and Gill Partington contributed many wonderful things to this project, and best of all, a lot of bookish hilarity. I am grateful to the eighteenth-century research community in Oxford, and for the conversations with colleagues elsewhere: Melanie Bigold, John Gallagher, Larry Klein, Valerie Rumbold, Nick Seager, Amy Solomons, and Mark Towsey, and particular thanks to Michael Edson and Alice Leonard for their rich exchange of ideas around error and misreading. Early sections of this book were written and researched pre-pandemic, with the generous hosting of Juan Christian Pellicer at the University of Oslo, Jennie and Luca Grillo at Notre Dame, Ben Card and Eve Houghton at Yale, and El Collins and Fraser Macdonald in Edinburgh. I was greatly helped by librarians and curators at the Beinecke Library, the Bodleian Library, the British Library, the National Library of Scotland, Hertford, Queens, Wadham, and Worcester college libraries, Somerset Heritage Centre, Kendal Archives, Lancashire Archives, and the National Trust team at Townend. I could not have finished the book without the erudite and resourceful assistance of Kate Allan, Adam Bridgen, Alice Huxley, James Graham, Kathy Keown, Rayana Prakesh, Edward Taylor, Niamh Walshe, and Carly Watson. Thank you to Ben Tate for bringing up Bonamy Dobrée in the first place, and for the wonderful team at Princeton for publishing me. Finally, love and thanks to my family, as ever.

# READING IT WRONG

# Reading It Wrong

## AN INTRODUCTION

This [allegory] will puzzle the Commentators of the next Age, for even
in ours we can hardly guess at it.

        —*THE MEDLEY*, 27 NOVEMBER 1710

none but Fools can Laugh heartily without knowing whom they Laugh at.

    —*THE FEMALE TATLER* 60, 23 NOVEMBER 1709

WHAT DID EIGHTEENTH-CENTURY readers really understand in what
they read? What do we actually know about how the uniquely, frustrat-
ingly tricksy forms of the period – the satires and coded fictions and
allegorical tales and pamphlets and sociable verse – landed in their own
time? *Reading it Wrong* explores the role of imperfect readers and misreading in early eighteenth-century literary culture. It looks at literature
from the point of view of readers who got it wrong, rather than those
who got it right, showing that Augustan literary texts were both ham-
pered and enabled by games of knowing and not knowing. All the works
considered here depended on the notion that many of their original
historical readers would not have had full understanding: they are
works which either attempted to address that fact, or play with their
imperfect readerly landings.

This is also a book about modern-day failings. It does not lament the relative paucity of knowledge in contemporary readers – that plaintive cry of so many critics and educators.[1] I am interested instead in the ways in which our own modern discipline and its investment in enlightenment and expertise hinders the recognition of ignorance, muddle, or incompetence. A critical and pedagogical focus on 'right reading' can make us peculiarly blind as modern readers to the existence, role, and benefit of reading wrong.

## Historical Contexts

I start from two linked but not often coupled aspects of early eighteenth-century literary culture. The first is the widely recognized reality that the turn of the eighteenth century sees a step change in the evolution of print culture: there is a surge in the numbers and kinds of books available, a crafting of new genres and forms of writing for new kinds of readers. We see this across the board: in the availability of classical works in translation; in the packaging of information and expertise in forms designed to appeal to the amateur reader, one who might not bring a university education or cultural or linguistic fluency with them. This is also, crucially, the era that invented generalist literary criticism. In many studies of the period, such development is commonly described as a socioeconomic progress narrative. It is a story about inclusion and new forms of writing, the culture of the coffee house, or the creation of the bourgeois public sphere, and the opening up of print culture to women writers and women readers, as well as to labouring class writers and their admirers.[2] This changing dynamic between readers, authors, and print can be traced back into the mid-seventeenth century. In 1642, the Church of England clergyman and poet Roger Cocks wrote that: 'Pamphlets, like wild geese, fly up and downe in flocks about the Countrey. Never was more writing, or lesse matter [...] *There is no end of making many books*'.[3] He was commenting on the proliferation of printed opinion surrounding the English Revolution, a political crisis which unleashed voices and words on a scale hitherto unseen in English culture. While the number of publications died down after the immediate heat of the civil war debates, the busy culture of printed political dialogue and opinionizing that it had generated was there to stay. Changes to the legal framework of publishing with the lapse of the Licensing Act in 1695 drove up publication rates, as the number of printers and publishers was uncapped, and restrictions on imported books went unenforced.[4] A growing and hungry market for printed books created a demand for new authors and new forms of writing.

All these changes meant that the world of print looked profoundly different in the early eighteenth century to the way it had less than a century before. One historian claims that the numbers of items in print increased by a factor of ten after 1640, from an average of 300,000 volumes a year from 1576 to 1640 to two million or more between 1640 and 1660.[5] Another notes that there are records of 848 published titles from 1640; just two years later, this had more than quadrupled to 3,666.[6] There was a rise of 270 per cent in titles between 1641 and 1660. We can discern the appetite for debate and current affairs in the evolution of the newspaper. In 1641, the first newspaper trading in English domestic news appeared – less than three years later there were twelve. The rise continued over the course of the civil war period.

As the practice of writing moved away from aristocratic patronage and towards a busier, more populous, and often anonymous print marketplace, it created opportunities, but also profound anxiety – an anxiety resonant of the early twenty-first-century rise of digital culture. It has become normal to compare the advent of the internet with the invention of the printing press, but we might better make the comparison between the online media shift and the commercialization and expansion of print in the early eighteenth century. Both periods of innovation have posed challenges to users and legislators over the authority of the printed word and its credibility. Generic innovation, an uncertainty about the ownership of content, and the role of anonymity are features of digital and of early commercial print circulation. What's more, an uncertainty about how to write for an unknowable and unpredictable mass audience, and the problems created by what we now call 'context collapse' are features of both eras, and they have shaped the terms of writing and engagement in some strikingly parallel ways.

The changes in consumption of the early eighteenth century were not confined to a rise in print volume or the derestriction of certain kinds of material. The seventeenth and early eighteenth century also witnessed a rise in the number of potential readers in the nation. By the end of the Stuart period, the English had achieved a level of literacy unknown in the past and unmatched elsewhere in early modern Europe.[7] The evidence of historical literacy is complex – many could read but not write, and so using signatures to evidence competence is tricky. Literacy also varied enormously according to social class and geography. The historian David Cressy has shown that overall literacy rates for men during the 1640s were 30 per cent, rising to 58 per cent by the 1740s. For women, the corresponding dates show a rise from 10 per cent to 32 per cent.[8] As this suggests, there was a steady rise in literacy, and the growth was stronger among women. The population was growing too. In 1696, the population of England was 5,118,000 – by 1756 it was 6,149,000.[9] There were more people and there was more money to spend: British GDP rose by approximately 246 per cent (compared with 80 per cent in continental Europe). Correlating the rise in literacy with population growth, and an upward trend in disposable income reveals the remarkable growth of the English reading public over the course of the late seventeenth and eighteenth centuries.[10] In 1700, the English reading public aged fifteen and above was about 1,267,000. By 1756, it was more like 1,894,000.[11] And all those people had better and better ways of accessing books – the improvement of transport networks across the country, the development of the Post Office, and the role of coffee houses and, later, libraries were all crucial to the growth of readers and reading in this period.

## Forms of Confusion

The second historical phenomenon of the period that is crucial to its culture of misunderstanding is the peculiar flourishing of densely referential literary forms that relied on reader interaction. The proliferation of ironic, coded, and allegorical works – of satirical forms dependent on shared understandings of subtext – means that rarely in the history of English literature has there been a body of texts so dependent on readerly interpretation to achieve an authorial vision. And rarely has there been a readership both in a dramatic state of flux and newly encouraged to interpret imaginative writing on their own terms. So what did these new and diverse readers find in front of them? One of the distinctive features of many works of the period is the hiding of names, places, and identities through a variety of textual and typographical features that signal almost instantly the clandestine or concealed nature of the text's meaning. Pages were pockmarked with half-written words and names, sometimes indicated through an initial and final letter, sometimes only a dash or series of asterisks. The use of palpably fictitious names such as 'Myrmillo', 'Horoscope', or 'Celia' forced readers into interactive engagement, asking them to supplement the text with their own knowledge of the setting or figures involved. Fictional works signalled their allegorical nature from the preface on, usually without spelling out the exact nature of the allegory. Contemporaries mocked the way in which such veneers of subterfuge became a way of spicing up otherwise unremarkable content. *The Female Tatler* observes that the combination of knowing and not knowing the identity of a subject of gossip made the revelation all the more alluring:

> it is very easy by giving them Ingenious Nick-Names, and pointing at something or other remarkable about them, to let every body that is not a Stranger to the Town, know whom you mean without naming them, or being very particular; and when thus the Picture is drawn to the Life, whatever is writ underneath must be true, when the Hints that must make 'em known, are finished, put upon them what Scandal you please, it will go for Current.[12]

Other writers claimed that the meanings were hidden but self-evident:

> We have several Ways here of abusing one another, without incurring the Danger of the Law. First, we are careful never to print a Man's Name out at length; but as I do that of Mr St——: So that although

every Body alive knows whom I mean, the Plaintiff can have no Redress in any Court of Justice. Secondly, by putting Cases; Thirdly, by Insinuations; Fourthly, by celebrating the Actions of others, who acted directly contrary to the Persons we would reflect on; Fifthly, by Nicknames, either commonly known or stamp'd for the purpose, which every Body can tell how to apply.[13]

Print forms used typography not to clarify content but to obscure it. Here, for example is the title page to a 1704 verse satire entitled *The M——'d C——b; or, the L——th. Consultation* (figure 1).[14] What on earth does this mean? It has no meaningful title, yet, although the key terms are blanked out, they do not appear to conceal names or seditious content: 'M——d' stands in for 'mitred', 'c——b' for club or cabal, and 'L——th' for Lambeth. The denial of disclosure is used to create an impression of controversial content rather than genuine protection of identity. There is no information about the author, nor publisher. Its two epigraphs tantalize with suggestions of treachery and vengeance but rely on some classical knowledge to achieve this. The first, famous quotation, 'Et tu Brute?', is Caesar's line to Brutus on realizing his betrayal, while the second quotation, 'Acheronta Movebo', comes from Book VII of Virgil's *Aeneid*: 'flectere si nequeo superos, Acheronta movebo' ('if Heaven I cannot bend, then Hell I will arouse').[15] It is a form of paratext, which, like so much of the literature of the period, demands a lot of its readers at the point of entry. The pages which follow sustain this playful withholding of meaning with repeated references to 'm——d' bishops and 'L——th'. And they also supplement it with a scattering of blanks to disguise names:

Can W——r tell with Prophetick Vein,
When'er he'll be L——d Almoner again?
Can Gl——r, Br——l, Zealous O——rd know
The happy Time when they shall not be so.[16]

*The M——d C——b* is a satire relating to a very specific political issue, in this case debates over religious conformity during the early years of Queen Anne's reign. It uses occluded words and names as a way

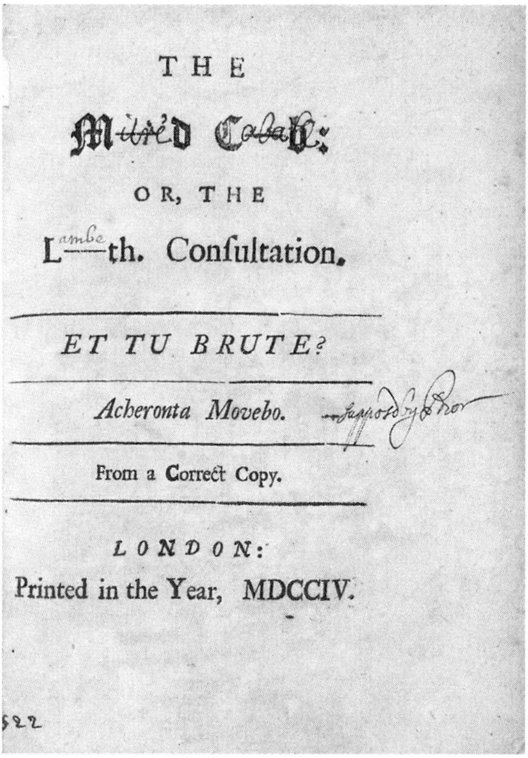

THE

M——'d C——b:

OR, THE

L——th. Conſultation.

*ET TU BRUTE?*

*Acheronta Movebo.*

From a Correct Copy.

*LONDON:*

Printed in the Year, MDCCIV.

FIGURE 1. *The M——'d C——b: Or, The L——th. Consultation* (London, 1704), title page. William Andrews Clark Memorial Library, University of California, Los Angeles, *PR.3291.M682.

of signalling politically risky content and creating an interactive game for its readers, who are forced to complete identities in order to make meaning from the semi-complete text. Such ludic strategies are also used in very different kinds of works. *A Pipe of Tobacco: In Imitation of Six Several Authors,* a 1736 poem by Isaac Hawkins Browne, is a comic exercise in pastiche in which Hawkins Browne imitates six contemporary authors, attempting to hymn the virtues of a tobacco pipe with all the stylistic parody and bathos that that entails.[17] The imitated authors are not anywhere named in the text, so it is left to the reader to firstly work out the intended subject, and secondly, how the resulting imitation relates to their previously published work. One annotated

copy in the William Andrews Clark Memorial Library helpfully provides the identities of the six: Colley Cibber, Ambrose Philips, James
Thomson, Edward Young, Alexander Pope, and Jonathan Swift.[18] The
reader's literary knowledge is gratified (or not) by the identification of
the imitated authors, and the joke only works if those identifications are
made.

Different again is a work such as the Welsh poet Jane Brereton's *Poems
on Several Occasions* (1744), a collection of occasional verses 'written for
the amusement of the author, and three or four select friends'.[19] This
collection of sociable verse declares its origins in Brereton's local Wrexham social circle, and the content is heavily autobiographical. According to the preface, the poems were not designed for publication: 'only a
few can be said to be prepared for Publication, as they were to make
their Appearance in a feigned Name'. The contents of the volume both
grant the reader access to the genteel friendship group, and withhold it.
There are poems such as 'Epistle to Mrs *Anne Griffiths*', 'On seeing Mrs
*Eliz. Owen*, now Lady *Longueville*, in an embroider'd Suit, all her own
Work', and 'On Mrs *Sybil Egerton's* singing an Anthem in *Wrexham*
Church' which clearly allude to episodes from the local life of the author. Alongside these there are titles which obscure identity, but which
also allow those identities to be easily guessed: 'To *J—n M—r*, Esq';
'To Miss *W—ms*, Maid of Honour to the late Queen'; 'To Mr *Y—ke*'.
Here the interactive game of the presentation seems designed to create
an impression of special access to a private world of a friendship group.

Yet at the same time as these forms of occluded meaning proliferated,
authors also mocked their contemporaries for being absurdly suspicious.
They laughed at their attempts to unpick the words in front of them, and
charged them with galloping away with their ingenious hermeneutics,
turning the most ordinary words and phrases into hidden codes. In
*Gulliver's Travels* we hear of a particular type of reader who is

very dextrous in finding out the mysterious meanings of Words,
Syllables and Letters. For Instance, they can decypher a Close-stool
to signify a Privy Council, a Flock of Geese, a Senate, a lame Dog an

Invader [...] When this Method fails, they have two others more effectual which the Learned among them call Acrosticks and Ana-grams. *First* they can decipher all initial Letters into political Mean-ings. Thus *N.* shall signify a Plot, *B.* a Regiment of Horse, *L.* a Fleet at Sea. Or *secondly* by transposing the Letters of the Alphabet in any suspected Paper, they can lay open the deepest Designs of a discon-tented Party. So, for Example, if I should say in a Letter to a Friend, *Our Brother* Tom *hath just got the Piles*, a Man of Skill in this Art would discover how the same Letters which compose that Sentence, may be analysed into the following Words; *Resist;——a Plot is brought home, The Tour.* And this is the Anagrammatick Method.[20]

It was all very well for Swift to mock these kinds of over-elaborate inter-pretations, but slightly ironic in the context of his own works, which continue to test our abilities to discern their purpose and topical focus. What is, for example, Swift's real aim in *Gulliver's Travels*? The fact that there are well-developed schools of 'hard' and 'soft' interpretations of the final book shows little consensus on the overall meaning of the text, while *A Tale of a Tub*, a satire in defence of the Anglican church, was read in its own time either as an endorsement of religious heterodoxy, or as being a game with no clear purpose.[21]

All the examples discussed above represent creative forms which needed decoding, which were dependent on shared forms of knowl-edge, on shared interpretative strategies. In his essay 'What is the His-tory of Books Revisited', Robert Darnton observed that 'of the many kinds of reading that developed in early modern Europe, one that I think deserves special attention is reading as game-playing. You find it everywhere, in libels, novels, and literary reviews, which constantly in-vite the reader to penetrate into secrets hidden between the lines or beneath the text'.[22] Yet, as suggested above, such forms emerged at a moment at which the game itself was changing, in which shared bonds and understandings were under pressure.

This book explores what happens when tricky books collided with a transformed marketplace and a changing readership eager to engage with literary texts. It shows how a combination of hyper-referentiality and a shifting dynamic between authors and readers created a particularly acute sense of puzzlement and confusion around the meaning of books and who ought to be able to read them. We don't often stop and wonder what effect these changing points of access and conditions of reading had on readerly competence, on the contracts between author and reader, and on the texts produced. Yet such shifts in print culture and readership are crucially related to the nature of reading and perceptions of reading, and this in turn fed the literature of the period. The history of reading, as well as the evidence of copies of books and of individual reader responses, offers us ways into better understanding how this all played out. *Reading It Wrong* draws on eighteenth-century discussions of the challenges of reading and interpretation, examining how readers were advised to negotiate partial comprehension, looking across the fields of scriptural, historical, and aesthetic understanding. Through a series of examples, we can see the impact that imperfect reading had on the literary works of the time. Rather than seeing the densely allusive and often recherché texts of the eighteenth century as a closed circuit of communication which we have to try to tap into, we might instead recognize the degree to which the literature of this period flourished in a climate of partial comprehension and a playful confusion of meaning. Many of the major works of the period depended on the fact that their readers wouldn't know all the answers. Some, like Pope's *Dunciad*, derived their satirical energy from such partial comprehensibility. That poem is not based on a readership that knows everything. Rather, it is dependent on a more flawed and intellectually vulnerable audience, one that has been trained to feel wrongfooted. Other works, like the social verse of the period, used their readers' partial knowledge of particular individuals and contexts to build a sense of exclusivity, or intimacy.

The critical neglect of this cloud of unknowing is partly a product of disciplinary and professional bias towards right reading. In our critical focus as editors, critics, and teachers focusing on correct or good interpretation, we haven't been able to recognize the many ways in which misreading is productive – it is generative of argument, intimacy, and social cohesion. Our dominant models for thinking about ignorance – shame and silence – equip us poorly for framing partial understanding or misunderstanding in positive ways. The existence of a complex and mixed model of reading and readerly inclusion does not sit well with the ways we teach, edit, and describe this period, all of which, for different reasons, tend towards hypothesized notions of an ideal reader. In thinking again about the role of misunderstanding in the literary culture of the period we can start to move beyond assumptions about paradigmatic ideal readers who have tended to dominate accounts of the period, and instead see the historical, social, and creative value of imperfect reading. We can also move beyond a crude distinction between elite and non-elite readers: as this book shows, the culture of partial knowing was widespread, complex, and not solely determined by class and income.

## Evidence

The material and anecdotal evidence of reading in the early eighteenth century shows us a complex picture of reception. Marginalia on eighteenth-century texts demonstrates that Augustan literary forms generated multiple forms of engagement. Most of the time we don't know the identities of individual annotators and can only guess at what their marks (or absence of marks) mean. But the collation of anonymous multiple marginal responses to works of the period display a proliferation of interpretation and a lack of consensus over the 'right' meaning. One detailed study of 149 different copies and all the various printed keys of Dryden's satirical mock Biblical poem *Absalom and Achitophel* shows that there were almost as many different readings of some individual characters in the mock biblical satire as there were annotated copies.[23] And within this sea of guesswork there were some readers who had only a very partial grip of the figures and places referenced in the allegory: one copy of Dryden's poem, in the library at Townend farm in Cumbria, has only five names identified on its pages.[24] My small-scale comparisons of Samuel Garth's *Dispensary*, or Pope's *Dunciad*, or Delariviere Manley's *The New Atalantis*, confirm a pattern of varied, partial, and inconsistent application – contemporary readers entertained a much wider range of referentiality than we acknowledge on paper or in teaching.[25] The material evidence of individual annotators of poems with blanked out or fictional names shows that very few readers were able to complete all the hidden identities in a poem.

Letters and diaries offer further evidence of the mixed reception of new works. There is frequently a sense of bewilderment at texts that we now accept as part of the literary innovation of the period. A member of the Ottley family, relaying a first encounter with Jonathan Swift's *Gulliver's Travels*, was both impressed and confounded by what he read in his four-volume edition:

> In these tracts are the strangest facts related that ever enter'd the Brain of man to forge, & the Alphabet as strangely distorted in feigned languages and inexpressible words; in short the whole is so unaccountably odd, yet wrote with a great deal of learning, & surprising Genius.[26]

On her first dealings with John Gay's *Beggar's Opera*, the diarist Gertrude Savile spluttered that 'it was impossible to expect anything so odd and out of the way', while the trainee lawyer Dudley Ryder commented of Gay's earlier satirical play *The What D'Ye Call It*, 'It is thought he had some design to reflect upon some authors by it, but to me it seems as if he had no design at all but to write something very new and out of the way'.[27] And here is the Swiss theologian Jean Le Clerc talking about Jonathan Swift's prose satire, *The Tale of a Tub*: 'an odd game ... goes on throughout the book, where we often do not know whether the author is making fun or not, nor of whom, nor what his intention is'.[28] This uncertainty was not just the preserve of those at a distance from the author. Jonathan Swift wrote to his close friend and collaborator Alexander Pope in July 1728 on reading an early printed version of the *Dunciad*: 'I have long observ'd that twenty miles from London no body understands hints, initial letters, or town-facts and passages; and in a few years not even those who live in London'.[29] He wrote to John Gay about his *Beggar's Opera*, 'I did not understand that the Scene of Locket and Peachum's quarrels was an imitation of one between Brutus and

Cassius till I was told it'.[30] John Arbuthnot wrote to Swift discussing *Gulliver's Travels*: 'Lewis [close friend and political ally] Grumbles a little at it & says he wants the Key to it'.[31] And having got themselves an explanatory key to a work, early readers were not necessarily sure what *that* meant: 'His Excellency our Governour Burnet has also obliged me with the *Dunciad*, and a Key to it: But whither the Key be written by a Friend or an Enemy I found something difficult to determine'.[32]

Across all the examples discussed in this book, acts of misunderstanding are found among very different types of readers. Sometimes misreading seems to be related to access to knowledge, and to class and gender, as, for example, in the Somerset writing master John Cannon's transcriptions of Latin he did not understand, or Ann Wolferstan's seemingly irrelevant listing of classical rulers in her edition of Juvenal. And sometimes it appears unconnected to social status: those we might expect to know the answers just didn't, like the figures at the political heart of Queen Anne's reign who were unable to unpick Delariviere Manley's recently published *New Atalantis*. And sometimes readers just had a strange sense of how best to understand things: the customs officer William Musgrave amassed pointless arcane biographical and genealogical detail in order to gloss secret histories of the early eighteenth century.

Two things are worth clarifying at this point: *Reading It Wrong* uncovers many different modes of reader engagement, from ignorance to wilful misinterpretation to uncertainty and muddle. There is an important distinction to be made between deliberate and accidental misreading, between having no answer to a puzzle, and having one different to that intended by the author. However, what all these modes have in common is that they are imperfect responses, and not part of a history of good historical reading with which we have become more familiar. And the second point is that while the transformation of print culture and the expansion of readership in the early eighteenth century clearly opened up many newly challenging textual encounters, it is not possible to describe misreading as a product of a single set of circumstances. It is, however, possible to see that much of the literature of the early eighteenth century created, depended upon, and suffered from acts of imperfect reading and interpretative confusion.

As the quotations and examples above suggest, there is much evidence of imperfect reading in this period: anecdotal evidence, material evidence of annotation, and history of reception. But it is important also to acknowledge the challenges posed by the evidence. As lots of critics have observed, the history of reading is generally the history of writing, of using textual marks to piece together something that is by its very nature impossible to capture. The commonest marking on a page is no marking. Or pen trials. We have to work quite hard to reconstruct reading habits from the slim evidence base of used books and pages. Does marginal annotation represent what readers did know, or didn't know? Sometimes it seems to indicate an absence of knowledge. For example, the National Art Library's copy of Jonathan Swift's edition of Pope's *Dunciad* contains a few markings by Swift (or perhaps Thomas Sheridan, who later owned it), but what was it that they registered on those pages about the Scriblerian masterwork?[33] The volume has got two annotations: next to the line 'Something betwixt a H*** and Owl' a handwritten note identifies H*** as 'Heydegger', clarifying that the opera manager Johann Heidegger is the intended recipient of this slur. And next to the line 'Sore sighs Sir G***' they have written 'Sir Gilbert Heathcoat', referring to the merchant and Whig politician. Heidegger and Heathcote were definitely not the only identities that either reader would have spotted in Pope's poem. It's much more likely that they were the ones they didn't get, and later found out. Another copy of the 1743 *Dunciad* only has one annotation, next to the line 'Behold yon Pair, in strict embraces join'd', which the reader has marked as 'Tom Burnet and Col Ducket'.[34] Why does this impossibly difficult work have only one annotation? Was this a reference that eluded the original reader? It may be that marginal glosses used to identify figures and references tell us more about an absence of comprehension than they do about what readers did know. But what seems more common is that early modern readers do not often use their marks to indicate a lack of comprehension – they are much more likely to mark a book with supplementary information or correction. So they might write the name of an author on the title page of a pamphlet of anonymous satire, and summarize its contents below, as in the case of a copy of Defoe's *Shortest-Way with the Dissenters* whose title page bears the note 'Madam, this villainous tract was written by Daniel De Foe, a furious scribbler for the Whiggs with a wicked design to Blacken'.[35] Or they filled in the blanks in a printed page even when the meaning was absolutely clear and in no need of clarification: a copy of a work entitled *A Pair of Spectacles for Oliver's Looking-Glass Maker* (1711; figure 2), probably owned by the historian and collector Narcissus Luttrell, shows him busily filling in all the omitted letters from words which were completely uncontroversial and obvious, such as 'H——e of L——ds' or 'D' for (Duke) and 'K' (King).[36] Or, in a state of uncertainty over a precise identification, they list the possibilities: one owner of a copy of Pope's *Epistle to Bathurst* (figure 3) noted that 'old Cato' was 'Sir Edward Hungerford' while another later annotator added 'or Sir Edward Seymour Bart'.[37]

Other readers acted like amateur textual critics, comparing different versions of a work and transcribing variants, as the Hardman family did with their 1733 copy of Alexander Pope's *Essay on Man*.[38] Copies of works are commonly marked up with their owners' observations on printing errors and misquotes, misattributions, or cross references with other reading. The owner of *Rocks and Shallows Discovered: Or, the Ass kicking at the Lyons in the Tower*, writes at the end of the pamphlet: 'Thanks to my Patience, I am at last arrived to the *last* page of his Discourse, where the Author being sensible of drawing near his End, does not justify, but *freely acknowledges* all his *Mistakes*'. They complain next to a particular passage: 'these 2 words clashing so soon together & all ye Nonsense in this Pamphlet is in Imitation of the Author in his Discourses'.[39] The annotator of an edition of Jacob Tonson's *Miscellanies* uses their notes to attribute verses to unnamed authors, and to copy in supplementary verses to create a fuller collection.[40] A reader named William Fletcher uses his comments on a copy of *Aesop's Fables* to correct the verse to make it scan more smoothly, commenting in the margins 'trochaic verse' and 'anapestic'. On one page, next to a correction of the translation is written 'a mistake deserving correction'.[41] The owner of a copy of Pope's *Works* evidently decided to use their marginal space

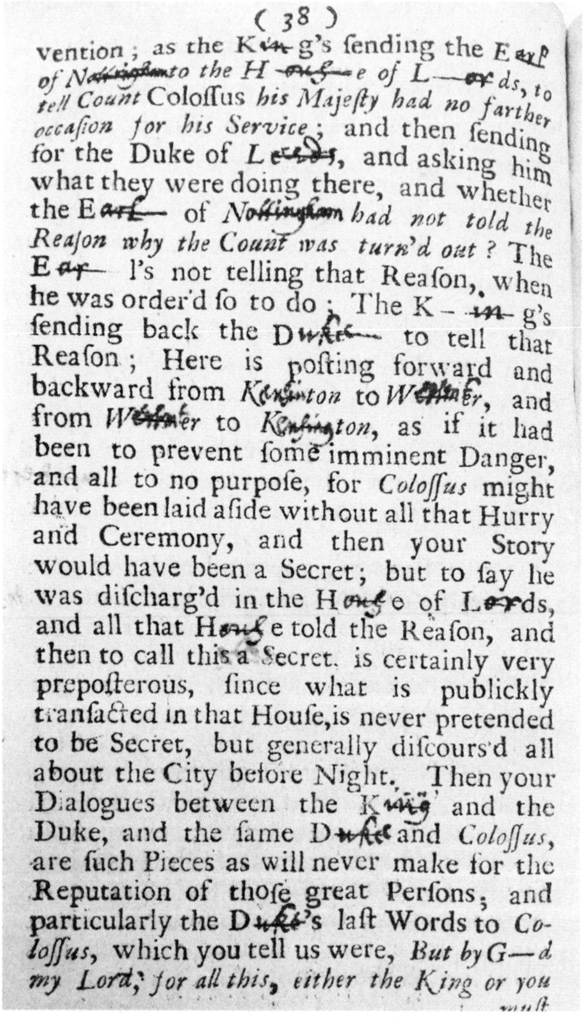
( 38 )
vention; as the K—ing's ſending the Earl of Nottingham to the H—ouſe of L—ords, to tell Count Coloſſus *his Majeſty had no farther occaſion for his Service*; and then ſending for the Duke of L—eeds, and asking him what they were doing there, and whether the Earl of *Nottingham had not told the Reaſon why the Count was turn'd out?* The Ear—l's not telling that Reaſon, when he was order'd ſo to do; The K—ing's ſending back the Duke to tell that Reaſon; Here is poſting forward and backward from *Kenſington* to *Weſtminſter*, and from *Weſtminſter* to *Kenſington*, as if it had been to prevent ſome imminent Danger, and all to no purpoſe, for *Coloſſus* might have been laid aſide without all that Hurry and Ceremony, and then your Story would have been a Secret; but to ſay he was diſcharg'd in the Houſe of Lords, and all that Houſe told the Reaſon, and then to call this a Secret, is certainly very prepoſterous, ſince what is publickly tranſacted in that Houſe, is never pretended to be Secret, but generally diſcours'd all about the City before Night. Then your Dialogues between the King and the Duke, and the ſame Duke and *Coloſſus*, are ſuch Pieces as will never make for the Reputation of thoſe great Perſons; and particularly the Duke's laſt Words to *Coloſſus*, which you tell us were, *But by G—d my Lord, for all this, either the King or you* must

FIGURE 2. *A Pair of Spectacles for Oliver's Looking-Glass Maker* (London: J. Baker, 1711), Beinecke Rare Book and Manuscript Library, Yale University, College Pamphlets 906 9, p. 38.

to set Pope right about his claims for the superiority of classical languages over English: where Pope had written that Greek and Latin 'became universal and everlasting while ours [is] extremely limited both in extent and duration' the annotator comments 'but neither is used in

[...]hall then Uxorio, if the ſtakes he ſweep,
Bear home ſix Whores, and make his Lady weep:
Or ſoft Adonis, ſo perfum'd and fine,
Drive to St. James's a whole herd of Swine?
Oh filthy Check on all induſtrious skill,
To ſpoil the Nation's laſt great Trade, Quadrille!

Once, we confeſs, beneath the Patriot's cloak,
From the crack'd bagg the dropping Guinea ſpoke,
And gingling down the back-ſtairs, told the Crew
"Old Cato is as great a Rogue as you."
Bleſt Paper-credit! that advanc'd ſo high,
Shall lend Corruption lighter wings to fly!

* *Beneath the Patriot's Cloak.*] This is a true Story, which happen'd in the [...]
King William, to an eminent unſuſpeſted old Patriot; who coming out
Back-door from having been cloſeted by the King, where he had received a [...]
of Guineas, the Burſting of the Bag diſcover'd his Buſineſs there.

FIGURE 3. Alexander Pope, *Of the Use of Riches, An Epistle To the Right Honourable Allen Lord Bathurst* (London: J. Wright, 1732 [1733]), British Library, C.59.h.9.(4.), p. 4.

any Nation nor Living in any one except by Grammars & Dictionaries: which omit the Pronunciation.'[42] A woman identifying herself as 'Eliz Robinson Jun.' marked her copy of *The Grove; or a Collection of Original Poems* (1721) only very slightly, making a correction to the translation in Lewis Theobald's translation of the Greek poet Musaeus's *Hero and Leander*, 'Her ~~rosie~~ lilly Fingers with dumb Transport prest', and 'snatch'd her ~~rosie~~ lilly hand away'.[43]

We can also find evidence of readers who complete missing information, and as they do so, they replicate the same habits of omission in their annotations that they found in the printed original. An anonymous reader of John Dryden's 1680 comedy *Mr Limberham: or the Kind Keeper* clearly understands that the reference to 'Fleckno' in the dedication refers to the playwright Thomas Shadwell, and in the margin writes 'alias Sh—well'.[44] From whom are they hiding this disclosure, and why do they feel the need to hide it? Perhaps the habits of concealment and indirection so prevalent in the literature of the time rubbed off on readers in ways that don't necessarily make logical sense now. It is hard to characterize all these discrete interventions collectively, but as an overall picture, it is easier to find readerly self-assertion than readerly doubt. However little they knew, eighteenth-century readers often wanted to show they knew it.[45]

Letters and diaries show a similar pattern – readers don't tend to show off their ignorance. The Sussex shopkeeper Thomas Turner left multiple volumes of detailed diaries, tracking his reading habits and his responses to individual texts. He was reading some sophisticated works and he was not a sophisticated man.[46] His evaluative comments give insights into the ways in which he understood major works, and he frequently offers up his own judgements on the books he has encountered. Across the five volumes of diaries we learn what he made of works ranging from the *Odyssey* and *Iliad* to *Paradise Lost*, to Richardson's *Clarissa* and Shakespeare's *Merry Wives of Windsor* and *King Lear*. It is intriguing that Turner only very rarely says that he has not understood what he is reading, that it is beyond him, or that he has misinterpreted it: 'Tho. Davy supped with us and stayed near 3 hours with us. I also read Bally's poem on the wisdom of the Supreme Being, which I think is a very sublime piece of poetry and almost too much so for my mean capacity. But as I find the author's views are good, I do, as I am bound in duty, like it very much.'[47] 'Read part of Locke's *Essay on Human Understanding*, which I find to be a very abstruse book.'[48] We might also note here the way in which appreciation is not dependent on full comprehension: George Bally's poem is approved of because its author's views are approved of, despite the fact that Turner isn't quite sure he understands it.

The diaries of other non-elite readers are similarly unforthcoming on the problems of understanding. John Cannon, a self-taught ploughboy and shepherd turned scribe and notary living in the Somerset levels in the first decades of the eighteenth century was a wide reader.[49] With minimal formal education, he cannot have grasped all the allusions and classical tags in the contemporary satires and literary works that he cites, but nowhere does he state this, or register any doubt about his interpretative abilities. This habit of omission may be particular to the aspirant reader: in the letters of elite readers we tend to find more examples of uncertainty. There is also a gendered element to the admission of ignorance – eighteenth-century women's correspondence often reveals an anxiety about a lack of knowledge or understanding, particularly of scholarly or theological subjects. But it is worth bearing in mind that we may be looking for signs of habits and responses that readers were reluctant to commit to paper.

## Understanding Misunderstanding

If we accept that, despite these evidentiary challenges, readerly incomprehension was a widespread phenomenon in the early eighteenth century, we might wonder how it was understood in its own time. Contemporary explanations for the gap between authorial intention and readerly understanding were varied. As we have seen, *The Female Tatler* declares that cloaked references were comprehensible to 'every body that is not a Stranger to the Town'. This idea that country readers, or those outside a particular metropolitan social group, were those most likely to struggle with occluded meaning is also evident in the prefaces to allegorical works and secret histories, which commonly blamed the interpretative lack in readers on geographical location. The preface to *The court-Spy; Or, Memoirs of St J–M–S'S* (1744) observed that:

> Some *Country* Readers, indeed, may be at a loss to explain the *Characters*, introduc'd in the Place of those *Names* that were in the Original; which, for certain very *important* Reasons, he did not chuse to publish'.[50]

Other texts were prefaced with material suggesting that doubt over their meaning might be cleared up through consultation with others: they are suggestive of a world of sociable exchange of information that the reader might need to engage with in order to access meaning. *The Secret History of Arlus and Odolphus, Ministers of State to the Empress of*

*Grandinsula* (1710), for instance, a thinly fictionalized account of the change of ministry under Queen Anne, contains a 'Word to the Reader':

> If upon the Perusal of the Title-page you find your self in the dark, whisper the first Honest Gentleman you meet (whom you will now easily distinguish by a certain new Life in his Looks) and you will be set right in a moment.[51]

It's worth considering that although many of the dominant historiographical narratives of this period have focused on the ways in which spheres of knowledge and understanding were opening up through the democratization of literature, or the spread of enlightenment values, this was also a literary culture in which muddle and uncertainty were at the heart of the reading experience. And that context was in itself generative of much of the literature of the period. We can see this both in the proliferation of forms of print designed to demystify the acts of interpretation and meaning-making, either through generalist literary criticism or keys to satirical works. And we also see it in literary forms which played with readerly comprehension, from the tantalizing references to coterie circles of sociable verse, to the ironies of works such as *Tale of a Tub* or the *Dunciad*, to the blanks, asterisks, and allegories of countless poems, fictions, and prose pamphlets of the era. These texts were built to encourage readerly misunderstanding as much as their authors were frustrated by it. They often depended on a readership that didn't or couldn't know all the answers. As this book shows, the response of contemporary readers shows very varied forms of engagement and comprehension. In the flourishing of misunderstanding or uncertainty in this period we find positives. A shared sense of not understanding among readers could be a form of community building.[52] It also seems clear that the act of encouraging readerly confusion or incomprehension was a desired effect in many literary contexts, helping to support a sense of a coterie, or an argument about cultural decline. Rather than seeing incomprehension as a form of failure, we could also recognize it as a generative force, producing new works, new editions, and new forms of engagement. In examining the reading histories of texts which are neither time transcendent nor universally understood in their own time, we gain transformative, historically nuanced insights into the big questions of literary history: meaning-making, intention, interpretation, access. This book puts the evidence of the printed reception of literary texts alongside the archival evidence of their material form and the marks made by their early readers to open up a lost history of misunderstanding.

The book falls into two halves. The first part explores the changing nature of readerly expertise and the intellectual contexts that have shaped how we think about misunderstanding. We begin with the present moment, and the way literary criticism, pedagogy, and editorial practice have positioned ideas of the 'good reader'. The second chapter examines perhaps the most universal form of reading in the eighteenth-century – religious and biblical reading. The notion of 'sola scriptura', that the good Protestant reader could find salvation through the Bible alone, placed enormous pressure on the individual to work out God's meanings. In an era of increasing textual democratization, scriptural decoding and unlocking offered an influential model for interpretation. In the third chapter we encounter the nature of access and expertise in classical knowledge, looking at how neoclassical in-jokes worked for the many eighteenth-century readers with mixed literacy in ancient languages. What did it mean to be an expert – what did it mean to be a good reader in the context of profound debates about the Ancients and Moderns and how to interpret words of the past? The fourth chapter takes us to the matter of literary criticism, and the move towards amateur, generalist, and polite appreciation of literary works enabled by contemporary periodicals and other print publications. Each one of these historical sections illustrates a profound shift in ideas about where knowledge comes from, who owns it, and how it might be used. Together they form an essential bedrock for thinking about how understanding and misunderstanding operate in the literature of the period.

The second half of the book explores the consequences of the culture of misunderstanding and misreading for literary texts. Chapter 5 explores the interactive puzzles of topical political satire, and the evidence of historical readers who can show us how the interpretative games of elusive verse forms might have played out in practice. Chapter 6 focuses

on the various ways hidden or allusive meaning was used to create intimacy and exclusivity in the social verse of the period. Chapter 7 examines the use of code, allegory, and the key in the popular scandal narratives of the period, and what this meant for matters of authorial
responsibility and interpretative authority. And what about when
all this went wrong? Chapter 8 shows what could happen when a book
landed disastrously and was read in ways that were damaging to its
author. In the concluding chapter we arrive at Pope's *Dunciad*, perhaps
the high-water mark of playfully obscure satire in this period. Reading
that mock-heroic poem in the context of so many forms of reading it
wrong, we see we are all Pope's dunces.

# 1

# The Good Reader

At present gross general misunderstandings are certainly poetry's worst enemies.

—I.A. RICHARDS, *PRACTICAL CRITICISM*

IF WE ASSUME that historical readers did not suffer from ignorance, confusion, or muddle at the sight of the works they saw before them, we are probably mistaken. Their 'wrong reading' is a part of the story of the literary culture of the period. But surely we have moved beyond the idea of 'right' and 'wrong' readings? I write this book at the back end of over a half-century of critical-theoretical debate which has repeatedly emphasized the plural nature of reading – and the polysemous potential of the literary text, in which multiple, unintended readings are constantly possible and desirable. To talk of 'misreading' in this context seems to drag us back into an age of fixed intentionalism, within which it is the critic or reader's job merely to seek and articulate the purpose of the text as its author intended. And the idea of calling out another reader as having 'got it wrong' is unacceptable for different reasons. Bruce Robbins states,

> These days, to call out wrongness or falseness or badness is to risk being accused of condescension. The desire to make such accusations is taken as a mark of unacknowledged privilege. It's understood as

likely to hurt someone's feelings. People prefer to play it safe. They hesitate to make such critical judgments.[1]

None of us believe in or criticize wrong interpretation anymore. Or do we? What I want to consider in this chapter are the often-unacknowledged ways in which scholars, editors, teachers, and readers remain committed to models of 'right' reading, and what the implications of that might be. I think that many of us still teach, analyse, and edit the historical texts we work on in the assumption that their contemporary political and cultural referentiality was understood by most historical readers in their own time, and that the people struggling to piece together the jigsaw puzzle are the benighted folk who came after them, disorientated by their temporal distance from the prime movers.

## Maps of Misreading: A Critical and Pedagogical History

It is not true that criticism has been blind to the pleasures of misinterpretation. There are various kinds of literary misreading that critics from across the theoretical spectrum have been ready to acknowledge and explore. So, for example, there is sustained critical interest in forms which purposefully challenge the intention or significance of a work. Harold Bloom's *A Map of Misreading* (1975) begins with the claim that 'Reading [. . .] is a belated and all-but-impossible act, and if strong is always a misreading [. . .]. Poetic strength comes only from a triumphant wrestling with the greatest of the dead, and an even more triumphant solipsism.'[2] Through his pantheon of (almost entirely male) 'strong readers' – Milton, Emerson, Browning, Wordsworth, and Keats – Bloom shows us a pattern of struggle within poetic inheritance, a form of revisionary allusion which enables writers to forge their own identity through a personal negotiation of their literary precursors. Bloom declares that Books I and II of *Paradise Lost* (1667, revised 1674) are a misreading of Book II of Spenser's *Faerie Queene* (1590, revised 1596): 'a powerful misinterpretation of Spenser, and a strong defense against him. [...] Milton rewrites Spenser so as to increase the distance between his poetic father and himself'.[3]

Deconstructionists, phenomenologists, and political philosophers have all turned their attention to the semantic gaps enabled by misunderstanding. In *Blindness and Insight* (1971), Paul de Man links together a group of related concepts – error, misunderstanding, blindness, and misreading – to describe a deconstructive reading of literature, one which engages with the blind spots and errors of the literary text in order to expose the text's unwitting, unintentional insights. He writes in praise of error, arguing that there is truth in mistake 'as the sun lies hidden within a shadow, or truth within error'.[4] The political philosopher Jacques Rancière has written of the nature of literary misunderstanding, arguing that gaps in understanding are central to the nature of language itself – and thus of literature and its appreciation.[5] We might too consider misreading as part of Paul Ricoeur's 'hermeneutics of suspicion': the practice whereby critics read between the lines of the text, and often against the grain, showing the things that those works omit and the internal contradictions that they cannot express.[6] This again is a habit of critical misreading that finds meaning in what is not said, not known, by the original author or reader. But, ultimately, each of these models uses error or misunderstanding to produce a superior or more insightful substitute reading, one that can only be revealed by the sophistication of the critic.

The kind of unintended misreading that I am interested in is a different thing. This is not misunderstanding as a fruitful appreciation of the gaps and silences in a text, nor its multiplying horizons of semantic possibility. What I want to focus on is misreading in the form of doubt and confusion – the historical evidence of people not understanding the literary texts of their own time, and registering this in their own words and marks. If we were to choose to develop a reception history of the text which showed a history of readerly confusion and incompetence, what would we do with that, what place might it have in our pedagogy, our editing, our history of reading?[7]

In some ways it is not that surprising that the history of literary criticism should be focused on the importance of the correct reading: who doesn't, after all, want to be right? It would be folly to say that we should try harder to be wrong, or that the mistaken interpretations of the past should be embraced as superior to the correct ones. But if we want to understand better how complex works played out in their own time, and how we might reconcile a history of interactive literature with the actual evidence of reader response, we need to be more alert to the practice of reading wrong. To do so means, among other things, being aware of the disciplinary models that shape our predilections for right reading. Teaching has long been built around a model of expertise through which dissemination converts the ignorant into the educated – a Socratic method in which the student finds the error in themselves. Centuries of pedagogical models have reinforced a hierarchy of knowledge in learning environments which reinforces the expertise of the teacher.[8] Students are guided to build a correct interpretation or understanding which is modelled by their teacher, the 'primary knower', who leads the discussion; the teacher asks questions and shepherds the group towards the best answers, leaving little room for those perceived to be incorrect or uncomprehending. Interestingly, this approach has been questioned in recent educational theory. Classroom case studies have shown the value of collective discussion of a greater range of viewpoints – and a very mixed set of understandings–which creates a shared ownership of eventual interpretative conclusions, rather than the scaffolding of correct interpretation that is the norm in classroom discussion.[9] Students might come to understand the text more fully, but without feeling that they had been corrected by a primary knower. Such a model enables struggling readers to assume a role as 'possible knowers', repositioning their lack of expertise as a form of collective debate over interpretation.

   Yet it remains the case that in English Literature, we are working within a discipline which has long been committed to the idea of the good reader.[10] In his 1929 *Practical Criticism*, I.A. Richards describes his experience of giving his students poems with no title, author, or any external information, and then letting them use their own experience and emotional state to produce individual meanings. He did not do this to show how each student responded in different or interesting ways – he did it to show how wrong they could go. *Practical Criticism* is an empirical study of inferior readings, in which Richards used the critical responses generated by unidentified texts to show the range and depth of textual misreadings achieved by both students and literary critics. It was a book that attempted to define what kind of training and knowledge was necessary to explain and understand a literary work. Its methodology was to deploy a series of examples of bad readings to construct a thesis about how good reading worked.

In his summary remarks at the end of the book, Richards introduces a section called 'Critical Fog' in which he deals directly with the need for comprehension of the meaning of a literary text.

> Our current reflective attitudes to poetry contain an undue proportion of bewilderment. It is regarded too often as a mystery. There are good and evil mysteries; or rather there is mystery and mystery mongering. That is mysterious which is inexplicable, or ultimate in so far as our present means of inquiry can explain it. But there is a spurious form of mysteriousness which arises only because our explanations are confused or because we overlook or forget the significance of what we have already understood. And there are many who think that they are serving the cause of poetry by exploiting these difficulties that every complex explanation presents. [. . .] At present gross general misunderstandings are certainly poetry's worst enemies. And these confusions have been encouraged by those who like to regard the whole matter, and every detail of it, as an incomprehensible mystery – because they suppose that this is a 'poetic' way of looking at it. But muddle-mindedness is in no respectable sense 'poetic', though far too many persons seem to think so. What can be explained about poetry can be separated from what cannot; and at innumerable points an explanation can help us both to understand what kind of thing poetry in general is, and to understand particular passages.[11]

We are reminded, reading this again, of how closely aligned the birth of literary formalism is with the notion of 'correct reading'. Richards is impatient with hazy 'mystery mongering'. His model of critical practice is based on the supreme importance of explanation as a corrective tool to the muddled apprehension of the inexpert reader. And even as later critics sought to alter the New Critical emphasis on the text alone, they did so by reemphasizing the importance of an accurate form of reading. In *Validity in Interpretation* (1967), E.D. Hirsch defended hermeneutic theory against the relativism and subjectivism he perceived at the heart of New Critical approaches, and articulated a series of principles of what he saw as valid interpretation. He too is on the side of right meanings. He concludes that

> despite its practical concreteness and variability, the root problem of interpretation is always the same – to guess what the author meant. Even though we can never be certain that our interpretive guesses are correct, we know that they *can* be correct, and that the goal of interpretation as a discipline is constantly to increase the probability that they are correct.[12]

This focus on establishing right readings can be traced through later twentieth-century critical debates about interpretation and the validity of the critical response. Reader-focused criticism might seem to create a critical space within which the non-expert or mistaken reader can find a role. One of its key practitioners, Stanley Fish, takes issue with the notion of the 'affective fallacy', and the claim that the variability of readers renders any exploration of their responses *ad hoc* and relativistic. Yet, once again, his emphasis is ultimately on the need to establish the parameters for an acceptable reading and to show how these are created by institutional context (rather than by the formal characteristics of the poem). He mocks critics who believe in a 'determinate meaning', and he lambasts a reductive obsession with 'the truth' that he sees in New Critical interpretation:

> The truth lies plainly in view, available to anyone who has the eyes to see; but some readers choose not to see it, and perversely substitute their own meanings for the meanings these texts obviously bear.[13]

But his quibble here is not so much with the idea that there *are* right readings. His point is that those meanings do not come from the text itself, but rather, from the institutions around it. It is the origin of the rightness that is at issue, not the importance of focusing on rightness in the first place.

Fish uses the evidence of the intellectual-structural context within which the critic or reader is operating to understand what generates meaning. But, at the base of it, his model of interpretive communities is committed to the notion of right reading. As his critics have noted, he is strong on the importance of the reader's role but less adept at historicizing that reader, or seeking empirical evidence for different historical reading practices. So what about critical models which offer a more historically nuanced way of understanding the reception of older texts? The sustained ascendancy of historicism as an approach to the literary works of the past has shown how an attentive recovery of the cultural, political, religious, and social conditions of the author and early reader's time can enable us to understand a plausible contemporary meaning of the literary work. The high level of political and topical referentiality in early eighteenth-century literature has secured pole position for historicist approaches. But even here, there is an emphasis on producing a correct, hyper-informed interpretation of the work. In 'Context Stinks' (2011), Rita Felski argues that historicism is founded on a fallacy that seeks to displace the text, reader, and author in favour of the critic's superior sense of context:

> What the literary text does not see, in this line of thought, are the larger circumstances that shape and sustain it and that are drawn into the light by the corrective force of the critic's own vigilant gaze. The critic probes for meanings inaccessible to authors as well as ordinary readers, and exposes the text's complicity in social conditions that it seeks to deny or disavow. Context, as the ampler, more expansive reference point, will invariably trump the claims of the individual text, knowing it far better than it can ever know itself.[14]

In Felski's analysis, this assertion of context is inadequate as a way of explaining the ways in which texts can be both resonant and affective across time. While her interest is in the ways in which Bruno Latour's actor network theory might enable critics to retrieve the centrality of the text itself, her account of historicism as a vindication of scholarly

prowess is useful in understanding why we might be so addicted to belief in a fixed meaning.

And if we dig deeper into the field of eighteenth-century studies,
across the changing critical fashions of the twentieth and twenty-first
centuries, there seems to be an ongoing assumption that the early readers of eighteenth-century texts had a pretty clear idea of how to interpret
them. In his 1959 study, Bonamy Dobrée describes an early reader's appreciation of Pope's satirical poem, *The Rape of the Lock*:

> So many lines or passages are echoes, adaptations, or parodies of
> pieces that the 'polite' reader of the day might be expected to know.
> He would for example recognize Statius in 'Where wigs with wigs'
> and Dryden in 'The conqu'ring force of unresisted steel'. He would
> be conscious that he was expected to understand the mockery of the
> epic form and its various points, the invocation, the sacrifice, the
> games, and so on, and to compare what he read with at least the *Dis-
> pensary*, if not *Le Lutrin* and *La Secchia Rapita*. All would seem to him
> of merely local reference. When, it may be, he read 'whether the
> nymph . . .' he would, probably, particularize the image, or if he were
> solemn, regard it as a criticism of the maids of honour at Court.[15]

Dobrée is confident that early (male) readers understood very clearly
all the reference points of the poem, even if in his eyes, their smaller-
scale reading limited the semantic range of a literary work. A similar
sense of confidence in the capacity of eighteenth-century readers to
both understand and engage with the intentions and premises of the
satires of the period is also evident in David Worcester's pre-war study
of satirical practice.[16] Worcester's account assumes an alignment between authorial intention and readerly comprehension, and he uses this
mutual comprehension as the basis for his understanding of the culture
of the period, and the writer-reader contracts that underpinned it. He
argues that forms of satire which were dependent on their readers supplying an implied meaning could only flourish in an era in which those
readers both possessed a good understanding of rhetorical norms and
enjoyed a stable notion of the organization and ideals of political society. But, with those in place, the exchange of opinion from author to

reader was pretty straightforward: 'The author first evolves a criticism of conduct [. . .] then he contrives ways of making his readers comprehend and remember that criticism and adopt it as their own'.[17]

## The Eighteenth Century: Perspectives on Satire

Such speculative interest in historical reader response was knocked into abeyance by the formalist approach to satire which dominated eighteenth-century studies of the 1950s and 60s.[18] New Criticism and the practices associated with it saw a proliferation of rhetorical theories of satire which emphasized the self-contained aesthetics of satirical writing – internal logic, rhetorical structure, and dramatic form – and in doing so, as Dustin Griffin has argued, tended 'to separate the work from the author who produced it, the world out of which it grew, and the audience towards which it was directed'.[19] Thus Alvin Kernan asserted that great satire has a general nature that transcends each individual instantiation. 'It should be possible', Kernan writes, 'to define in very general terms the essential satirist, those traits, attitudes, passions, which every author of satire brings together'.[20]

In the wake of New Critical approaches, and the advance of new historicism and cultural materialism, the notion that (elite) eighteenth-century readers were able to understand the satires they held before them returned with new emphases. In the more theoretically inflected accounts of the 1980s, an emphasis on the hidden ideological agendas of early eighteenth-century writers produced accounts of the literary culture of the period which saw readerly inclusion and exclusion as determined along class and gender lines.[21] In this formulation, critics explored the way in which – while new forms of writing purported to be inclusive – some classes of readers were deliberately kept out of the literary sphere or their aspirations were clearly demarcated. With this came a corresponding implication that there was a social and intellectual elite who remained in the know, or at least the level of their comprehension was not questioned. Brean Hammond's *Professional Imaginative Writing in Britain* (1997) saw Addison and Steele's *Spectator* (1711–12) as 'widening the scope of the aesthetically enfranchised but carefully drawing new boundaries'.[22] Hammond shows the way in which Addison, in his essays on the Pleasures of the Imagination, opened up discussion of the appreciation of beauty while reinforcing the social barriers that would prevent full entry to aesthetic appreciation. Allon White and Peter Stallybrass's Bahktin-influenced *Politics and Poetics of Transgression* (1986) examined the role of the carnivalesque in eighteenth-century literature and society, but again there was a tendency to reaffirm a politics of interpretation as a form of segregation in the writing of the period.[23]

More recent work on satire has continued to presume a degree of mutual understanding between author and intended reader. Michael Seidel explains John Dryden's satiric achievement thus:

> Attack is something the satirist does; wit is something the audience understands. Dryden adds something very important to the spirit of satiric opposition. He allows the satirist – through the literary manipulation of style and tone – to make accomplices of his readers. Attack can even arrive in a package marked as praise, if readers are sensitive to all the ironies that language can provide.[24]

And here is Ashley Marshall in a copious and in many ways impressive survey of eighteenth-century satirical practice: 'most Carolean scribal satire was designed for a fairly specific coterie. I suspect that members of that audience often had a pretty good sense of what the satire was doing and to whom'.[25] She refers specifically to manuscript satire in the later seventeenth century, but elsewhere there are similar assumptions about how poems worked for their readers: 'readers are not likely to appreciate – buy, read, enjoy – satire that does not communicate anything to them'.[26] Discussing Defoe's political satire, again, without any specific evidence of how those readers responded, she asserts that: 'his concept of satire is largely audience rather than target based. He [...] often addresses a specific audience in an effort to expose his enemies and to provoke unsettledness or anxiety on the part of like-minded readers'.[27]

The *Oxford Handbook of Eighteenth-Century Satire* (2019) contains forty-one essays on different aspects of the form during the period, and while the collection has many strengths, it is notable that none of the essays explore the empirical evidence of what actual readers made of satire in this period.[28] Although some of the essays' authors acknowledge that the intentions of a satirist were not always met by a receptive audience, there is more commonly, as with so many critical accounts of the period, a generalized sense of readerly competence.[29] So we find claims that the genre of satire attempts to elicit 'the painful shock of readerly self-recognition'; that 'the task of identifying and correlating [Dryden's satirical intention] falls to the reader'; that 'it is through the reader's laughter thus provoked that [Pope] achieves his goal'; that 'the reader is encouraged to imagine some of the scenes' in satirical prints; and that '"general satire"' – 'attacking whole descriptions of men and women, if not the entire human species' – 'turns the reader's attention uncomfortably towards the satirist's motives and purposes'.[30] These are all hypothesized models of reader response, imagined ideas of the way texts landed in their own time. They presuppose successful, knowledgeable acts of reading – and many satirical works will have found those responses. But not all of them did. Such accounts of satirical texts offer us a model of reflected comprehension, in which our assumption of historical readers' understanding is linked with a validation of our own critical prowess.

It may be that the cognitive turn in literary studies will enable fresh attention to be paid to the possible varieties of response. Robert Phiddian has argued that the notion of the death of the author 'had liberatory consequences in many ways, but it made an understanding of satire hard to articulate'.[31] In dismissing the idea of authorial purpose, theorists and critics have struggled to account well for satire because in doing away with ideas of intention, we lose the central purpose of the genre: 'satire does need to be construed as purposive, as intentional. To construe a text as satirical is to construe it as making a point'.[32] Phiddian looks to alternative disciplinary models from social science, which might help to realign satire with the issues of purpose and response that are at the heart of the form. He concludes that greater interest in the empirical evidence of diverse response would enable us to 'pursue the actual effects of satire – often limited, or hit-and-miss, often counterproductive, seldom directly successful.'[33] As I have been arguing in this chapter, it seems that our own discipline's privileging of technically competent acts of interpretation has left us little able to explore the historical evidence of diverse responses to satiric stimuli.

## A History of Good Reading

I have quoted a series of influential studies of the period to show that even the best critical accounts have rested on an untested assumption of competence – a hypothetical sense of the reciprocal dynamic between authorial intention and reader complicity. We might expect that the emergent, and now established, history of reading would offer more room to consider the variability of readerly interpretation. Yet it seems that here, too, there has been a focus on good or exceptional exemplars, and the history of reading has often been the history of right reading. Important recent work on error in early modern and medieval studies has deepened the field, but overall it could be said that the history of reading is skewed towards a history of enrichment and affirmation, confirmations of the way we ought to read – not so much how we *have* read.[34] Very often the history of early modern reading is based on extraordinary readers like the Renaissance polymaths John Dee and Gabriel Harvey, whose marginal annotations to their works illustrate for us the complex intellectual life of an informed reader and their range of reference, offering illuminating examples of the ways in which books were read right, read richly, by their early readers.[35] The work of Lisa Jardine and Anthony Grafton, Heidi Brayman Hackel, and Bill Sherman has done much to show us how early modern readers were guided in their practice by classical habits of commonplacing and indexing.[36] In the marginal annotations of early modern readers, we can see recurring patterns: adversarial commentary, supplementation of the text with other sources of authority, correction, amplification, and marking up of *sententiae*. There is an emphasis in much of this work on the active role of the reader, and the degree to which a good reader corrects, improves, and enacts the work before them. So, for example, when Sherman lists the categories of annotation that he has found in marked books, none of them include signs of getting it wrong or registering incomprehension.[37] It is not that there is no attention to misinterpretation: we have several engaging case studies of historical figures who seem to misread deliberately the texts before them. Geoff Baker's work on the commonplace book of the Catholic William Blundell, Kevin Sharpe's account of Sir William Drake and his notebooks, and Carlo Ginzburg's influential research into the heretical Italian miller Menocchio all offer models of readers who read wrongly, or repurposed materials in order to suit their own agenda.[38] And as discussed in the introduction, it is true that much evidence suggests a bias towards affirmative or supplementary marginal commentary rather than marking of doubt or uncertainty. Yet, as we shall also see in the next chapter, there is historical evidence of printed advice to students which recommended marking up passages which were unclear in sources ranging from university manuscript accounts from the mid-seventeenth century, through to the printed directions of eighteenth-century advice guides to students. It seems like we have been so busy trying to learn about how historical readers were supposed to have read, what they took to be a model of good reading, that we have rather neglected the fact that many of them were imperfect or flawed readers.

And then if we look at work on the history of readerly engagement in the eighteenth century, so well documented by Heather Jackson's two studies on marginalia, we find a different kind of problem. Jackson describes a shift in the eighteenth century towards a different kind of reader response. She argues that, in the first phase of the history of marginalia in English, a habit associated with scholars and textbooks filtered through to other kinds of books, readers, and reading modes. This process continued and was accelerated in the publishing boom of the eighteenth century. Late eighteenth-century marginalia were typically evaluative, personal, and designed to be shared, and personal applicability came to shape marginal notes. Yet Jackson's case studies again tend to be exceptional readers, who show what, to her, makes for good marginalia – intelligibility, wit, historical significance, and creative symbiosis. Again, this is a history of reading, brilliant though it is, that has little space for the uninformed, superficial, or mistaken reader. This is how Jackson writes about the expansion of the reading public with the advent of the steam press in the early nineteenth century:

> There is no denying that some of the fears of educators and connoisseurs about the effect of the mass market in books after about 1820 were realized during the nineteenth century. Standards of production did drop. Ill-prepared readers got their hands on materials not intended for them. Besides the learned, the Aquinases and Casaubons and Bentleys of their day, readers with no special competence took it upon themselves to criticize their books from the margins in annotations that are pedestrian for the most part, and sometimes worse – careless, ignorant, or abusive.[39]

Jackson has a clear idea of the kinds of readers who count and those who don't. Readers with 'no special competence' seem not to be part of what we read marginalia for. In these exemplars of the history of reading, there is little room to think about ignorant, confused, or mistaken readers, who don't fit neatly enough into the kinds of stories we want to tell about intellectual or cultural history. Is there a positivist bias in interpreting annotation and book use, a tendency to focus on knowledge at the expense of absence and ignorance?

I have argued that narratives and case studies of historical readers have focused on superior or correct reading experiences. It could be said that we have reverse-engineered our own desire for certainty of interpretation onto the readers of the past. A tendency to neglect the historical evidence of a lack of knowledge has also shaped the way we publish and edit historical works. The goal of scholarly editing is to clarify and amplify the meanings of the texts we work on – to showcase the rich political, cultural, religious, and social context out of which they emerge. But again, that process tends, in its comprehensiveness, to suggest a degree of knowledge that cannot always have been present for contemporary readers. Martin Battestin described the purpose of literary annotations as 'to recover for the reader, as briefly and objectively as possible, all essential information (and only essential information) necessary to render the author's meaning wholly intelligible'.[40] It is a definition which presents many questions – not least what is 'essential' and what is not – but for the purposes of this argument it is problematic in its assumption both that the author aimed to be fully intelligible and that readers were fully able to understand the whole of the text. Modern readers confronting the dauntingly referential works of the early eighteenth century now need to be bolstered with an armoury of historical and cultural context in order to begin to unravel their complex and ingenious wit. The extensive annotations to editions such as the Longman annotated editions, the California *Works of John Dryden* (1956–2002) or the Yale *Poems on Affairs of State* (c. 1960–80) offer them all these tools, enabling every reader to become an expert. But, as we shall see in later chapters of this book, in seeking to provide and pin down certain meanings in the playful and elusive works of the eighteenth century, conventional editorial treatments may often miss the mark of the original text.

What I hope to show in this book is that a new attentiveness to imperfect readers and readings might offer us a more historically nuanced perspective on the question of meaning and intention in the works that we read. There are some models for this kind of approach. As we have seen, critics have drawn attention to the way in which other disciplines, notably political science and studies of cognition, might offer some insights into the value of exploring reading responses as diverse and sometimes flawed. Recent literary critical and editorial work presents additional illumination. Michael Edson's study of 'the annotator as ordinary reader' uses the example of a late eighteenth-century edition of the satirist Charles Churchill to raise questions about the place of accuracy and relevance in modern explanatory editing, arguing that the emphasis on accuracy can lead to historically inaccurate readings. He shows the way in which an 1804 edition of Churchill's works reflects the understanding not of an expert reader, but of the popular information, gossip, and salacious revelation that was circulating about Churchill at the time. That edition, he argues, presents a model of explanation that is both correct and not correct: not correct in that many of the facts are untrue and non-verifiable, but correct in that it offers the context within which Churchill was familiar to his early readers. And so, Edson argues, 'precisely because they seem so inadequate by modern standards, the notes in early editions offer clues to non-specialist reading habits in the past.'[41]

Others have also noted the intellectual fallacy of modern annotation. In an essay on the editor and annotator, Ian Small observes that 'the role that the individual is required to take is that of an ideal, perfectly knowledgeable, and competent reader; a reader for whom all textual allusions and all possible meanings are simultaneously available. Of course, the problem is that no such reader exists'.[42]

Catherine Nicolson's recent study of *Reading and Not Reading the Faerie Queene* uses the single focus of the poem to explore a history of uneven and imperfect landings. Nicolson shows the way in which the difficulties of the *Faerie Queene* – its obscurity, the density of its allusions, its topical references – 'conspired to make it an ideal object of academic research'.[43] We have come to value highly a poem that validates the expert reader, and Nicolson's task is to look to other kinds of responses, aligning herself with 'readers short on understanding, skill, objectivity, patience, learning, curiosity, broadmindedness, sophistication, and all of the other intellectual virtues with which we tend to associate literature in general and *The Faerie Queene* in particular'.[44] Such thinking about alternative responses extends beyond early modern studies. In a 2004 essay on 'Uncritical Reading', Michael Warner draws attention to the normative effects of particular kinds of critical reading practice at the expense of the many other responses to a text practised by readers across time.[45] In *Paraliterary* (2017), Merve Emre examines the history of twentieth-century 'bad readers', which she defines as 'individuals socialised into the practice of readerly identification, emotion, action and interaction'.[46] Rejecting models of aesthetic 'pure' appreciation, she focuses on the more worldly forces and institutions which have shaped reading habits, creating generations of bad readers who have their own history in the story of post-war literature. All these approaches seem to me to offer models for thinking beyond the Good Reader.

We have seen here that many of our key scholarly activities are modelled on versions of right reading that don't reflect early encounters with the works we study and teach. They are particularly out of step with the satirical and coded texts of the late seventeenth and early eighteenth century. Gaining a greater sense of the role – and creative potential – of imperfect reading offers a new perspective on the interactions among reader, author, and text, and, in particular, how that dynamic worked in the interactive texts of the early eighteenth century. It also gives us more purchase on the peculiarity of this historical and cultural moment. The heyday of English satire was a period which saw many of the contexts of literary publication change radically: anonymous print publication, new authors, new readers, and unknown and unknowable circuits of textual transmission. All these factors complicated readers' ability to 'make sense of' the works they held before them. And at the same time, those works habitually forced readers to make their own meanings, to fill in the gaps and use inference to work out purpose and intention for themselves. Exploring the history of misunderstanding and misinterpretation in this context helps us to see the literary culture of the period as less clear cut than we might assume, even in forms which seem to be predicated on known or fixed meanings. There is of course a contradiction in this project: in seeking to acknowledge a history of imperfect reading, aren't we replacing one kind of 'answer' to the past with another? Is it ever possible to let go of the impulse to explain, clarify, fix, or ultimately secure a good interpretation of what we read? It may not be possible to escape the seductions of rightness, but it is surely time to look at the value of reading wrong.

# 2

# The Christian Reader

But yet to read it is not all. *Legare & non intelligere, negligere est.* To read and not to understand, or not to heed, is to neglect. Such reading of Scriptures is to dishonour God and them.

—JOHN GEREE, PREFACE TO NICHOLAS BYFIELD, *DIRECTIONS FOR THE PRIVATE READING OF THE SCRIPTURES*, 1648

*Si non vis intelligi, debes negligi.* [if you don't wish to be understood you deserve to be neglected.]

—ORIGIN DISPUTED, QUOTED BY JOHN LOCKE, *AN ESSAY CONCERNING HUMAN UNDERSTANDING*, 1690

THE QUOTATIONS above offer two radically different ideas about how to approach textual difficulty and understanding. The first is advice given by the Puritan preacher John Geree in his preface to a popular early seventeenth-century guide to reading the Bible.[1] The passage lays bare the difference between literacy and comprehension: there's no point in reading without understanding, and, in the context of the word of God, a merely passive acquaintance with the text is disrespectful and irreligious. The second, possibly apocryphal, quotation is said to be St Jerome's commentary on reading Persius.[2] It's a vein of thinking which emphasizes plainness and transparency, a no-nonsense view that if a writer can't express themselves clearly, they don't deserve to be read. Together they set up a framework for debates over clarity, interpretation, responsibility, and the good reader within the context of Christian devotion.

So what have they got to do with the muddle and play of literary texts? To understand how interpretative competence might have been viewed in the late seventeenth and early eighteenth century, we need to look towards these reference points, distant as they might seem from the world of blanked-out names and playful insinuations found in so much secular reading in the period. Immersing ourselves for a moment in the world of scriptural exegesis, we find readers encountering some of the key issues at stake in a culture of misreading. The Bible, the most read and known text in contemporary society was a site for profound, often agonized debate about who could read, and how they interpreted what they encountered. It is through the literature of religion that we encounter key themes of secular reading: the interpretation of irony and metaphor, the challenges of an author whose intentions were often unknowable. This was intrinsically connected to the history of Western Christianity, since for many early modern readers, the relationship between reading and understanding was fundamentally linked to Christian salvation. The Protestant emphasis on individual apprehension and interpretation made each reader responsible for their own eternal spiritual destiny. Moreover, every amateur, imperfect reader mattered equally – it was not enough to discount those who were not expert. And so, while the stakes were very different for those approaching Scripture to those puzzling over the latest political lampoon or sociable *jeu d'esprit*, it is within the context of religious reading that we find some indicators of the ways in which a combination of obscure writing and broadened readership affected reading and print culture. We also see some of the fullest explication of contemporary ideas about understanding the book in hand.

As the consideration of scriptural puzzles expanded beyond a narrow group of hermeneutical specialists, responsibility fell on the individual to become a 'good reader'. In discussion of religious reading there is often explicit discussion of how a non-expert reader might unlock a text with a hidden or inaccessible meaning, and how they should deal with their lack of understanding, their inability to pick that lock. Printed advice on biblical interpretation was frequently pragmatic, advising how to make use of parallels, allegories, and types, and it bears comparison with the approach demanded by secular literature published in the late seventeenth and early eighteenth century, which also needed unlocking and application to a world outside the frame of the book. We see the way in which Bible publishing led the way in innovating forms of apparatus for aiding comprehension which would later be mirrored, adapted, and exploited in more secular works.

The reading of Christian Scripture framed key debates about interpretation and access to the text. There was a central paradox: the Bible was both utterly straightforward and plain, and yet at the same time capable of generating multiple meanings. Was it the task of the reader to find within themselves the key to its significance, or was this to be gained by talking to others? If Scripture seemed incomprehensible, whose fault was that – was it down to a lack of hermeneutic sophistication, or the failure of language itself, or possibly even God's inability to make Himself clear? How was one to understand multiple interpretations of the same text? The Bible offered various ways of addressing misunderstanding in the period, but they were often contradictory. While the challenge of *sola Scriptura*, or 'the Bible alone', is at one level fundamentally different from the interpretative questions raised by the satirical topical works and fictional models discussed elsewhere in this book, the epistemological questions arising from scriptural encounter provide an essential background for thinking about models for puzzled comprehension. The proliferation of commentary on 'what to do when you don't understand' that we find emerging from debate about Scripture offers a primary site for understanding the tensions among education, access, authority, class, and textuality in this period. Moreover, some of the proposed solutions offered to students and other puzzled readers – active engagement, notetaking, supplementary commentary, and social consultation – are strategies that we find reflected in secular discussions.

The seventeenth century was a critical period in the popularization of arguments about scriptural interpretation. The religious and political controversies of the mid-seventeenth century oxygenated debates about the interpretation, use, and application of biblical texts.[3] While biblical hermeneutics might once have been the preserve of the learned and erudite, by the end of the seventeenth century such issues were being communicated to a far broader audience than ever before.[4] There was an explosion in accessible discussion of the nature of biblical scholarship and its relevance for the lay reader.[5] Works such as *Clavis Bibliorum* (1649), claimed to be 'for the help of the weakest capacity in the understanding of the whole Bible'.[6] Similarly, *A Key to Catechisms* (1682) offered 'easie and familiar help for the true and right understanding of the principal Substance of all Catechisms whatsoever. Suited to the Meanest Capacities and the Weakest Memories'.[7] 'Weak capacity', 'meanest memory': as we can see from these telling phrases, the literature of scriptural advice was explicit about the existence of poor reading habits, and about the need to cater to them.

Debate about how to control or guide religious reading for the lay Christian was not new. From the point of the publication of the first Bible in English in the sixteenth century, discussion of reading of the Scriptures had been fraught by dilemmas at the heart of Protestant ideology – the tension between the individual reader's ability to read and understand the word of God for themselves, and the need to guide that interpretation to avoid heresy and error. The circulation of the Bible and access to it was inflected by religious divisions: the statutes of Henry VIII had promoted public access to the various authorized versions of the Bible, but later legislation attempted to wrest back control of the readership and interpretation. During the Reformation, Bibles were translated and printed in English so Scriptures might be directly available to the individual. Under Queen Mary, the printing of English Scriptures was banned, and Protestant reformers were forced into exile on the continent, leading to the printing of the influential English language Bible in Geneva. As this suggests, the very fact of considering the Bible to be the main source of divine authority was itself contested.

Further division arose with the growth of biblical scholarship during the seventeenth century. The relatively recent recovery of ancient biblical manuscripts, combined with humanist scholarly approaches to the text promoted intense dispute among Catholic, Protestant, and non-conformist readers over approaches to Scripture. While many of these disputes were sectarian in origin, they ultimately weakened the idea of the Bible as a single, authoritative, and unchallenged source of divine revelation.[8] Thus the pursuit of the truth of the Bible was less likely to reveal consensus on its divine legitimacy than a sprawling mass of pathways through the text that could be seen as undermining any single meaning. As one author complained, 'another cause of the multiplication of extravagant opinions and sects, in Christianity, has been the arbitrary practice of giving different senses to the same passages of the Bible'.[9] This kind of hermeneutic pluralism reached far beyond the scholarly elite. Conversations about the historicity of Biblical texts, their language and application, began as partisan and scholarly printed disputes, but by the end of the century they had filtered through to the lay reader. Pamphlets, journals, and sermons debated even the most sophisticated matters of philological and critical concern.[10] So what we see in the history of biblical interpretation and publication in the seventeenth and early eighteenth century is in many ways a reflection of the conditions of secular literary culture. In both cases, texts based on allegory, metaphor, and hidden meaning demanded readerly unlocking. And those texts were also increasingly consumed by a broadened reading public who might not have access to the expertise to enable easy decoding.

## Easy or Hard?

Many of these scholarly and increasingly popularized debates about scriptural reading centred on the correct way to interpret the Bible, and on how to use the emerging new scholarship to advance an understanding of God's word. Religious groups struggled to reconcile the historical specificity and vulnerability of the received text with its universal application as a form of revelation, and fought among themselves over the correct interpretation. But it's not as though the Bible was straightforward in the first place. What was the lay reader or ordinary clergyman supposed to make of what they found? On the one hand, Scripture was God's word and designed by Him to teach the individual reader the crucial truths of Christian belief. The Anglican clergyman and scholar Francis Hare emphasized the importance of scriptural revelation:

> Let us put no Fetters on Mens Understandings, nor any other Bounds to their Enquiries, but what *God and Truth* have set. Let us, if we would not give up the *Protestant Principle,* that *the Scriptures are plain and clear in the necessary Articles;* declare *nothing* to be necessary, but what is *clearly revealed* in them.[11]

Yet on the other hand, this description of the whole text of Scripture as 'plain and clear' was obviously not quite accurate. Hare follows his words on the clarity of Scripture with an acknowledgement that the Bible's meaning was not always brilliantly lucid, and ends up with an almost comic tautology: 'Next to the understanding a Text of Scripture, is to know that it can't be certainly understood'.[12] He encapsulates the problem facing religious communities that both had to believe that God had made plain his meaning in the words of the Bible and yet also accept that that meaning was in places difficult to retrieve. Even the simplest parts of the Bible were dependent on some analogical explication – the gospels were supposed to be plain – and yet Jesus spoke in parables, while Mark 4:12 alluded to the need for some extra level of interpretation and application that people 'hearing they may hear, and not understand'. Other parts of the Bible were really tricky. The Pauline epistles were notoriously obscure: they needed to be known and interpreted – but yet they were not 'plain'.

We can see this doublethink about the Bible as both plain and obscure ricocheting across the commentary of the period. In his *Vindication of the Divine Authority* (1692), an introduction to lay and ordinary Bible reading practices, William Lowth argues that of course God knew what he was doing when he revealed his truths in the form of Scripture: 'for God to communicate his Will by Writing, implies nothing in it but what is Natural and Easie'. To doubt the truth of this, he says, would be to doubt God's skills as a communicator: no one would argue 'that God cannot order a Book to be writ in as intelligible a manner, as men can indite it when they are left to themselves'.[13] Others took a similar line. John Williams writing *Of the Perspicuity of Scripture* (1696) assures his audience that though there may be difficulties in reading the Bible 'they are nothing', he insisted, 'in comparison to the plain Texts of it; and which no more hinder us from understanding the plain, than the Spots in the Sun prevent us of the Light of it'.[14]

But then there was the other side of the argument – all those who pointed out the dangers posed by the bits of the Bible that were truly hard to penetrate. Some writers justified their biblical exegesis by reminding readers how easily a false interpretation might lead one into big mistakes:

> The letter of Scripture suffering various Interpretations, it is plain that Error may pretend to Scripture; the antient Fathers being likewise dead, and not able to vindicate themselves, their writings may be wrested, and Error may make use of them to back itself; Reason too being byassed by Interest, Education, Passion, Society &c.[15]

Many readers conveyed personal uncertainty about the application of particular texts. One of these was the philosopher John Locke. In the *Essay on Human Understanding* (1690), he expressed impatience with the elaborate exegetical gymnastics demanded by the obscurities of historical texts: 'Therefore in the reading of them [historical authors], if they do not use their Words with a due clearness and perspicuity, we may lay them aside, and without any injury done them, resolve thus with ourselves, *Si non vis intelligi, debes negligi*.'[16] So far, so matter of fact. But sometimes one was under an obligation to understand. In his essay on the 'Understanding of St Paul's Epistles', the philosopher conceded the difficulty of comprehending scriptural passages which clearly could not be ignored. He wondered how any reader might understand the purpose of St Paul's letters: 'though I had been conversant in these Epistles, as well as in other Parts of Sacred Scripture, yet I found that I understood them not'.[17] For Locke, there were a number of 'Causes of Obscurity' in the text. Some of this he attributed to the intimacy of epistolary form: it was common that 'a well Penn'd Letter which is very easy and intelligible to the Receiver, is very obscure to a Stranger, who hardly knows what to make of it'.[18] As we shall see in a later chapter, the dynamics of intimacy and inaccessibility suggested here in texts written for a known addressee and read by a stranger were a key feature of much of the sociable verse of the period. And so too, as Locke found, was the case with Scriptural letters. Within the Pauline Epistles, the general difficulty of the Hebraic idiom of New Testament Greek was compounded by St Paul's idiosyncratic style and intellectual temper. It was up to the reader to read carefully. Locke emphasized the need for attentive study, because 'if [the style of St Paul's discourse] be neglected or overlook'd [it] will make the Reader very much mistake, and misunderstand his Meaning, and render the Sense very perplex'd'.[19] The stakes were high, and we can see here Locke attempting to navigate within his works between two rather different approaches towards difficult Scripture: on the one hand, if it wasn't written clearly, it wasn't worth bothering with. Yet on the other, the devout Christian also bore an obligation to read right the word of God: Edmund Calamy, author of the popular *Clavis Bibliorum*, emphasized that Christians must 'read *them* [the Scriptures] *with* a godly trembling, *for feare least like the spider, they should suck poison out of those sweet flowers*, & wrest the Scriptures to their own destruction, as they that are unstable and unlearned do'.[20]

Another reader who expressed his struggles with biblical interpretation was the Catholic Royalist, William Blundell. Blundell was the head of a recusant landowning family living at Crosby Hall in Lancashire. Loyal to his faith and the Stuart monarchy, Blundell experienced exile and repeated imprisonment during his long life. He was also a compulsive reader and writer: as a Catholic he had less formal education than his Protestant peers, but his surviving notebooks show an appetite for knowledge acquisition, and an ongoing desire to learn new languages and understand the political issues of his day through wider reading.[21] His various surviving notebooks record a range of information, from drafts of letters to notes on contemporary politics, the weather, travel logs, and the weights of family members. Also within the Blundell collection are two commonplace books, a two-hundred folio 'Historica', and a four-hundred folio 'Adversaria'.[22] Across these sheets, in often random order, Blundell registered his thoughts on his reading matter: the Historica was primarily used for historical materials, and the Adversaria for religious works.

Reading and notetaking offered Blundell a place to develop and maintain his religious beliefs, but his engagement with the texts he read, and in particular the Bible, was not straightforward. In his notebooks he registered a sense of the practical failings that might prevent him from being a good Catholic, worrying that he didn't have the capacity for sound theological debate. So, for example, in response to the Italian church historian Sforza Pallavicino's account of the ecclesiastical Council of Trent he notes that 'I question my own ability, whether I do rightly understand these matters, as well as some other higher points which are handled in our Authors work'.[23] Fascinatingly, he comforted himself that he was not alone in his struggles with comprehension, which he identified as being at the heart of scriptural interpretation. He compared his efforts to comprehend God's word with those of the Apostles, who could not understand some aspects of Scripture until Christ explained them. He also noted that Saint Augustine himself had admitted that large sections of the Scripture were beyond him: 'The Apostles, till Christ opened their senses, for ye Understanding of ye Scriptures could not understand them and St Augustine confesseth that there were many more things that he understood not than that he understood'. [24]

Blundell was alert to the interpretative challenges of the Bible: the Adversaria contains a number of sections entitled 'Scriptura Difficultis', which dealt with what Blundell called 'the many appearing incongruit-yes and other hard things to be found' in the Bible.[25] He remarked that 'The Apocalypse is full of inexplicable wonders; ye 20 chapter is particularly hard to be understood, and was ye occasion of ye Millenarie or Chiliasts'.[26] What seemed to him especially difficult to understand in reading the holy text was all the contradictions within it: so, for example, in Matthew 23:9 we are told 'Call no Man father upon the earth', yet in Matthew 19:5 it is recorded that 'Man *shall* leave father & mother & cleave to his wife'.[27] In his sections on scriptural difficulty he compiled lists of contradictory indicators in scriptural texts. He puzzled over how one was to understand that 'in John 3:2 it said plainly that Jesus baptized: yet chp: 4:2 it is sayd *Jesus did not baptize but his disciples*'.[28] He commented that 'The Jewes [?] used Scripture against Christ. See John 7. V. 41–52. See John 5:31 & compare it with 5.14 it appeareth a plain contradiction, concerning Christs testimony of him self being true & not true'. [29] In his book he asked himself questions he could not answer: 'What is ye sense of Corban: Matt 15:5?' [30] He was greatly concerned about the evidence of worthy figures who seemed to defy biblical teachings: he cites instances in which individuals claimed to have seen God's face, and yet 'it is els where sayd that one canot see God and live, yet it seems by sondry texts that he hath been seen by mortall eyes'.[31] But rather than criticizing God's word, Blundell evidently felt that it was his own failing that prevented him from accepting the apparent errors in the Bible. Were he a better Christian and Catholic, he would not be drawn to noticing these contradictions, since 'the devinest & best men' would unquestioningly accept all that was contained within the text.[32]

## Navigating Incomprehension

So how was a reader supposed to deal with a state of incomprehension? Part of William Blundell's response to not understanding Scripture was regular rereading of the Bible. He developed a special method to remember the Apostles' writings, in which he used a verb to signify the contents of each chapter.[33] And his notebooks clearly provided him with a space in which he could think through the things he found difficult, a kind of intellectual confessional. Other readers could take advantage of the practical guidance available on how to remedy a deficit in understanding. One recommended strategy was effective notetaking and the marking up of passages of difficulty. As discussed earlier, although the study of marginalia and annotation has tended to focus on the use of marks as signs of positive engagement with a text, it seems that there was also a role for specific forms of notetaking to signify struggle and incomprehension. Instructional guides provide some evidence of printed and manuscript advice for readers on how to record their queries. In his *Directions*, Nicholas Byfield offered the following guidance:

> Now for the manner of using these rules, I think thou mayest profitably follow these directions. First, make thee a little paper book of a sheet or two of paper, as may be most portable: then write upon the top of every leaf the title for that thou wouldst observe in reading [...] As for example, would I observe all the hard places, which in reading I have a desire to know the meaning of.[34]

If one were to follow these instructions, one would produce a book of queries which could be remedied through further reading and consultation. The emphasis on recording readerly difficulty is also reflected in the kinds of headings that were to be used for collecting examples. At the back of the *Directions* was a list of things to look for and mark up in reading, and alongside the thematic points, the index lists: '12. Hard places that I would fain be resolved in the meaning of them, 1 Cor 15.29, Revel. 20.4'.

The advice about how to mark up passages of uncertainty was addressed to all levels of literacy. John Geree, whose prefatory comments on use also appear in the *Directions*, advises those who cannot collect written notes to make particular kinds of strokes in the margin of the book. He imagines someone telling him 'I cannot write, and therefore these directions for noting speciall places are not usefull for me, because they require a mean that is above the compasse of my qualification'. The response given is 'Those that cannot write, can yet make marks' and for those who cannot read themselves, to seek the assistance of others:

> they must seek a supply of this defect by others, as blinde men doe. If this defect be in housholders, either the husband may use the help of the wife, or the wife of the husband, or both of a childe, or at least of a servant to read to them.[35]

Some readers clearly took all these practical instructions on practical measures to rectify incomprehension to heart – a British Library copy of Byfield's *Directions* shows lines and crosses in the margin where there is discussion of the practical response to a lack of knowledge. This reader has marked up in particular both the lines on the importance of understanding ('Legare & non intelligere, negligere est. *To read and not to understand, or not to heed, is to neglect*') and the passages which advise the marking up of passages of obscurity, as well as the recruitment of other readers to help those who cannot read.[36]

Such advice to identify unclear passages was not exclusive to scriptural reading. A mid-seventeenth-century manuscript guide for students at university, seemingly copied from a source in Emmanuel College, Cambridge, also advises students to make a special notebook with which to record passages in their reading with which they had difficulty.[37] The document, which has been cited as indicative of educational practices during the period, may give insight into common practices for the uncomprehending reader.[38] The author of the 'Directions', Ralph Holdsworth, explains:

> Let this be your manner of Reading them; Gather into a paper book all the Phrases and Idiotisms which you know not allready; Whether they be such as consist in single words, or sentences; with the English signification & use as you go along. This study you may think tedious but the benefit will be a sufficient Requitall.[39]

In the plan specifying the month of September's academic study of the Greek New Testament, Holdsworth again refers to this paper notebook: 'Those words which are most difficult or seldom met with, set down in a paper-book for that purpose'.[40] It is very clear that this notebook for queries is not the same thing as a commonplace book, a compilation which is rather, as Holdsworth clarifies, for collecting 'all the Remarkable things you meet with in Historians, Orators, or Poets, as you find them Promiscuously'.[41]

While there were clearly some readers, like William Blundell, who created subsections within their commonplace books for matters of textual difficulty, it seems that in both the examples above authors recommended a particular material form for the collection of reading queries, namely, a paper notebook, possibly hand-made, which might become its own collection of questions separate from the kind of textual compilation in a commonplace book. The history of reading has leant heavily on the commonplace book as evidence of reading practices. It may be that if we are to fully understand historical reading practices and, in particular, appreciate how readers engaged with material that they did not understand, we may have to explore additional forms of archival evidence, such as notebooks of queries as described here, many of which are less likely to have survived than the traditionally conceived commonplace book. While some authorities – such as Byfield – recommend marginal notes as a response to reader uncertainty, it is clear that this wasn't a universal assumption, and that students may have collected their queries in manuscript items that either don't survive or are not studied.

One of the things that's also worth noting about the reading of Scripture in lay settings is the many different roles that religious books played within the life of a family or individual. The combination of kinds of content we find on the marked pages of Bibles and books of Common Prayer is a salutary reminder of the mixed literacy, sophistication, and focus of readers of this period. Many Bibles and prayer books were used as repositories for other kinds of knowledge, from family trees to recipes to childish doodles or lists. So in looking for evidence of the interpretation of biblical text within individual copies, we are as likely to find marginalia which reflect the rich array of social and domestic functions performed by a copy of the Bible or a Book of Common Prayer. These were the books most likely to be held in every home, passed down from one generation to another, and they were also the places where essential family information was kept.

The Blanshard family collected together their copy of the Book of Common Prayer, along with two other Anglican devotional texts, *A Companion to the Altar* and *The Whole Book of Psalms* and bound them with a very fine green Morocco gilt tooled leather, with a matching box. On the upper and lower endleaves of the Book of Common Prayer are the records of all the births, marriages, and deaths of many generations of the family.[42] The binding suggests it was a very special item for this family – but was that because it was devotional, or because it contained all the family records? Alongside such genealogical content, the pages of a Bible were used for countless other purposes: Anne Wolferstan's 1679 copy of the New Testament bears her ownership inscription, 'Ann Wolferston hir booke may the 22 1680', written when she was a young child growing up in Statfold Hall in Staffordshire.[43] It also contains her father and uncle's inscriptions, followed by a series of letters of the alphabet. Someone, perhaps the uncle, has written 'A b c d e f g h I' after his signature and below this, in an erratic child's hand, we see Anne has copied out the letters. This book was being used to teach handwriting, or literacy, as well as for devotional purposes. The copy is also marked up throughout with passages underlined which seemed particularly important, and the front blank pages of the volume contain notes on the various texts preached at church. Finally, at the back of the book the empty leaves are used to record the length of the space between the kitchen door and the buttery door, along with the transcription of an advert for a specialist to cure deafness. There's a lot going on here: this book's readers are registering their engagement with multiple forms of knowledge, with varying degrees of sophistication. Another example of the variable levels of interpretative nuance evident within a single copy is a 1670 Bodleian copy of the Book of Common Prayer, bound together with an edition of the Authorized Version of the Bible.[44] There is no ownership inscription. The work has the phrase 'For ye new Brevor Bib'. written on the title page, and then within it, there are scattered pencil markings. These marks do not suggest an expert or particularly well-informed reader: next to a passage in the Book of Numbers 11:25–26, which describes God granting the holy spirit to the seventy elders, enabling them to prophesy, a reader has written the word 'WISDOM' in uneven capitals.[45] The only other significant marks are some amateur pencil drawings of scenes from the text in the margins.

In other kinds of religious texts we find readers attempting to summarize complex arguments in ways that show an intellectual grip rather different from that found in the work itself. A copy of Richard Allestree's *The Causes of the Decay of Christian Piety* (1674) at Townend house in Cumbria demonstrates the way in which Benjamin Browne, an early eighteenth-century yeoman farmer has systematically gone through the book, creating marginal glosses for its content.[46] These notes offer key words which reduce the main text to what is effectively a soundbite. In a section on divine power and God's evangelical gifts to Christian believers, Browne has written 'God helps'. [47] Elsewhere Richard Allestree offers his readers a rather dense discussion of historical examples of divine fury: 'So verifying even in a literal sense the Apostles affirmation, Heb. 12:29, Plutarch tells us when Fabius sackt Tarentum, he took not away their Images', followed by some phrases in Greek. Next to this, Browne writes the words 'fire' and 'Impiety'.[48] It seems as though he is using his notes to mark up key themes, in ways that do not always map on to the intention of the passage they accompany. Other topics identified in the margins are 'Churches' 'Hypocrisy', 'Hope' 'God & his people', 'excellency of things promised', and 'wiles of Satan'.[49] At one point he writes in large letters 'The Creator of Christian Religion' down the side of the margins at a right angle to the text.[50] These are notes which seem designed not to correct or dispute the content – which is the case with much marginal annotation in this period – but to reduce it into an easily navigable set of topics in ways probably not intended by the original author. Browne's annotations both here and in his copies of literary works, described later in this book, offer a fascinating insight into how complex printed texts might have been received and understood by non-elite readers, and what they perceived their role as interpreters to be.

## Print Solutions

Reader annotation was one response to the words of Scripture. Another was the use of the paratextual elements of printed forms of the Bible to aid comprehension. Most of the standard printed (and, more importantly, 'authorized') editions of the Bible were prefaced with short guides 'to the Christian reader' or the 'diligent Christian reader', which invoked the duties of careful and orthodox study. As editors and printers sought to present a clarified Bible for their users, the layout of the text became increasingly elaborate. Paratextual materials multiplied as a form of guidance and interpretative scaffolding for readers. The Geneva Bible was full of graphic interventions designed to aid

comprehension. Over the course of the sixteenth and seventeenth centuries, the introduction of page numbers, chapter headings, cross references, and concordances across a range of printed Bibles ensured that
the text was mediated for its readers through bibliographical features
which were designed to make the book easier to handle, read, and understand.[51] Yet at the same time, such textual additions also provided a
site for the staging of hermeneutic disputes between Catholics and
Protestants, Calvinists and Anglicans. The marginal annotations,
glosses, and summaries all offered a way in which editors and commentators could guide and shape the reading experience. And as they did
so, their interventions played out internecine interpretative battles, particularly between wings of the fractured Protestant church in this
period. Far from merely clarifying content for readers, the glosses of
sixteenth- and seventeenth-century Bibles presented defensive moves,
designed to head off incorrect interpretations by spelling out instead
what the Bible should signify. There was commonly a negative slant to
this commentary, in a body of explanatory material often dedicated to
showing what something did not mean, as much as what it did mean. [52]
Thus the elucidation of understanding was polemically bound up with
the representation of misunderstanding.

There are parallels here with the secular literature of the Augustan
period. Works such as Pope's *Dunciad* used their apparatus both to
clarify how to read the text and, at the same time, to show all the foolish
ways in which it might be misread. And we can see similar forces of
textual generation at work: just as the Bible grew more printed paraphernalia to accommodate misunderstanding and aid comprehension,
so too secular works generated more printed material. Editions of classical texts spawned acres of footnotes and learned apparatus in which
complex historical arguments were waged, dwarfing the original text;
Swift's *Tale of A Tub* was repackaged with supplementary footnotes
parodying its own detractors; scandal narratives, such as *The New Atalantis*, acquired printed keys to identify contemporary figures. Looking
across both religious and secular reading, it becomes clear that the forgotten history of misunderstanding was a key driver in the proliferation
of print in the early eighteenth century.

At the same time that the Bible itself swelled to accommodate extra explanation, we also see the rise of ancillary works designed to explicate its content. Some guides to lay scriptural study recommended particular works to aid the struggling reader: Samuel Blackwell, author of *Several Methods of Reading the Holy Scriptures in Private Seriously Recommended to Consideration* (1720), suggested 'Bishop Hall upon the hard Texts of the whole Divine Scripture' and added: 'If in the Use of these, and other Commentators and Criticks, special Reference shall be had to that Catalogue of Difficulties in Mr. *Fenton's Apparatus*, p.120 &c. it may be, it is hoped, of no small Advantage'.[53] One of the potential downsides of reading ancillary or companion works was that they might fuel the proliferation of meaning rather than clarifying things. People read their Scriptures, then a commentary on the text, then another, and by the end of it they were trying to navigate a whole sea of competing meanings. Puzzling over complex theological questions, Alexander Beresford writes to John Locke: 'Some of these Texts, which I have interpreted differently from Dr. Williams, I am pretty sure I have interpreted rightly. Some indeed I doubt of, but even as to those what I have here sett down do seem to me more suitable than any other interpretations that have yet occurrd to me'.[54]

If the Bible was difficult to interpret overall, the notion of figurative representation and application was especially tricky for readers. It seems to have lent itself to the image of the key that might 'unlock' inaccessible content. The idea of a 'key to meaning' was not exclusive to devotional matter – allegorical literary works had used them as a guide to interpretation. However, the growth of accessible non-specialist biblical commentary during the later seventeenth century created a more widespread use of the key in relation to scriptural explication. Edmund Calamy explained in his prefatory address to *Clavis Bibliorum*:

> *The Rabbins say, that there are* four Keyes *that are in Gods keeping.* The Key of the Clouds, The Key of the Wombe, The Key of the Grave, The Key of Food. *I may adde that there is a* fifth Key also in Gods bestowing, *which is* the Key of the Scriptures. *The God that made these books, can only* un-riddle *these books.*[55]

The idea of God as a riddle-maker, a forger of double meanings, is at the heart of another multiply published guide of this period, Benjamin Keach's *Tropologia: A Key to Open Scripture-Metaphors* (1681). *Tropologia* offers instruction on the way in which the figurative language of Scripture should be approached, and Keach began by acknowledging that Scripture abounded with truths presented in an opaque way:

> Tis obvious to every one's Observation, that the Holy Scripture abounds with *Metaphors, Allegories,* and other *Tropes* and *Figures* of Speech. Similitudes are borrowed from Visible Things; yea, heavenly Things are often called by the very Names that material or earthly Things are called, which is not to obscure or hide the meaning of them from us, but to accommodate them to our Understanding.[56]

What Keach offered the reader was ways of unpicking these figures of speech, which he broke down into paraphrases, allegories, types, and metaphors. He created tables showing the ways in which earthly metaphors both were like and unlike divine intention. It is interesting to see that figurative language was dealt with in a fairly instrumental way. Addressing the metaphor of 'The Word of God Compared to Light', Keach explained that:

> *In handling this* Metaphor *we will* (1.) *Shew what* Light *is.* (2.) *Give its various acceptations.* (3.) *Run the Parallel, and largely open the Properties of Gospel Light; Concluding with Practical Improvements upon that and some Dependant and Collateral Points.*[57]

The language here focuses on the extraction of meaning: 'handle', 'show', 'run the parallel', 'open the properties'. In this context, interpretation is shown to be an almost mechanistic exercise. Many of the examples in *Tropologia* rested on the difference between the words on the page and their application or, as Keach put it, describing Allegory: '*when one thing is said, another thing is understood*'.[58] But having accepted that there was a whole world of double meanings present in Scripture, one of the challenges was how to know whether something was *meant* to be unpicked or not. The guide aimed to assist those without expertise in hermeneutics or rhetorical theory to understand multi-layered texts, but there was a problem in identifying what needed decoding. There were, Keach said, some schoolmen and purported experts who sought to create hidden or secret meanings where none were intended, and to draw out of Scripture an exposition that was completely unfounded: 'This is indeed unsafe, and is justly reprovable; for this makes clear Scripture dark, and obtrudes Meanings on the Words never intended by the Spirit'.[59] Yet on the other hand, there were many examples of intention cloaked in figurative language in which it was the reader's job to tease out the intended meaning:

> An Exposition of *Allegorical* Scripture is the opening and expounding of some dark Scripture, (wherein the Mind of the Spirit is couched and hid under Figures, &c.) making it plain and edifying, by bringing out the Sence according to the meaning of the Holy Spirit in the place, tho at first it seems to bear no such thing. So *Mat.* 13. Christ expounds that Parable or Allegory, [. . .] calling the *Seed* the *Word*, and the *Sower* the Son of Man, &c. This way of expounding such dark Scriptures is both useful and necessary, and was often used as edifying by our Lord Jesus to his Disciples. Now 'tis this we speak of, which teacheth how to draw *plain Doctrines* out of *Metaphors*, *Allegories*, &c. and not to draw *Allegories* out of *plain Histories*.[60]

The distinction is confusing, as it must have been to early readers – how were they to know what was 'drawing plain Doctrines out of Metaphors' and what was 'drawing Allegories out of plain Histories'? And once Keach got onto the detail of how particular metaphors worked, it was even more bewildering. He tries to explain the image of leaves and flowers:

> A [*Leaf*,] because it easily falls and withers, carries the notion of vileness and vanity, Job 13.25. But in regard the leaves of some Trees are always green, under the similitude of such a Tree, eternal Life is described, Ezek. 47.12.
>
> [. . .]

A [*Flower*] denotes prosperity, Esa. 5.24. See Job 15.33. Job 30.12. But because a *Flower* is easily cut down, and withered, it is put for any thing that is, frail, uncertain or transitory, Esa. 28. 1, 4.[61]

Was a leaf the sign of vileness and vanity, or of eternal life? Was a flower an emblem of prosperity or uncertain frailty? In both cases, the image had extra-textual significatory value. The words on the page were clearly supposed to adumbrate another layer of meaning, but those words could point in markedly different directions.

These discussions of the impenetrability of biblical text also extended to the challenges of irony. It was commonly recognized that the Bible contained doublespeak. Anthony Horneck, the author of *Delight and Judgment, or the Great Assize . . . a Discourse Concerning the Great Day of Judgement* (1705) argued that there were many occasions on which

> those Sentences which sound like Exhortations, are perfectly Ironi-cal, or spoke by way of *derision*, as if we should say to a Man, *Go play the Fool, burn they Finger in the Candle, and see what thou wilt get by it*; whereby we do not mean that he should do so, but do rather express the silliness and simplicity of the thing, to make him avoid it: And such Ironical Expressions, or mocking Exhortations are very fre-quent in Scripture.[62]

Thomas Blackwell, the author of *Schema Sacrum, or, a sacred scheme of natural and revealed religion* (1710) showed the ways in which God himself sometimes deployed irony to convey his message. He alighted on one particular example of Ecclesiastes 11.9: '*Rejoyce, O Young Man in thy Youth, and let thy Heart chear thee in the Days of thy Youth, and walk in the Ways of thy Heart, and in the Sight of thine Eyes; but know thou, that for all these things, GOD will bring thee unto Judgement*'. Blackwell claimed that this 'grave and weighty Ironical Expostulation' showed that 'GOD justly Mocketh at Sinners, for the Unaccountableness of this Choice.'[63]

An emphasis on the divine uses of irony was also used in secular contexts to reassure those who feared that the use of figurative or non-truthful language was morally unacceptable. In a pamphlet on the ethics of lying, the Bristol clergyman Charles Brent argued that God himself practised this form of deception in exceptional circumstances: 'where a just occasion is given to be severe, and the expression is natural and pure, this way of reprehending with an Irony has great force and pungency with it, and is so far from being unjustifiable, that we find it sanctified by the unerring word of God'. Quoting from Genesis, he offered God's words to humanity after the fall in support of this point: 'Behold the Man is become like one of us, to know good and evil'. In this instance, Brent explains, God was saying the exact reverse of what he meant. But just in case that might cause readers to think of the Lord as duplicitous, he assured them that God was

> far from Lying too; for by the manner and turn of the expression, 'tis very evident, he intended both to speak, and to be understood in a quite contrary sence; his design was to awaken their hearts to a due concernment at their mistake; and, to do this, a direct and dry assertion would not have been so effectual[64]

It was a truly complicated business. Such discussions of the hermeneutics of biblical irony show an appreciation of the didactic value of double meaning, but also an awareness that it might need explication. As we shall see, a puzzled sense of 'I know this means something else, but what is that, and how should I interpret it?' was characteristic of many readerly responses to the satirical and allusive literature of the early eighteenth century, and the unstable forces of irony are visible everywhere, from novels to political pamphlets to verse satire.

## Social Comprehension

Keach's *Tropologia* is only one of several guides to unlocking the meanings of scriptural metaphor and allegory. Titles such as *Clavis Bibliorum, Clavis Cantici: A key to Catechisms* (1682), and *Clavis Cantici: An Exposition of the Song of Solomon* (1668) all drew on the idea that God's word needed releasing by the reader in order to have application to the individual's own life and experience. They are evidence of the ways in which uncertainty or concern about the right meaning and application of the text generated ancillary publications offering solutions, keys, or guidance on how to interpret. One of the answers to not understanding was evidently a growth in printed materials – a supplementation which offered both clarity, and, as *Tropologia* showed, further amplification of difficulty. But print wasn't the only solution to interpretative questions. The advice given in the prefatory pages of the Geneva Bible was to consult printed sources and after that to ask others for help with clarification:

> Take opportunities to
> Reade intepreters, if he be able
> Conferre with such as can open the Scriptures Acts 8. V.30, 31 &c
> Heare preaching, and to proue by the Scriptures that which is
>     taught, Acts 17 v.12.[65]

This suggestion of a social solution to a lack of understanding – that interpersonal consultation and discussion might be the answers – is present elsewhere in advice literature of the late seventeenth and eighteenth centuries. Byfield's guide to understanding Scripture counselled readers to collect their queries in a notebook, and then to ask relevant authorities for assistance in their resolution: 'As for example, would I observe all the hard places, which in reading I have a desire to know the meaning of, that so when I come into the company of Preachers, or able Christians, I might have profitable questions to propound: I would set it down thus'.[66] And a recourse to personal, social connections is also present in the mid-seventeenth-century manuscript 'Dr Merryweather's Directions to Students':

> Out of all Authours of note draw out hints for Discourse, and Questions
> upon Difficulties speculative or Practicall, which insert into small
> portable Paper Books, that you may never be at a loss for something
> whereby to draw out usefull communications, from Men of eminent or
> solid Learning & Piety, when at any time you fall into their Company.[67]

It's hard to gauge from this extract whether the 'hints and questions' referred to were to be manufactured as social prompts or were genuine uncertainties – but either way we see how a state of interpretative doubt could be seen as a form of social connection, and perhaps flattery. Marginal annotation might be a form of personal interaction between one reader and another, guiding towards correct forms of interpretation. A copy of the nonconformist John Owen's 1655 *Vindiciae Evangelicae,* a lengthy refutation of Socinianism, bears evidence of multiple hands, probably belonging to members of the Ryland family of Birmingham – prominent Unitarians and supporters of Joseph Priestley. The book shows them intervening and commenting on the text over an extended period of time during the century or so after the initial publication.[68] We can see from one cursive hand a concerted effort by a father to direct the reading of his son. The annotator, possibly John Ryland, has covered the margins with various intemperate comments and outbursts from 'Trifling nonsense Socinus!' to 'Adam was a Great Baby' to 'Ridiculous Grotius', but his words are evidently not designed merely for his own edification.[69] He writes next to Owen's discussion of false and sophistical interpretation of Scripture 'Mind this Son John', and against references to the false ways of Socinians 'Mind this my son John', 'Mark this', 'NB', 'NB', 'Mind this', and 'Here Stop'.[70] In places the annotation becomes one half of a conversation: 'My Son be a solid Scholar for Christs Sake! purely to serve and defend his Cause'.[71] As this example shows, marginal annotation could operate as a form of guided reading, in this case, shepherding young John towards the right application of the text.

This sociable and communal nature of incomprehension is certainly reflected in other secular contexts – early eighteenth-century familiar letters are full of pleas for help in resolving puzzling satires or works with hidden meaning. A 1697 letter from the Irish writer William Molyneux to John Locke is illustrative of numerous similar exchanges between friends and acquaintances:

> I have by me some Observations made by a Judicious friend of Mine on both Sir R. Blackmores Poems; if they may be anywise acceptable to Sir R. I shall send them to you; they are in the Compas of a sheet of Paper. And were it proper, I should humbly desire you to procure for me from Sir R. the Key to the Persons Names in both his Poems; Most of the first I have already; and a great Many in the second; but Many I also want which I should be very glad to understand.[72]

Sometimes we can see these conversations about meaning staged on the annotated pages of a text. One copy of Jonathan Swift's *Tale of a Tub*, a notoriously confusing satirical work, offers material evidence of the way in which readers might exchange explanation and acts of decoding between themselves.[73] The *Tale* is particularly interesting in the context of questions of scriptural hermeneutics because it is a work which showcases the follies of misreading of the Bible through allegory, while at the same time being famously misunderstood by its early readers. Readers transcribed points of interpretation into their own copies of the book, glossing the allegory and adding information that seemed to them central to understanding the satire. Or not. Ben Browne of Troutbeck marks at one point in his copiously annotated copy: 'I can't conjecture ye meaning of this tho' 'tis capable of sevrl Interpretations'.[74] The first printed key to the *Tale* did not appear until 1710, but it is clear that manuscript keys were in circulation before this point, which offered slightly differently phrased glosses on Swift's satire.[75] From another example, now in the Beinecke Library at Yale, we can see the way in which the exchange of information about what Swift's satire was supposed to mean became a kind of social currency.[76] A 1705 copy of the fourth edition presents its owner's transcriptions of his friend's annotations of the *Tale*.[77] On the blank inside front leaves the owner has written:

> These observations which I gott from a friend I thought so just and so agreeable to the authors design in writting this [. . .] that I have with very little alteration transcrib'd 'em as he gave 'em.[78]

The annotations, which often bear close similarity with those in the other surviving annotated copies, bear a personal tone: 'If I am nott mistaken this is in ridicule of ye too much affected simplicity of ye Kirk of Scotland'; 'as I think in imitation of a canting way'.[79] Within the marginal comments, we can see varying degrees of confidence in the friend's interpretations. Many of the notes in the margin seem to be transcriptions of the 'key' given by the friend. He indicates for example the allegorical references to 'Luther or Calvin' or symbolic representations of the Catholic love of image worship.[80] Elsewhere he notes points of approval, and it is unclear whose words these are: 'Here I can't chuse butt declare my admiration of Dr Swift in this passage for I don't believe ever any thing was ridicul'd with more Spirit'.[81] Yet there are some moments in which the owner clearly thinks his source has got it wrong and misread the text.[82] Early on in Swift's discussion of the brothers' dress, the annotator signals in the margin his doubts over the allegorical interpretation offered by the friend's key (figure 4):

> My friend with his pardon & leave has ta'en all this disputation about Suits in too literall a Sense for in my opinion it's to prepare us for what he is gooing to Say aboutt the Roman clergy who turn'd Every thing both in morality & in Religion to a vain ceremonious Shew.[83]

At the end of the book, with its incomplete Conclusion, the owner writes

> The Tale and my friends observations end att once, I've only difer'd from him in my applying all the Qualifications of the renowned Jack in a very Strict Sense to the Calvinist as most consonant to the author's design of their character, if any thinks itt more applicable to some other Sect, for my part I shall admire his dexterity & think him every bitt as good att handling ye Text of this book as Lord Peter that of his father's testament.[84]

This reader is one who sees very clearly the parallels between the challenges posed by the 'handling' of religious texts and those presented by Swift's allegorical prose satire, as he comments of his friend: 'I shall admire his dexterity & think him every bitt as good att handling ye Text of this book as Lord Peter that of his father's testament'. For this annotator, scriptural and secular decoding are closely aligned, and the world of biblical hermeneutics is very much comparable with the demands of the secular allegory offered up by Swift. The copy as a whole also offers a remarkable insight into the ways in which information and interpretation were a social currency which had particular value in a world of allegorical works and hidden meanings. The act of collaborative solution was probably part of the fun of the work itself, like doing the crossword with a partner or in a group. It seems important to consider that although some forms with hidden or cloaked meanings might seem to be

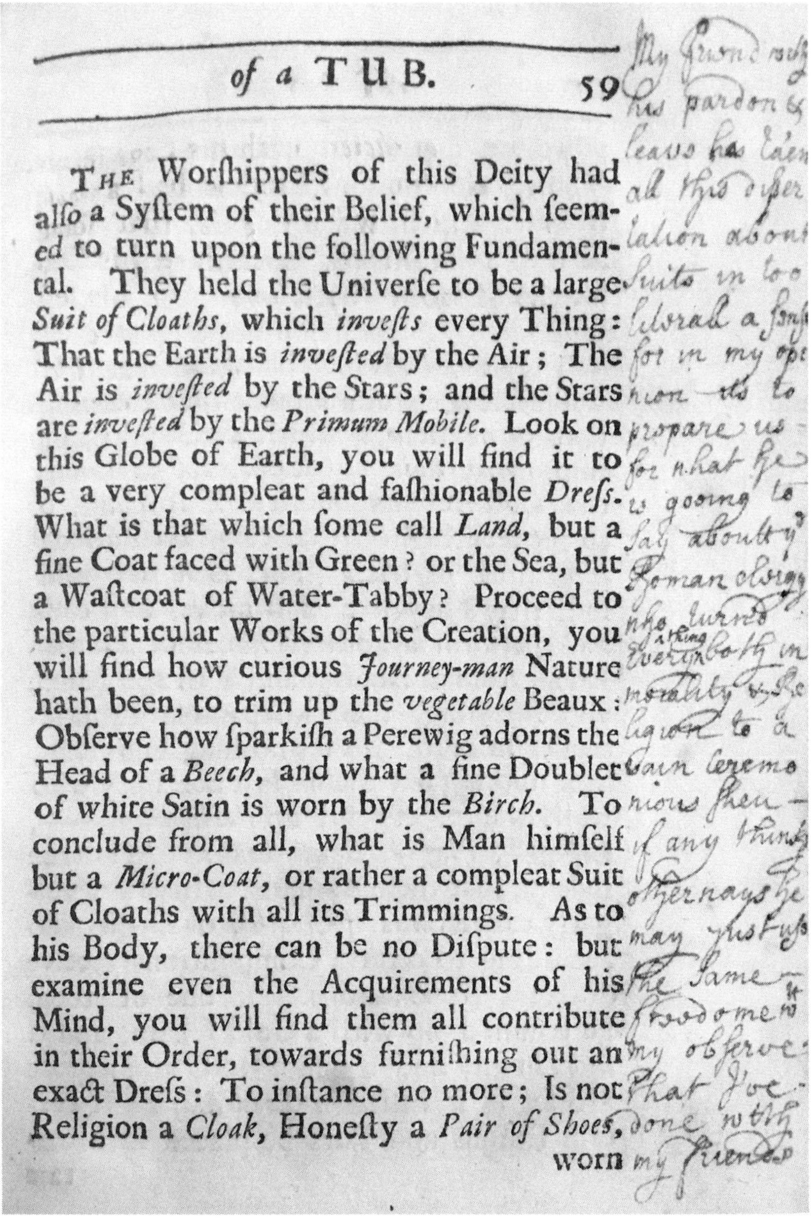

THE Worshippers of this Deity had
also a System of their Belief, which seemed to turn upon the following Fundamental. They held the Universe to be a large
*Suit of Cloaths,* which *invests* every Thing:
That the Earth is *invested* by the Air; The
Air is *invested* by the Stars; and the Stars
are *invested* by the *Primum Mobile.* Look on
this Globe of Earth, you will find it to
be a very compleat and fashionable *Dress.*
What is that which some call *Land,* but a
fine Coat faced with Green? or the Sea, but
a Wastcoat of Water-Tabby? Proceed to
the particular Works of the Creation, you
will find how curious *Journey-man* Nature
hath been, to trim up the *vegetable* Beaux:
Observe how sparkish a Perewig adorns the
Head of a *Beech,* and what a fine Doublet
of white Satin is worn by the *Birch.* To
conclude from all, what is Man himself
but a *Micro-Coat,* or rather a compleat Suit
of Cloaths with all its Trimmings. As to
his Body, there can be no Dispute: but
examine even the Acquirements of his
Mind, you will find them all contribute
in their Order, towards furnishing out an
exact Dress: To instance no more; Is not
Religion a *Cloak,* Honesty a *Pair of Shoes,*
worn

FIGURE 4. Jonathan Swift, *A Tale of a Tub. Written for the Universal Improvement of Mankind. The Fourth Edition Corrected* (London, 1705), Beinecke Rare Book and Manuscript Library, Yale University, Osborn pc265, p. 59.

aimed at an 'insider' with a superior level of interpretative skill or knowledge, the state of not understanding could also operate as a form of connection between readers.

The reading of the Bible framed questions about access, interpretation, and the role of misunderstanding within early modern print culture. While secular contexts – such as rhetorical education or classical theories of historiography – clearly informed contemporary concepts of the application and use of knowledge and exemplars, the discussion of religious reading was unique both in focusing on all kinds of literacies and in considering readerly difficulty as a matter requiring explicit guidance. The figurative and instructive function of stories, images, and types found in Scripture is comparable with much of the satirical literature of the early eighteenth century, which also relied on processes of analogical application in order to fulfil an intended purpose. Both kinds of text taxed their readers with making meaning. And in the proposed solutions to incomprehension – notetaking, supplementary guides, asking others – we gain insight into the ways in which readers approached difficulty, and the ways in which that difficulty might connect them together.

# 3

# The Classical Reader

I generally understand every thing I read, all but what's *Latin,* and
that I skip.

—'T.G.,' THE FEMALE TATLER, NO. 81, 9–11 JANUARY 1710

I am very sensible, *MADAM,* of the absurdity to speak Latin in a Ladies
presence, but I am sure you understand it; and for the sake of those
who do not, I will translate them after my way, that is somewhat
Paraphrastically.

—MATTHEW MORGAN, DEDICATION TO *A POEM
TO THE QUEEN UPON THE KING'S VICTORY IN
IRELAND, AND HIS VOYAGE TO HOLLAND,* 1691

NOWHERE ARE we more reminded of our distance from Augustan
readers than when we see the evident pleasure they took in the reworking and replaying of classical texts. It's pretty hard now to enjoy the
ingenuity of Horace speaking through the mouth of a coffee-house
gentleman, or Ovid rerun through contemporary rakish eyes. But
those neoclassical pleasures were also complex in their own time. Substantial critical and editorial work has revealed the depth and brilliance
of classical perspectives in the literature of the period and the degree to
which major and minor writers drew on and were inspired by ancient
models.[1] Many of these accounts have focused on elite male readers,
assuming those groups to be well versed in classical literature and

language in an era of bilingualism.[2] In his introduction to early eighteenth-century literature, Bonamy Dobrée described the writing of the period as dependent on knowledge of the Ancients, 'a scale of reference which the poets expected the reader to be able to share'.[3] But what exactly could these poets expect their reader to know?

The classical culture of Augustan England is complicated by the very varied legibility of the ancient world to contemporaries, and in exploring the limits of such knowledge we can begin to see that the question of what one needed to know in order to read well was a complex one. The evidence of primers, school syllabi, and correspondence all show us that there were many different levels of familiarity with classical culture. This chapter starts by exploring what this complex picture of literacy meant for female and non-elite readers in the period and how it might have shaped their encounters with classical references and classical texts. It then turns to a different context for thinking about understanding: the heated debates among elite readers and contemporary satirists over reading the works of the past. This was a period in which there was little agreement on what expertise even meant. What did you need to read the classics well? Intellectual debates about the Ancients and Moderns were shaking up ideas about who read best, and many of the works arising from that debate sought to promote insecurity and muddle. It follows from all this that our modern lack of familiarity with classical pretexts should not blind us to the fact that neoclassicism was not straightforward or assured in its own time. The hundreds of works that drew on ancient culture did so within a context in which literary and linguistic competency was highly variable, and in which the very notion of being a good reader of the past was a source of contention.

## Knowledge, Print, and Translation

As we know, the early eighteenth century saw a massive expansion of print, an explosion created in part by a desire to appeal to, and capitalize on, those without traditional education: women, the middling sort, and the culturally aspiring. This had profound implications for many aspects of literary culture, and in particular it drove a huge growth of translation, imitation, and paraphrase in this period: the English Short Title Catalogue lists over 7,600 titles published between 1700 and 1800 that include 'translated' as a keyword.[4] Translation meant many things. Vernacular renderings of Latin and Greek texts ranged from literal translations to loose reworkings to even looser paraphrases or imitations, and within these traditions it was possible to see the correlation between modern and classical texts from many dimensions. At the same time, the thriving genres of the period – the epic, mock-epic, pastoral, georgic, and satire – were all based on an implicit understanding of classical genres from ancient sources to neo-Latin forms, and their proponents often exploited the potential parallels and discrepancies between ancient and modern times. Yet many of the newer readers coming to these works were not reading the classics in the original, but in translation, or with a partial knowledge of Greek and Latin; their sense of the relationship between ancient culture and their own was often founded on texts already mediated by modern, English voices.

Translation was not the only printed aid for those lacking the skill or confidence to approach Latin and Greek texts. There were also halfway houses between original Greek or Latin and vernacular English: works which offered readers the opportunity to read classical works in the original by offering a form of linguistic hand-holding, taking them through a piece word by word. So, for example, *Clavis Virgilianæ: Pars Prima. A Numerical Key to the Bucolics of P. Virgilius Maro* (1715) advertised itself as a numerical key to Virgil, 'Shewing by Figures Answering to each Word in every Line, in what Order they ought to be taken, so as to Construe into good Sense; in a Method so easy, that a Learner of the meanest Attainment in the *Latin* Tongue, may be enabled to Construe his Lesson with Ease and Pleasure to himself'.[5] Although the title page suggests that the book is for the use of schools, the preface addresses itself to those outside the Master's pedagogical care, including 'those that not having that Advantage, would either add to what they have learned at School, or recover what by disuse they have lost'.[6]

This emphasis on utility in the development of works which aimed to make unfamiliar and potentially intimidating spheres of knowledge accessible is part of broader patterns described elsewhere in this book.[7] As we have seen, the growth of popular introductions to biblical interpretation put hermeneutics into the hands of semi-skilled laypeople, and, as we'll also find, the *Athenian Mercury* or the *Spectator* offered guidance in aesthetic and cultural matters for the uninitiated. A work such as *Clavis Virgilianæ* provided a service for those seeking to read classical Latin.[8] Numerous other titles addressed other forms of knowledge, previously the domain of the university-educated scholar. As John Gallagher and others have argued, the sixteenth and seventeenth centuries had seen a boom in education outside established institutions – a rise in autodidacticism and private educational provision – with the publications attendant on this:

> The vibrancy of early modern England's educational economy could be seen in the educational lectures given in coffee-houses, the private schools springing up and offering instruction in handwriting and arithmetic, and the growing number of women's boarding schools teaching pastrywork or needlework alongside music, deportment, and languages. Language-learning was central to this changing educational culture: it brought vernacular teaching to new audiences in new spaces, and relied on the labour of those often excluded from more prestigious educational environments, such as immigrants and women.[9]

By the middle of the eighteenth century, it was possible to find introductory, digested accounts of more or less any area of intellectual life, including classical languages and literature – forms of knowledge once thought synonymous with being a formally educated gentleman. These introductory works give us some insight into the varied levels of classical literacy enjoyed by readers. In her influential *Essay to Revive the Antient Education of Gentlewomen* (1673), Bathsua Makin – herself an experienced teacher, former royal tutor, and prodigious polyglot – argued for women's capacity to learn and offered common-sense advice on the kinds of books that might help young women learn grammar and classical languages.[10] Her summary of the kind of syllabus she was advising – and in fact, that she offered to teach at her newly founded school in Tottenham High Cross – gives some sense of the limits of classical competency in an aspirant student of this kind. She recommends a simple course of learning a thousand sentences in six to nine months, and dismisses the idea that students might try to learn a whole language and its grammar:

> To Construe the *Grammar*, and to get it without-Book, is at least the task of two years more; and then, it may be, it is little understood, until a year or two more is spent in making plain Latin. My Reader, it may be, thinks I have forgot, or purposely omitted to allow time for these things, without which nothing can be done.[11]

Having dispensed with the idea of learning the whole language, she explains the pointlessness of extensive study:

> to commit the very *Accidence* and *Grammar* to memory, requires three or four years, sometimes more, (as many can witness by woful experience) and when all is done, besides *declining Nouns*, and *forming Verbs*, and getting a few words, there is very little advantage to the Child. This being supposed, it's not likely Children of ordinary Parts should in so short a time be improved in any competent measure in the Latin Tongue.[12]

Children 'of ordinary parts' would not much benefit from declensions and verb conjugations, and besides, there was the danger that even after all this, students would still not have much to show for it:

> If we should dance that wild-Goose-chase usually led, it would require longer time; ordinarily Boys learn a Leaf or two of the *Pueriles*, twenty Pages of *Corderius*, a part of *Esop's Fables*, a piece of *Tullie*, a little of *Ovid*, a remnant of *Virgil, Terence*, &c. and when all this is done, they have not much above half so many words as this little *Enchiridion*, the *Janua* [her favoured pedagogical model], supplies them with.[13]

Bathsua Makin's accounts remind us of some of the realities of classical knowledge below an elite level during this period. Nodding acquaintance with the major works of a few celebrated authors and a thousand sentences will have been the limits of many early eighteenth-century readers' knowledge, placing a ceiling on their ability to understand all of the complex and playful commentary of many of the imaginative neoclassical works of the period. Surviving schoolbooks from middling sort students offer some indicators of the nature of language learning at school level: the Brownes of Troutbeck in Cumbria, the family of yeoman farmers, not only left behind a collection of annotated books in their farmhouse, but also an extensive collection of papers, account books, and diaries. Among these are some of the schoolbooks of the early eighteenth-century Brownes and their near neighbours in the village, the Birketts. It is not yet clear where the children went to school: there was the famous grammar school at Hawkshead, but it seems more likely that the boys went to a more local school at Windermere or Bowness or even Troutbeck itself.[14]

The notebooks of Ben Browne Sr (b.1664) and George Birkett (b.1711) show us the ways in which their classical education might have worked and what its limits were.[15] Both notebooks are centred on inscribing pairs of Latin and English phrases taken from classical Latin literature – from Horace, Virgil, and others (Browne) and from Terence (Birkett). In Browne's notebook, dated 1680, when he was 16, these phrases are labelled *phrases collectae*, while in Birkett's, which must have been compiled some forty years later, they are *formulae loquendi*. This focus on classical phrases rather than grammatical exercises or non-classical texts reflects the humanist grammar school curriculum that had developed during the sixteenth century: after covering the rudiments of grammar, this primarily centred on teaching Latin through classical texts, because this was the best way to teach good Latin style.[16] Horace, Virgil, and Terence were standard school authors. It seems most likely that both notebooks were compiled in school contexts, or at least following familiar school practices. Browne's book suggests that he was given English sentences that were designed to be translated into Latin using phrases from a particular classical text. The errors within the pairing of phrases show an uneven grasp of the Latin: so, for example, 'The Scotts cames [*sic*] in swarmes. Scoti angliam ut æstivis effusus nubibus irrupuere'. The phrase 'ut æstivis effusus nubibus' is from Georgics

4.312–13, although the reference to Scots is not from Virgil.[17] The Latin given here is incorrect – it omits a word from Virgil ('imber' ('storm') after 'nubibus') that would make this accurate. This appears to be an attempt to say 'the Scots broke into England like [a storm] pouring from summer clouds', embedding the Virgil phrase in the translation. Birkett's work shows less evidence of active translation: we see him copying Latin and English from a single printed source, most likely *Terence in English. Fabulæ Comici Facetissimi et Elegantissimi Poetæ Terentii Omnes Anglicæ Factæ*, a work with translations of Terence into English by Richard Bernard. It was first printed in 1598, most recently printed in 1641, and designed as a Latin teaching device.[18] Birkett's verbatim copying of sections of the text suggests that he thought it was valuable to copy down these phrases, but not that he was necessarily able to translate independently by himself.

The kinds of limited skills evident in both Bathsua Makin's schooling and the Troutbeck notebooks was nonetheless something that many middling parents and aspirant students wanted to acquire. Tuition in the classics was part of the education on offer to students in a range of non-elite contexts: the *Post Boy* of September 1700 contains an advertisement for a school near Somerset House on the Strand offering education in 'the Rudiments of the Latin, French and English Tongues, Writing and Arithmetick' at ten shillings a quarter, or twelve pence a week; while '[a]pprentices, and such as are grown to maturity, may be instructed in Arithmetic, &c. Suitable to their Trades and Employments, between 5 and 8 these Winter Evenings'.[19] There were evidently multiple competencies among eighteenth-century readers, depending on the speaker's age, gender, origin, and occupation.[20]

It follows from this that if we encounter the witty, learned, heavily referential neoclassical satires of the early eighteenth century and read them assuming that they were immediately and wholly accessible to all their first readers we are probably wrong. Early eighteenth-century readers cannot necessarily have been secure in their ability to understand the books they read, and they were not necessarily encouraged to feel secure. In the judgemental margins of works of the time, readers commonly mock their contemporaries' linguistic failures. The Catholic

William Blundell, whose commonplace books appear in the previous chapter, was unable to attend university because of his faith, and he professed his own poor Latin. However, this didn't stop him from repeatedly commenting upon errors and infelicities in the authors that he read and creating sections in his commonplace book in which to list examples of bad Latin.[21] He regularly calls out 'pityfull latin', and having noted 'sondry faults' in Thomas May's *Breviary*, a history in Latin of the English civil war and parliament, he went on to comment that 'It is very remarkable that the English in this age have no great tallent in writing latin prose'.[22] Alexander Pope's copies of pamphlets by contemporary writers are also peppered with snarky comments about his rivals' lack of learning. His edition of the anonymous *Gulliver Decypher'd*, a critique of Swift's prose satire, contains a mean little list of its author's malapropisms and typos, including the mistranscription of βασιλευς as ΒΑΣΙΛΙΣ.[23] In his copy of Matthew Concanen's *A Supplement to the Profund* (1728), Pope again laid into an adversary's lack of Greek. In his work, Concanen had questioned Pope's erudition, and in his notes on the *Supplement*, Pope went to town in exposing his adversary's limited classical knowledge, writing of Concanen 'his remarks and his observations proceed almost all from his own ignorance of ye Greek'.[24] The reality was that Concanen was a barrister, later Attorney General of Jamaica, and had in all likelihood more extensive university education than the Catholic Pope (Concanen's early life is unknown). Calling out another writer for substandard learning served the dual purpose of discrediting the publication and shoring up Pope's own contested credentials as a translator of the classics.

A sensitivity to a potential lack of classical fluency was particularly evident in relation to female writers and readers. Periodicals of the time poked fun at women who wanted acquaintance with classical culture but lacked the language to master it. *The Censor* of April 1715 sketched a satirical portrait of a lady who loved to listen to Greek:

> She has indeed a great many odd Humours, and innocent Vanities, which it would be ridiculous to offer at correcting in One of her Age; tho' I am in some hopes of getting off from a Task she has oblig'd me

to perform for these Ten Years together, which has been to read to her an Hour once a Week out of some *Greek* Author. 'Tis true, she does not understand a Tittle of my Lecture, but admires it for a fine sounding Language; and Madam *Dacier* her self cannot be in more Transports than my *Cousin* is upon my reading of *Homer*: When any one rallies her upon this Subject, she only replies, she has as much Reason as the Ladies who are pleas'd with *Italian* Opera's.[25]

A letter to the *Female Tatler* of January 1710 also featured the avid female reader without classical learning: 'Ladies, I Am a Young Gentle-woman that take great delight in Plays and Opera's, and read the *Tatlers* both *Male* and *Female* as constantly as they come out. I generally understand every thing I read, all but what's *Latin*, and that I skip'.[26] Even in the formal and flattering contexts of dedicatory prose such constraints were acknowledged. An address to an aristocratic female patron in a panegyric from 1691 reads: 'I am very sensible, *MADAM*, of the absurdity to speak Latin in a Ladies presence, but I am sure you understand it; and for the sake of those who do not, I will translate them after my way, that is somewhat Paraphrastically'.[27]

Countless examples from women's correspondence of the period shows the gendering of this concern about comprehension:

> We separate after dinner till tea calls us together at half an hour after six, and then Homer's *Iliad* takes place; Miss Hamilton reads the notes and translates all the Greek words and passages as she goes along, with so much ease that the first day she read (till I looked over her and saw the Greek characters) I thought they *had been* all translated! The Dean now makes her read the Greek first, and so we have the pleasure of hearing that fine-sounding language, not without some mortification at not understanding it.[28]

> 'Yesterday a charming man dined here – a clergyman, his name Bighton, an enthusiast in botany [...] I sat by in silent admiration, like the lady who "loved to hear Greek though she did not understand it".'[29]

Voltaire writes to a correspondent: 'If you load this allegory with another allusion to the first book of Virgil, it will not be understood by the

women, and by the young trippers [coxcombs]. Even many men of letters in reading it will be at a stand for a little while till they remember
the passage of Virgil. [. . .] T'is not a single *emistiche* known by every
body that strikes a full light on the mind of the reader'.[30] And there were
those who recognized that a lack of classical literacy made other areas
of potential knowledge inaccessible to them. Elizabeth Bury, a self-
taught nonconformist diarist, reportedly rose at four every morning to
pursue studies in Hebrew, medicine, mathematics, French, music, history, divinity, and philology. Yet in an edition of her writings published
after her death, her husband wrote that

> She would often regret, that so many *Learned* Men should be so un-
> charitable to her *Sex*, as to speak so little in their *Mother-Tongue* and
> be so loath to assist their *feebler Faculties,* when they were any wise
> *disposed* to an accurate Search into Things curious or profitable, as
> well as others; especially (as she often argued) since they would all
> so readily own, *That Souls were not distinguishable by Sexes.* And there-
> fore she thought it would have been an *Honourable Pity in them to
> have offered something in Condescention to their Capacities, rather than
> have propagated a Despair of their Information to future Ages.*[31]

There were many readers, particularly women, without confidence
or facility in classical language and literature who nonetheless wanted
to engage in the worlds of cultural and literary debate, as well as the
worlds of knowledge opened up by linguistic fluency.[32] And the assumption of an ignorance of classical languages and literature, signifying
lack of access to higher forms of education, became a frequently employed sign of the common denominator.[33] While, as we have seen,
many texts were misunderstood by their readers in ways that cannot be
explained solely by factors of gender and class, these characteristics
were nonetheless influential in shaping responses to classical reference
points.

So what did these kinds of readers do when they encountered classical literature? Some of their responses can be traced in surviving marginal annotation and amateur writing. The books annotated by Anne
Wolferstan might give some insight into how ancient texts were

understood by the self-taught or informally educated. Anne Wolferstan was the granddaughter of the Staffordshire bibliophile Frances Wolfreston, a gentry reader whose sizeable book collection – a large proportion of which took the form of drama, romance, and fictional literature – has recently come to light across a range of British and American research libraries. As one of the largest surviving collections amassed by an Englishwoman of non-aristocratic status, Frances Wolfreston's books offer new insights into the history of early modern women's reading.[34]

Although Anne Wolferstan was only three when her grandmother died, she seems to have inherited both access to some of her books and an enthusiasm for recording her reading on the pages of her collection. Anne's annotations, like those of her grandmother, are suggestive of the ways in which amateur female provincial readers encountered literary works and the kinds of interpretation they performed – readings often at odds with the more scholarly or professional commentary cited in histories of the period. Wolferstan's inscribed copy of John Dryden's edition of the *Satires of Juvenal and Persius* (1693) gives us a glimpse of what that world of amateur classical reading might have looked like in late seventeenth-century Cheshire. Anne received the book at the age of twenty as a gift from a local physician, Phineas Fowke.[35] Like many women of her class and era, she was likely not to have been educated in Latin, but she would have studied classical literature and history. Dryden's translation was explicitly aimed at readers with a similar knowledge base: in the prefatory pages, he explains that he wrote for 'those Gentlemen and Ladies, who tho they are not Scholars are not Ignorant: Persons of Understanding and good Sense; who not having been conversant in the Original, or at least not having made *Latine* Verse so much their business, as to be Critiques in it'.[36] Further on in the volume, he goes on to address directly his female readers, reassuring them in the context of the misogynistic satire VI, a catalogue of the vices of Roman women: '*Whatever his* Roman *Ladies were, the* English *are free from all his Imputations*'.[37]

We might wonder what the young Anne made of this pointed commentary on female reading experience, or of Juvenal's cataloguing of female vice. In fact, her annotations offer us no idea on these matters.

What we find in her notes, which almost all precede the text itself, is evidence of the way in which she read the book on her own terms. She read it not as a literary rendition of familiar classical satire but as a series of references to classical history which could be cross-checked against other sources. Like the genteel female readers described by Amanda Vickery and Roey Sweet, Anne Wolferstan seems to have been schooled in classical history, rather than adept in classical languages.[38] Both sides of the flyleaf and the half-title page of her copy of Dryden's translation are covered in notes under the headings: 'The name of the 40 pagan emperours of Rome with their several mottos'; 'The names of the 32 Christians Eastearn Greeks & their Mottos'; and 'The Names of the 25 Western Franks with their several mottos &'. Why has she written this information on her satires? How does it help understand them? Her notes on classical history are taken from Mathias Prideaux's *An Easy and Compendious Introduction for Reading All Sorts of Histories* (1655, 1672), a work that described itself as a starting point for readers who wanted to know about history. In his preface, Prideaux, 'sometime Fellow of Exeter Colledge in Oxford', said that his introductory book was designed 'to lead thee to larger Volumnes'.[39] Anne seems to have used a run of pages of this encyclopaedic digest to gloss her copy of Dryden's *Satires*. It is not an interpretative response that provides us with much evidence of her understanding of the literary qualities of the translation, the texts themselves, nor their appeal for a young woman reader. It turns the satires into a series of references to classical history. Is this reading or misreading? It certainly shows that people read books in ways perhaps unanticipated by their authors, their approach shaped by class and gender.

My emphasis so far on the partial exclusion of women from classical culture should not obscure the fact that there were also many male readers who had, at best, a patchy understanding of the classics. There were the self-taught, those who had forgotten whatever they had learnt in formal settings, and those who had experienced the kind of limited syllabus described by Bathsua Makin and evidenced by the Brownes and Birketts of Troutbeck.[40] As we admire the assured classical joking of the early eighteenth-century literary canon, we should also be mindful of the experiences of those who half got the joke or the classical allusion, and the way many satires played with an anxiety about the right kind of learning. For a variety of reasons, the everyday use of Latin, the great *lingua franca* of the medieval period, was on the wane.[41] Despite the number of hours and years dedicated to Latin on the school curriculum, it was a complaint of educationalists from the mid-seventeenth century onwards that the considerable linguistic apprenticeship in schools guaranteed only a mediocre output in terms of pupils' abilities in written and spoken Latin, let alone Greek.[42] Even educated English readers were less likely to have fluency than they did a century before, and yet this is the era of the great love affair with classical translation, imitation, parody, and play.[43] Latin and Greek remained at the heart of university education and European culture throughout the period, but the assumption that, for example, even elite and well-educated English writers would continue to write in neo-Latin as a primary form of cultural exchange was unquestionably in decline.[44]

To understand reading wrong in terms of the classics, it's worth recognizing two competing forces at work in the early eighteenth century. One was the rise of neoclassicism, as seen in the zealous promotion of post-Restoration culture as a new Augustan age, the growth of interest in and access to classical texts, antiquities, and knowledge, the sense of emulative reverence of that past.[45] And the other force was the democratization of literature, which involved new readers and new points of access to the world of culture, including those without an extensive formal education. So it was that a period of intense interest in how the classics might be made to speak to contemporary society was one in which, for a range of reasons, the reader's linguistic competence could not be relied upon. Some of this disconnect between literary fashion and classical literacy can be seen in amateur writing. The surviving evidence of middling sort and self-educated readers of this period are scanty – we have far more sense of the ways in which elite readers encountered the literary culture of the period.[46] But even within the limited records that do remain, there are striking case studies of readers who seem to have wanted to be part of a world of witty jokes and classical allusion even though they were without the intensive formal education that we might assume to be essential to that engagement.

A particularly intriguing example of this kind of approach is John Cannon, an exciseman and writing master living in the Somerset Levels in the first two decades of the century. Cannon left behind an extraordinary illustrated manuscript journal (figure 5), recording his daily life, intellectual interests, and reading habits.[47] His carefully transcribed *Chronicles*, covering the period 1684–1733, reveal a man who, as his editor says, was hungry for knowledge, even if that knowledge often made him scornful of those around him who knew less than he did.[48] Cannon left school in his early teens and worked as a shepherd, reading books under hedges and gradually acquiring knowledge through subscription-order periodicals and newspapers: 'so from a schoolboy I became a plowboy, from a plowboy to an Exciseman, from an Exciseman a Maltster from a Maltster to an almost nothing except a Schoolmaster, so that I might be called the tennis ball of fortune or as the motto in the almanac'.[49] Cannon was sceptical of the idea of learning for its own sake:

Any artisan whatever, if he knew the secret and mistery of his trade may truly be called a learned man & the usefullest sort of learned men. For without them we might want the necessary accommodations of life & commerce with other nations, by which this island grows wealthy at home and formidable abroad, & such ought to be preferred with respect to the subsistence of a country before the polymathists that stand poring all the day in a corner upon a moth-eaten author and converse only with dead men.

[...]

There is not a simpler animal and a more superfluous member of a state than a mere scholar, a self-pleasing student who is *Telluris Inutile Pondus*.[50]

But despite scoffing at the superfluous and moth-eaten corners of scholarship, he was nonetheless keen to display his own learning throughout the *Chronicles*. There is no evidence of his knowledge of Greek, but Latin was a part of Cannon's literary and professional life, and through his transcriptions we can gain some insight into the importance Latin held for him, despite the fact he doesn't appear to have had

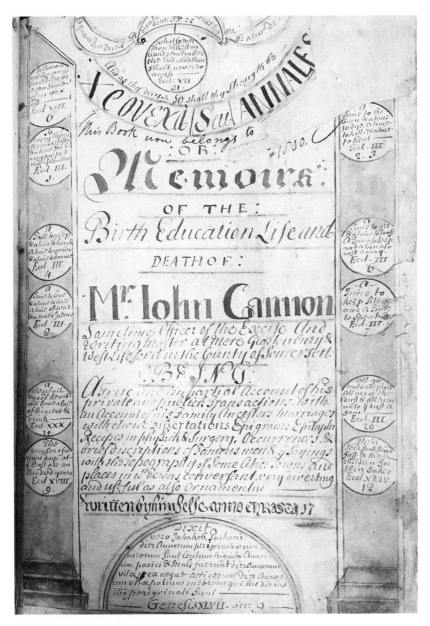

FIGURE 5. The title page from John Cannon's *Xρονεχα seu Annales*, 1741–42. Somerset Heritage Centre, Taunton, MS DD/SAS/C1193/4. f. ii. By kind permission of the Somerset Archaeological and Natural History Society.

much knowledge of the language. Cannon records that as a schoolmaster, he recommended a manual called Mr Garretson's *The School of Manners* (fifth edition, 1726). From this source he copied out in his *Chronicles* parallel columns of Latin and English, consisting of ninety-five Erasmian precepts concerning all aspects of conduct, from duty to God and parents to table manners, discipline, and social behaviour. The Latin in this transcription is erratic, and some of the translations are either mistakenly copied or bowdlerized. For example, No. 51, 'Coram aliis manum ad partem usitate velatam ne admoveas' ('Do not scratch your private parts in company'), is translated as 'Sing not nor hum in thy mouth while thou art in company'.[51] What's probably happened here is that Cannon has copied out the columns of Latin and English from Garretson, but he has misaligned them, not noticing that the translation doesn't match the original.[52] It's an example which shows how the elite use of Latin texts moved through the social scale – in this case Erasmian strictures first intended for courts and great households were here presented as a series of mistranscribed rules for Somerset schoolboys. Moreover, while Cannon wanted to draw on this educational material for his pupils, his own grasp of Latin does not appear to have been good enough to enable him to spot the mistranslation.

Much of what Cannon writes down in Latin and neo-Latin is copied from print sources. In June 1737 he takes from the *Gentleman's Magazine* an original 'peculiar Latin satire on the first Gin Act'; shortly afterwards he copies out neo-Latin enigmas, in the form of 'The true origin of Life and Death Griphology'.[53] Sometimes his transcriptions demonstrate fairly basic errors, once again suggesting that he didn't have a very functional knowledge of the language. A short section of biblical material from Zechariah 5:3–4 is reproduced in Latin and English, and shows confusion over some fundamental grammar: *superficium* for *superficiem*, *terra* for *terrae, consumam* for *consumat*.[54] Cannon doesn't have the linguistic skills to identify a third declension noun, a genitive form, or a third-person verb form. And elsewhere, as he copies out neo-Latin verse, he does not lay the lines out in the correct way: the elegiac couplets that he writes down are made up of alternating lines of hexameters and pentameters, in which the pentameters would conventionally have been indented. The fact that Cannon doesn't set the verse in this way when he copies the lines out, even though this practice was widespread in the manuscript and print culture of the time, further indicates a lack of familiarity. But, at the same time, the fact that the former ploughboy took it on himself to transfer all this material into his illustrated *Chronicles* shows that he wanted to participate in the kind of classical textuality that we tend to associate with elite university-educated groups. Latin is linked to authority and gravitas through the *Chronicles*: the neo-Latin poem Cannon transcribes is 'highly deserving of a place in my Memoirs'.[55] He copies out passages from the book of Ezekiel in Latin as a response to 'having been grossly abused' by Mary Down and William Nicholls, and although the surrounding pages of the journal are hurriedly written and scuffed, the biblical anathema he transcribes here to accuse his neighbours is meticulously copied out in a double column, with Latin on the left and English on the right.[56] Classical culture became, for him, a form of self-defence and self-fashioning, and this fits with habits elsewhere in the journal in which Cannon is interested in language and writing as a form of authority. In March 1738 he offers a summary of something called 'The Quaker's Tea Table, or Tea Spattered and China Scattered' – a four-part satire on modern luxury which he had copied for a neighbour.[57] This is followed by reflections on beer and wine drinking, with a Latin catalogue of their respective symptoms and diseases. In relation to this, he says he has couched the particulars 'under technical words, being more comprehensive [though] a little less intelligible to such persons who are [?not] at all likely to consider this subject as a physician'.[58] Latin forms part of a world of cultural gravitas alongside such technical terms, enabling Cannon to demonstrate his education and status.

## Augustan Parallels

The curious case of John Cannon and his Latin, more useful to him as a form of generalized cultural authority than a known language, speaks to the way in which readers handled broader forms of connection between contemporary and ancient culture. The past imbued the present with a seriousness that was highly valued. The arts of translation and imitation in this period worked in a similar way and depended on the ability not only to translate passages of text or recognize individual correspondence between figures and places, but also to grasp wider cultural parallels and comparisons. In the case of Cannon, this meant copying out text he did not fully understand to give credibility to his work. But elsewhere the broader cultural links were deployed in acts of translation and imitation. The impact of Pope's *Imitations of Horace*, or Samuel Johnson's *London* or *Vanity of Human Wishes*, rested on the reader's awareness of the original in its general significance, as well as a one-to-one correspondence between individual figures.[59]

Yet looking at some of the annotations to neoclassical works of this time we find readers whose approach to imitation signals a more limited mode of engagement. It is evident that not everyone came to anglicized versions of the classics with a holistic sense of the parallels between Augustan Britain and ancient Rome. One example of this kind of approach can be found in an anonymous reader's annotations to Pope's 1734 *Imitation of the First Satire of the Second Book of Horace*.[60] Pope's *Imitation* is a creative reworking of Horace's original, which takes the concept of the satirist's *apologia* found in the original and reworks it into a sophisticated defence of his own practice and articulation of his literary, political, and religious values. It draws not only on Horace's poem but on the *apologiae* of Juvenal and Persius.[61] Pope responds to contemporary criticism by offering a series of statements about who he is as a poet and what satire can achieve, at the same time that the text's facing page presentation of the original Latin and contemporary English draw attention to its author's facility in adapting his source. However, the reader of the Clark library copy does not seem to engage at all with the broader context, but instead reads the poem as a series of references. So, for example, they write 'Hervey' over the reference to 'Lord Fanny', gloss 'Sir Richard' as 'Blackmore', and clarify that 'Shippen' is 'William Shippen'.[62] Next to the line 'From furious *Sappho* scarce a milder fate', they have noted 'Generly applyed to Lady Mary W'.[63] Where there are lacunae in the poem, with letters substituted for blanks or asterisks, they fill in the correct names: 'B**ll' becomes 'Budgell' and

'M**o' becomes 'Marlbro'.[64] Pope's *Imitation* is a poem which establishes a complex set of correspondences between one culture and another, in which the voices of past writers are transmuted into a powerful form of self-positioning for the leading satirist of the age. But the annotations in this copy betray none of that: it is read as a guessing game that needs to be solved. While this is but a single example, it suggests that some of the interactive reading habits described elsewhere in this book, the habits of decoding and reference spotting, might have come to shape the way readers engaged with all kinds of literature, encouraging them to approach what they came across as a puzzle that needed unlocking.

## Who Are the Experts?

So far I have been distinguishing between those with expertise in ancient languages, and those without that skill, who might have enjoyed a partial fluency. For those in the latter group it must have been hard to access the full effect of texts which played with classical forms, references, and languages to make their meanings. Yet as elsewhere in the literary culture of the period, the difference between knowing and not knowing was still more complicated than this. Because what was expertise, when it came down to it? This was an era when the very nature of learned prowess was up for debate. As we have seen, the early eighteenth century was a time of profound change in the understanding of who had access to culture. And concerns about the right kind of reader and reading were also applied to the writings of the past, forming an essential context for thinking about what it might have meant to read well – or badly – at this time.

To understand the representation and practice of misreading during this era, we also need to explore the textual battlegrounds of the intellectual elite, which were littered with charges of misreading, ignorance, pedantry, and folly. The battle of the 'Ancients and Moderns' was a literary and historiographical controversy over the relative superiority of ancient classical culture and modern achievement. It involved rethinking not only the virtues of ancient and modern literary forms but also the ways in which they were understood and explicated. The role of the professional scholar – and a concurrent emphasis on specialist, historicist knowledge as a way of understanding older literature – are features of an academic approach that are now a norm, but which three hundred years ago proved fiercely controversial and distasteful to those educated in an earlier tradition of amateur, humanist approaches to the text.[65] The rise of the professional scholar prompted a host of anxieties and frustrations provoked by the handover of interpretative power from the gentleman amateur to the trained philological and textual editor. Who ought to have authority over the meaning of the past? What was a good reading of a classical text? Opinion was divided, and out of those divisions emerged not only a series of polemical skirmishes but also a series of satirical works which exploited a thematic preoccupation with interpretation and misinterpretation. The role of the scholar as guide and interpreter was mocked mercilessly in parodic acts of wilful misunderstanding which showcased the ways in which readers could get things hopelessly and gloriously wrong. Paratexts designed to clarify were used to increase muddle and misunderstanding. And the evidence of contemporary reception shows us that many historical readers were left behind – in the hall of mirrors of the satirical attack on pedantry there was considerable confusion about what was really meant and who knew best.

## The Ancients and Moderns

The Ancients and Moderns debate, or the 'Querelle des Anciens et des Modernes', began in France in the late seventeenth century. In some ways it opened up ideological divisions which had long been implicit in Renaissance humanism. The Renaissance rediscovery of the classical past, and its embrace of the aesthetics, morality, and rhetoric of those older cultures, was based in part on the idea that classical values were timeless, a benchmark against which modernity could be measured (and usually found wanting). But at the same time, the retrieval of classical art and literature also seemed to demand a fuller understanding of the culture from which it was produced, thus sowing the seeds for the

first forms of philological enquiry and the retrieval of historical information about societal practices. And that kind of knowledge often showed
how *unlike* modern times the Ancients really were.[66]

These two sets of ideas – the transcendent and the historically
specific – were clearly in tension with one another, and they began to
take concrete form in the opposition between a group of writers and
thinkers asserting the superiority and untouchable brilliance of ancient
achievement (led by Nicolas Boileau), and an opposing group who argued that recent achievements in science and scholarship could rival the
wonders of days past (as articulated by Charles Perrault and Bernard de
Fontenelle). Each side produced substantial treatises to justify their
position, and their beliefs were also reflected in editions and translations, in the material and textual presentation of classical culture. Representing the Ancients, Anne Dacier's influential translations of Homer
demonstrated her commitment to the moral and aesthetic qualities of
Homer's poetry. She dismissed the idea of the superiority of modern
achievement, as well as the Moderns' idea that to be fully understood,
Homer needed to be recontextualized in the pagan and primitive mores
of his own age. And, on the other side, Bernard de Fontenelle published
alongside his 1688 collection of pastoral poems a 'Discourse on the ec-
logue and nature of pastoral poems', in which he argued that classical
forms should not be mere pale imitations of the past, but be updated to
the age in which they were produced. As this summary suggests, the
debate was partly about competing attitudes towards the making of
meaning in books. Was it the editor or translator's role to show the enduring aesthetic qualities of a classical work? Or were they supposed to
be doing something rather different, more like textual archaeology, ex-
cavating the world from which a literature emerged, perhaps using conjectural emendation and other interventions to correct the errors in
transmission that flawed great works? Out of these very different views
of what it meant to read the past well emerged a literature preoccupied
with the ways readers of the literature of the past might get things
wrong.

The debates at the heart of the Battle of the Books were circulating
in the French academy during the final decades of the seventeenth

century, and they took pronounced form in England around the turn of the century with a series of printed spats about the authenticity of a set of classical texts known as the 'Epistles of Phalaris'. The story of that fight reveals a lot about changing ideas concerning who had knowledge and who didn't. The combatants on the English side of the Ancients were the diplomat and amateur man of letters Sir William Temple, accompanied by the aristocrat, student, and later politician Charles Boyle, and the 'Christ Church wits', a group of assembled men associated with Christ Church College in Oxford. On the side of the Moderns were the antiquarian William Wotton and the combative and influential classical scholar Richard Bentley. Their battle took place at many levels: it was about whether the 'epistles' of the sixth-century Phalaris were genuine or not; whether the modern world could rival the ancient one; who would know best the answers to these questions; and how they would know if they were right. But at the heart of it all lay a profound uncertainty about the role of knowledge and expertise in the modern world, and how it might best be mediated. This uncertainty is the bedrock on which much of the literature of the period depends.

William Temple initiated the English battle with the publication of his 1690 *Essay Upon Ancient and Modern Learning*, in which he refuted claims made by Bernard de Fontenelle and Thomas Burnet, who had argued that both culture and science bore evidence of progression in modern times. Temple was opposed to this notion, and his *Essay* argued that nothing could rival the Ancients in achievement in the centuries since the times of Plato, Aristotle, Virgil, and Livy. To pretend that more recent historians and scientists had achieved otherwise was utter absurdity – one might as well argue that:

> the Plays in *Moor-Fields* are beyond the *Olympick* Games, A *Welsh* or *Irish* Harp excels that of *Orpheus* and *Arion*; The Pyramid in *London*, those of *Memphis*; and the *French* Conquests in *Flanders* are greater than those of *Alexander* and *Caesar*.[67]

Temple presents a mock-heroic disjunction between the scale of old and recent achievements, arguments bound to rile his opponents. But amidst the bluster and confidence of Temple's claims there was one specific element that attracted the attention of Wotton and Bentley. This was Temple's apparent endorsement of the authenticity and brilliance of the letters of the ancient Greek king Phalaris. Little was known about Phalaris, but in keeping with his argument that the oldest books were invariably the best, Temple asserted that the Epistles had 'more Race, more Spirit, more force of Wit and Genius than any others I have ever seen, either ancient or modern'.[68] He knew that their authorship had already been questioned, but he claimed that the letters offered evidence enough in themselves:

> such diversity of Passions, upon such variety of Actions and Passages of Life and Government, such Freedom of Thought, such Boldness of Expression, such Bounty to his Friends, such Scorn of his Enemies, such Honor of Learned Men, such Esteem of Good, such Knowledg of Life, such Contempt of Death, with such Fierceness of Nature and Cruelty of Revenge, could never be represented but by him that possessed them.[69]

This argument was profoundly syllogistic – Phalaris was known only from the evidence of his supposed letters, but, Temple argued, the epistles were so good, they must have been by him. Despite the fact that the elderly diplomat read the epistles not in the original Greek, but in translation, he nonetheless felt able to dismiss the doubts earlier scholars had raised about the authenticity of the letters. Armed with confidence in his own literary evaluation, he used the epistles as a demonstration that the ancient works surpassed all modern imitations. As we can see, at the heart of this defence were unspoken assumptions about the nature of the act of reading and the quality of the reader. Temple thought that the text before him bore evidence of its historical authorship. And the tool which enabled him to discern this was his own inbuilt amateur sense of the literary qualities of the letters. The notion of a correct interpretation of the text was intrinsically linked to issues of class and social status; to read the classics correctly, one needed to be a gentleman, and the linguistic competence to understand the original language was secondary.

    This was not a defence that was going to persuade the sceptical scholar-philologists of his day, Wotton and Bentley. Following Temple's promotion of the virtues of Phalaris, a new edition of the letters appeared, from the hand of the Christ Church student Charles Boyle, under the title *Phalarides Agrigentinorum Tyranni Epistolae* (1695).[70] Though he had some classical knowledge, Boyle was not particularly well equipped for the task and lacked guidance. He laid himself open to the scholarly wrath of Bentley, the living embodiment of the modern professional classicist. Bentley was at this time employed as a tutor to Edward Stillingfleet, bishop of Worcester, with access to the finest libraries in the country. In 1697 Bentley published a 'Dissertation on the Epistles of Phalaris', which renounced both Boyle's translation and Temple's claims for the letters' authenticity. Bentley began by listing the inconsistencies and the anachronistic references and borrowings that meant that the letters had to be a forgery by another writer, probably writing centuries later. His commentary pulled no punches in illustrating his opponent's intellectual folly: 'A pretty Slip of our Sophist, who, like the rest of his Profession, was more vers'd in the Books of Orators than Historians, to introduce his Tyrant borrowing Money of a City, almost CCC Years before it was named or built'.[71] He mocked Boyle's translation of particular words, and he showed the ways in which his own philological expertise could more accurately date a text than any assurance of greatness of style: 'Every living Language, like the perspiring Bodies of living Creatures, is in perpetual motion and alteration; some words go off, and become obsolete'.[72] To add insult to injury, Bentley went on to demolish the *Epistles* on the very grounds of literary merit that had been the cornerstone of Temple's humanist defence. He attacked the letters as improbable and absurd, 'a scene of putid and senseless formality', full of 'silliness and impertinency [...] a fardle of Common Places, without any life or spirit from Action and Circumstance'.[73]

Bentley was a man with tendency to overkill; not content with a few damning pieces of evidence to persuade his readers of his superior authority, his objections and observations were relentless. This adversarial style was to characterize many of his printed interventions in cultural debate and shape the terms of public conversations. As we shall see, debates about good and bad reading and interpretation frequently centred on notions of education and politeness, and here too they formed part of the arsenal that was used against Bentley and the Moderns.[74] When the Christ Church wits responded to Bentley, and to Wotton's lengthier rejoinder, they framed their argument not only as a debate about Phalaris, but as a contest between two different types of reader: the wit and the pedant. One of Boyle's supporters, the clergyman George Smalridge, pronounced: 'This at least I am confident of, that all persons of quality and good breeding will declare against him, when it shall appear how clownishly and unlike either a gentleman or a scholar, he has treated Mr Boyle and Sir William Temple, who have something at least of both'.[75] Bentley had erred not only in his judgement, but also, and perhaps more importantly, in being the wrong kind of reader, 'unlike either a gentleman or scholar'.

When Boyle responded to Bentley's assault, he showed a distaste for the detail of his scholarship, dismissing in a sentence what now seem to us the essentials of the trade: 'to consult the several Editions, to collate the Manuscripts, to turn over Dictionaries, nay, and to make 'em', all seemed to him to be 'Noise about Trifles'.[76] In the end, Boyle asserted, 'for as much as I value Learning, I value Good Sense, and Common Civility More'.[77] According to his detractors, Bentley was a rude pedant, a nit-picking, self-important expert who brought scholarship into disrepute. The man of sense and wit, on the other hand, was a much more appropriate judge and reader of classical literature.

As this book shows, the landscape of early eighteenth-century print culture was riven with uncertainties about cultural authority and reading, and, in this case, the question was about wherein lay true knowledge and authority over the texts of the classical past. The Battle of the Books focused attention on what one was supposed to do when confronted with the classics and what sorts of skills best equipped a reader to make sense of them. It also exposed the complex relationships among class, education, and good reading, troubling any easy distinction we might want to make between elite and non-elite readers. Would the Temple model of gentlemanly *sprezzatura*, an impressionistic linguistic competence, combined with an earnest commitment to the humanistic values of the Ancients, do the trick? Or was it necessary to acquire the polyglot confidence and precision of a Bentley or Wotton? And if scholarship was to adopt these newer, more scientific forms of expertise, what would those layers of textual explication, appendices, emendations, glosses, and footnotes do to the classical texts themselves, the treasure houses of Western literature? Would their long-cherished true meaning and beauty get lost under the weight of pedantic commentary?

All these concerns fed the satire of the period and its recurring concern with over-interpretation, in which perceived acts of misinterpretation often generated forms of wilful misreading. The idea that there were libraries of arriviste experts manhandling ancient books merely to enhance their own status took firm hold in the creative imaginations of some of the most prominent satirists of the day. Pope, Swift, and John Gay began to produce works which mocked the art of scholarly interpretation, often by parodying the material forms of books – the indexes, glosses, and footnotes that came to embody the efforts of the professional scholar.

Much attention in both the printed polemic and the satires of the era focused on the nature and quantity of annotation of a work, and what this said about the role of the editor or translator. As those on the side of the Ancients saw it, the place of the annotator was to show the beauties of the literary work which they were presenting. So, for example, Pope's translation of Homer's *Iliad* offered appreciative glosses on the poetic qualities of his language and imagery: he explained to his readers that Homer excelled in his 'poetical fire', and that his job would be to show them 'how this vast *Invention* exerts itself in a manner superior to that of any Poet'.[78] This approach was very different from the textual-critical annotation favoured by Bentley. Bentley made his name as a classical editor with his 1711 edition of Horace, a lavish eight-hundred-page treatment of the Roman poet, his first work devoted to a single author and an entire text. The volume offered no literary or historical commentary, but instead consisted of a copious discussion of textual matters and proposed emendations.[79] There were three hundred pages devoted to Horace's text, and four hundred and fifty devoted to Bentley's annotations. Bentley's choice of author was particularly striking because, of all the ancient poets at this time, Horace represented genteel masculinity, a poet who offered elegantly rephrased commonplaces adaptable to modern conversation. Not only was Horace widely taught in grammar schools and by private tutors, but he was highly fashionable among adult readers.[80] By offering his own version, Bentley signalled, in one critic's words, that 'the pedantic, ill-bred barbarians were now within the gates of genteel culture'.[81] And, in contrast to the author he presented, Bentley's additions were far from polite. His preface gave a bullish defence of his methods and reasoning, and showed what seemed like delight in the prospect of a dustup with his detractors: 'I will overwhelm them with the weight of my reasons and the number of my examples, until at last I drag them by the neck into agreement with me'.[82]

Bentley's model of engagement with other critics was pugnacious, based on an unshakeable sense of his own rightness. And one of the ironies of his approach was that in its fixed sense of his own 'ingenium' as a form of communion with the dead author, Bentley in some ways resembled the Ancients. Like Sir William Temple, he was guided largely by his own sense of what the poet was saying. Both men believed that they had a superior understanding of the real meaning of classical poets, but they located their confidence in very different forms of authority: one literary, and one linguistic.

## Mocking Pedants

One of the consequences of this internecine battle between different models of expertise was that it highlighted the matter of how one explained things. Bentley's critics were struck by the abundance of information that he provided, sometimes wondering what the point of all this knowledge was, and what it added up to. The new kinds of copious philological and specialist information promoted by the modern classicist seemed to them to reflect the broader pattern of proliferating print that was a concern of the time. So part of the critique of the new scholarship was not just about over-interpretation or misinterpretation, but also about how to navigate an abundance of textual explication. Bentley's opponents mocked the very act of explanation, and their approach can clearly be traced in the many literary works of this period which use their apparatus, their presentation, and their interactivity to explain and confuse at the same time. The numerous satires on learning, pedantry, and the act of misreading that emerged with such vitality in the first decades of the eighteenth century, from the *Memoirs of Martinus Scriblerus* to *Gulliver's Travels* or Gay's *Three Hours After Marriage*, grew out of this interconnected set of changes in the perception of knowledge, readers, and types of books.

One of the most notable is Swift's *Tale of a Tub*, with its allegory of the three brothers whose exegesis of their father's will represented the fortunes of the various strands within the Anglican church. Although it was the religious reflections that provoked most concern in his contemporaries, Swift's connected assault on the pretensions of modern learning was a clear jibe at modern scholarship. Within the *Tale* itself, wrapped around the allegory was a parody of contemporary authorship, in the form of the digressive narrator whose abstruse and endlessly proliferating commentary mocked the self-important digressions of the modern author. With its prefaces, appendices, footnotes, excursions, and introductions, Swift satirized the pedantry of the modern scholar. In a 'digression upon digressions', a digression 'concerning critics', it was clear that part of the intellectual folly that Swift was aiming at was the way in which editors and critics interpreted and presented the texts they read. At one point, the narrator notes that the arguments of the Moderns have been so effective that there is a 'grave Dispute, whether there have been ever any *Antients* or no', a *reductio ad absurdum* of the modern denigration of classical achievement.[83] The narrator's pretentious fetishizing of the conditions of the original manuscript, with his '*sic hiatus in ms*', was directed at the modern philology that had inspired the quarrel between Temple and the Moderns.

These arguments about ancient and modern were often embodied at the level of the material text: that is, through the satiric deployment of the machinery of scholarship – the index, the footnote, and the appendix. The forms through which the reader was encouraged to make meaning of their text were part of the satire of the period. In *Tale of a Tub*, Swift mocked the self-aggrandizing nature of editorial commentary and apparatus. The 1710 edition of the *Tale* became an interactive satire, containing within its new footnotes excerpts from William Wotton's criticism of the first edition, judiciously selected to show Wotton at his most pedantic and obtuse.[84] Wotton's 'Observations Upon the Tale of a Tub' started life as a fairly cogent series of objections to the moral and religious implications of the *Tale*. But in redeploying Wotton's words as part of his revised version of the satire, Swift comically presented them out of context, cutting and pasting so that they became emblematic of the modern critic's woeful misunderstanding of Swift's work.

This use of the apparatus of a work to satirize misinterpretation – in effect, to stage a misreading of the text – was to provide an almost limitless source of inspiration for Swift and his contemporaries. Again, the controversy over the authenticity of the epistles of Phalaris was a profitable starting point. When Boyle and his friends compiled their response to Bentley's attack on their scholarship and translation, they did so not only by accusing Bentley of being an unsociable pedant, but also by wittily mimicking the appearance of the scholarly commentary they criticized.[85] Boyle lampooned Bentley for his proliferating glosses, yet the margins of his reply to the scholar were so littered with allusions and notes, quibbles and additions in Greek and Latin, that they interrupted the main text of the argument, pushing the lines downwards and off the page. The paratext of Boyle's page made it very clear that the act of annotation could be a landgrab, an act of aggression towards the very text it commented upon – even if, in his case, both were by the same author. His satire was aimed both at authors and at the forms of books which aimed to create clarity for readers. Boyle was having none of it. He rubbished indexes and their readers as a particularly base form of intellectual activity: 'I take Index-hunting after Words and Phrases to be, next Anagrams and Acrostick, the lowest Diversion a Man can betake himself to'.[86] And later versions of the *Dissertations on the Epistles of Phalaris, and the Fables of Aesop Examin'd* included a satirical index which extended the joke. A four-page table, inserted at the back of the book, was the brainchild of the lawyer and writer William King. Entitled 'A Short Account of Dr. Bentley by Way of Index', it offered a guide to Bentley's character and intellectual predilections.[87] As part of the panoply of information-management tools used by the new modern scholars, indexes were seen with suspicion by many in the traditionalist camp. Condensing a work to a series of heads, or topics, was seen as a potentially dangerous and reductive sort of interpretation.[88] But indexes were also seen as a shortcut to actually reading a book. The index was both a digest of reading and a replacement for the real thing. And, in a parodic form, it could be used to showcase misreading. Unlike normal indexes, King's pages did not offer comprehensive coverage of all topics covered within the three-hundred page book, but were instead only a guide to the references to, and thoughts of, Bentley within the work, a reduction that signalled the narcissism that Boyle and his friends saw at the heart of the new scholarship. The entries have both a cumulative and a particular effect. Reading across the whole, we get a sense of Bentley the man. The mock index included entries such as:

Dr. Bentley's Civil Usage of Mr. Boyle
His Singular Humanity to
    Mr. Boyle
    Sir Edward Sherburne
    Foreigners
His dogmatical air
His Modesty and Decency in contradicting great Men.

We get a sense of a man who is vain, pugnacious, and given to over-assertion. And the most significant heading in the whole index – the one, it is implied, that would have been most important to Bentley himself – is left empty, void of content. The final entry in the entire index reads:

His profound Skill in Criticism. From the beginning to
THE END.

There is an implication that there is no evidence at all for Bentley's skills within the book. Perused on its own, the mock index offers a commentary on all the follies and rudeness of which Bentley was accused by his detractors. No one need read the whole three hundred pages of Boyle's work to arrive at this conclusion – the headings are enough. The idea of an interpretative guide which manages to mock, at the same time, the act of interpretation, the people who use the interpretative guide, *and* the text being interpreted seems a fitting place to end a consideration of the role of misreading within the cultures of classical knowledge. Far from being a world of gentlemanly certainties, the works and languages of the Ancients provoked ferocious battles about who really knew the past. Coupled with profoundly uneven levels of readerly knowledge, the opportunity for uncertainty, play, and muddle was immense.

# 4

# The Literary Reader

In the even read the 12th and last book of Milton's *Paradise Lost*,
which I have now read twice through and in my opinion it exceeds
anything I ever read for sublimity of language and beauty of similes.

— THOMAS TURNER, SUSSEX SHOPKEEPER

WHAT DID IT MEAN to be a competent *literary* reader? As numerous
critics from F.R. Leavis to Habermas have described, the burgeoning commercial print culture of the late seventeenth and early eighteenth
century saw the emergence of generalist literary criticism – the art of
amateur appreciation of the world of letters.[1] For the first time, periodical
essays, newsletters, and instructional guides began to offer frameworks
and a language with which non-specialist readers could articulate their
judgement of literary works. Everything you needed to know to read
secular literary texts in the right way was available, for a price, to a newly
engaged and aspirational reading public.[2] But that advice and information itself offered a complex negotiation of bookish understanding. It
was not just the elusive and puzzling satires, the allegories, and the romans à clef of the Augustan era that teased their readers with offering
and withholding comprehension. Early instructional literary criticism
also played with the sense of who knew, who ought to know, and who
would never know. And texts which were supposed to be reassuringly
inclusive could also promote interpretative uncertainty.

Diaries and annotations show us that by the middle of the eighteenth century, there were readers of all kinds who confidently pronounced their views on the literary merits of their books. John Periam, a small-time country squire and MP living outside Exeter, marked up his copy of Mark Akenside's *Pleasures of the Imagination* (1744) with comments on its aesthetic virtues, such as: 'noble & sublime', 'charming episode', 'a noble Description of a giddy, & youthful Imagination', and 'This section is most elegant & divine'.[3] Both the vocabulary and the amateur appreciation is that of a man versed in contemporary generalist literary criticism – his approach is not merely to record sources and cross-refer to other works (although he does do some of that) but to use a non-expert language of aesthetic evaluation to describe what he sees. Thomas Turner, a shopkeeper living in East Hoathly in Sussex, writes in similar terms of his wide literary reading: 'In the even read the 12th and last book of Milton's *Paradise Lost*, which I have now read twice through and in my opinion it exceeds anything I ever read for sublimity of language and beauty of similes'.[4] He says of *Hamlet*: 'After supper read part of Hamlet Prince of Denmark; think Hamlet's character extremely fine and on the whole think it a good play'.[5] Of Richardson's *Clarissa*, he declares: 'In the even my wife finished reading of *Clarissa Harlowe*, which I look upon as a very well-wrote thing though it must be allowed it is too prolix. I think the author keeps up the character of every person in all places; and as to the manner of its ending, I like it better than if it had terminated in more happy consequences'.[6]

At a rather different place on the social scale are the papers of Hugh Dalrymple Murray Kynynmound, (c. 1692–1741). Dalrymple was an advocate, the second son of the Hon. Sir David Dalrymple, of Hailes Castle in East Lothian. Here are Hugh Dalrymple's thoughts on his own qualification to be a literary critic:

When I speak of a Verbal Criticks Sphere, far be it from me to intend any derogation from the honour of so grave a Body, of which I myself am an unworthy Brother. For as any single action of John is proof sufficient that such a man as John existed, so any single Poetical act, were that but an Acrostick, denominates a Poet, and secures immortality in the Poets Plutarch, Mr Giles Jacob. In like manner a single emendation constitutes and gives the rank of a verbal Critick, and that I, tho' the meanest of that Tribe, am truly intitled to the dignity aforesaid, will clearly appear from this my following proper and personal Criticism, which I hope no man will be so brutal as to tell me was ever thought of but my self, Horace excepted.[7]

In his convoluted phrasing, Dalrymple acknowledges that literary criticism is a specialist business, but also that there is room for him to do it on his own amateur and elementary terms.

We have here snapshots of three men, from very different backgrounds, with a shared sense of qualification to speak of literary matters and to venture their own opinions on the nature of fine writing. None are poets, scholars, or literary critics. Their willingness to write and think in this way is in no small part to the huge change that occurred at the beginning of the eighteenth century when the works of Joseph Addison and others extended the idea of a literary public beyond the court, scholars, and social elite to include what Addison called 'the Town'. While there were those who maintained the idea that criticism should remain the preserve of experts, the democratization of literary appreciation was underway, and it would reshape the landscape of print culture and reading habits.

## We've Had Enough of Experts

After a lifetime as a poet laureate, eminent literary critic, and professional writer, John Dryden complained in 1696 that 'Criticism is now become mere Hang-man's Work, and meddles only with the Faults of Authors'.[8] These were not merely the words of an ageing man tired of his profession. Dryden's vocal exasperation with critical nit-picking had begun in this vein some two decades earlier, when he had characterized the work of his contemporaries as 'an Age of Illiterate, Censorious, and Detracting people, who thus qualified, set up for Critiques'.[9] In that essay, he had also spelled out what it was that a literary critic ought to be doing:

> I must take leave to tell them, that they wholly mistake the Nature of Criticism, who think its business is principally to find fault. Criticism, as it was first instituted by *Aristotle*, was meant as a Standard of judging well: The chiefest part of which is to observe those Excellencies which should delight a reasonable Reader.[10]

Not for Dryden the habits of irascible fault-finding practised (he claimed) by his contemporaries. His emphasis here is on literary criticism as a way of finding and praising what is good in a work – a habit of intellectual generosity that he claims originated with Aristotle. It is also a habit premised on the views of the expansive – but rather vague-sounding – notion of the 'reasonable reader', rather than the privileged insights of the expert. Once again, the nature of expertise was up for debate. Dryden is often described as the 'Father of English Criticism', and his series of essays written from the late 1660s through to the late 1690s on heroic poetry, dramatic verse, satire, and translation present a coherent body of thought about the values and technical features of various genres. He was to anticipate Joseph Addison and Samuel Johnson's literary critical essays, which offered non-technical generalist discussions of the values of various authors and their works, and which together opened up for the first time the idea that the appreciation of literary works ought to be accessible to a broader public. But although he claimed to be interested in the 'reasonable reader', Dryden's essays in fact read as though they were intended for a fairly erudite following. Many take the form of lengthy prefaces to his works, and use the publication of a play, translation, or poem as a springboard for the laureate's musings on the evolution of the form. His essays are formal, deferential, and tightly bound up in references to existing authorities. The earliest, *Of Dramatic Poesy* (1668), is a neoclassical dialogue featuring four fictional speakers – Crites, Lisideius, Neander, and Eugenius – who conduct among themselves a debate over the relative merits of English and French drama and classical and modern drama, arguing whether rhymed plays are better than those in blank verse. Later pieces martialled dense and often slightly rambling arguments, and seem to address a readership with enough education to navigate both classical and modern languages. 'Of Heroic Plays: An Essay' (1672) discussed, among other things, the role of magic in drama, the nature of the hero, the refinement of English poetic style, and the inferiority of the Elizabethan playwrights. It did so by way of an array of literary authorities. In the space of only a few pages, Dryden cites Ariosto and Tasso in Italian, Petronius and Horace in Latin, and Homer in Greek. His prefatory pieces were often addressed to aristocratic patrons and thus have a dual sense of audience: the nobleman whose work and erudition is to be flattered, and the reader who can bask in the sense of inclusion in a shared gentlemanly style. Dryden's turn of phrase often seeks to reassure readers of a common base of cultural knowledge: he repeatedly uses the inclusive pronoun 'we' to suggest that his readers share his extensive library of literary examples, and flatteringly cuts short a summary of a work because, of course, it is all too familiar. Dryden sought to shape his readers' interpretation of literature, but he did so from a fairly high base, working from the assumption that they came to his criticism well-versed in how to evaluate a literary text in several languages. In time his style would come to seem outdated: for all his professed desire to open up literary criticism beyond the world of crabby pedants, only a few decades later readers would find that Dryden 'writ more like a Scholar' and 'wanted that Easiness and Familiarity, that Air of Freedom and Unconstraint, that gentle and accomplished Manner of Expression which is more sensibly to be perceived, than described'.[11] As a starting point for thinking about the relationship between expert and inexpert literary readers in the period, Dryden is useful because his words frame an ongoing discussion about the role of expertise within secular, literary forms of reading. It is here that we find the origins of a debate about what it means to be a good reader, whether one might learn to be one, and how far the question of misreading and reading were class- or gender-based matters.

The term *criticism* at the end of the seventeenth century meant many things – it covered a whole raft of textually based disciplines, including history, geography, grammar, and philology – and the term *literary criticism* did not exist at all.[12] The evolution of all these forms of criticism was complex. But over the course of the late seventeenth and early eighteenth century there was a particular focus on the issue of what it meant to be a critic, what the qualifications were, and how one should address one's readership.[13] This focused on questions such as whether the critic should be polite or combative, or how they should display knowledge without bewildering the reader with detail – concerns we have also seen emerging in the field of classical commentary. And as with scriptural explication and classical translation, the era saw a proliferation of texts concerned with unpacking the mysteries of learning and culture for diverse readers. Yet, at the same time as this expansion, there was also a careful negotiation of who exactly got to determine literary value and meaning. Throughout this book we can see a dynamic of inclusion and exclusion: those who were in the know, those who were not. We will see texts which tease readers' desire for inclusion, play with their confusion, and misfire when they are misread. Literary competence was part of a wider cultural debate about who ought to know the answers.

A conversation clearly emerged at the end of the seventeenth century about what literary criticism was for. In tandem with this, the era also saw changing approaches to the way readerly opinions might be both formed and shaped by print media. Dryden's gestures towards a more inclusive model of literary reading may seem rather implausible in the context of the kind of criticism he wrote himself, but they were the sign of a changing relationship among new readers, authors, and new print forms in the sphere of secular literary texts. This rethinking of the packaging of cultural knowledge and the role of the reader is strikingly evident in one of the most innovative publications of the 1690s, John Dunton's *Athenian Mercury*, a twice-weekly broadsheet which appeared between 1691 and 1697. Dunton was an opportunistic publisher who, through the *Mercury* and its related publications *The Athenian Oracle* and the *Ladies Mercury*, developed his own brand of participatory journalism.[14] As the editor of the *Athenian Mercury*, he invited the general public to send in their questions, guaranteeing that he and his group of associates would answer them:

All Persons whatever may be resolved gratis in any Question that their own satisfaction or Curiosity shall prompt 'em to, if they send their Questions by a Penny Post letter to *Mr. Smith* at his Coffee-house in *Stocks Market* in the *Poultry*, where orders are given for the Reception of such Letters, and care shall be taken for their Resolution by the next Weekly Paper after their sending.[15]

The nature of this 'question-answer' project marked a significant shift in the dynamics of knowledge exchange, one in which the content was driven by the general reader, and the way in which the information was provided assumed very little prior formal knowledge of the topic on their part. Dunton and his associates had committed themselves to addressing all the questions sent in, however random. To provide the answers, Dunton rapidly assembled a little group of supposed experts, consisting of himself, plus his two brothers-in-law, and a philosopher, John Norris. He concealed the identities of the limited cluster of men involved, and instead fabricated a society emblem depicting a group of twelve worthies seated around a table, deep in learning. The author Charles Gildon was commissioned to write a history of this 'Athenian Society' (despite the fact that it was only a year old), and so bolstered the authority of the publication by suggesting that the knowledge emerging from it was the fruit of a neoclassical republic of letters. The group announced that it was going to 'answer the most Nice and Learned Questions which shall be sent us by the Ingenious of both Sexes'.[16] The periodical was, then, to be interactive, its content generated by the curiosity and enthusiasms of those who bought or read it.

The questions came pouring in through the Penny Post, and covered all the most pressing questions of life: on 14 May 1697, the group considered 'Which of the two is more constant in Love, Man, or Woman?' Their considered response was the following:

> *Answ. Virgil* and other Poets have accused Women, of a great Lightness and Inconstancy; Nevertheless, we are of Opinion, that Reason and Experience are Champions for them. Reason, foreasmuch as they are more Cold than Men, and the Nature of Cold is to be Tenacious.[17]

On 21 May 1697, we can see some of the range of expertise that was called for: 'What is the cause of the Generation of Monsters?'; 'How comes it to pass, that we do Love sometimes those whom we never saw?'; 'How is the Dew Ingendered?'[18] The society responded with brevity and admirably straight faces, dispatching their queries with economic dollops of natural science and common sense. Answering the question of 'Can we hear under Water?' the group replied: 'Yes, very well, as those that are accustomed to dive do relate and affirm. And Fishes themselves will slip away if a great Noise be made on, or near the Water. *Pliny* relates, that there were Fishes (in the Ponds of the Emperour of *Rome*) that wou'd come forth of the Water, being Called by an accustomed Name.'[19]

As the answers demonstrate, the *Athenian Mercury* showed its readers the way expertise might be deployed in applied situations. It both gave them answers, and showed the kinds of sources that were commonly used to form them. The utilitarian aspect of this knowledge was important: Virgil, the Bible, and the ancient philosophers were not a study in their own right, but were instead mined for their insight into matters of contemporary interest, from science to love to the natural world to human behaviours. In his *History of the Athenian Society* (1692), Charles Gildon described the way in which such publications made learning accessible:

> for One hour in a week is all the time, that is required to peruse them, and Two pence weekly sufficient to purchase those Papers, in which, every one may find the Marrow of what great Authors have writ on any curious Subject, with the improvement of many ingenious, and learned men upon it.[20]

The *Mercury* offered redaction and synthesis: the 'Marrow' of accrued knowledge on any subject raised by their curious readers. It, alongside other publications, responded to readerly doubt by packaging information in accessible, generalist terms. Though they were anonymous, the Athenian society gave advice that had an immediate bearing on the thoughts and experiences of the people reading it. The tone was affable, reassuring, and reliable – a long way from both the irascible critics described by John Dryden and Dryden's own model of deferential discussion founded on an extensive familiarity with the classics. The

Athenians were quite dismissive towards a pedantic, detail-focused culture of scholarly debate. Replying to the question of whether vision was caused by rays of light emanating from the eyes towards an object in sight, the Athenians declared: 'This hath been Antiently a very great dispute, and is so at this day among such as are self-conceited; and we will not trouble the Reader of this Paper with the long disputes of the one side and the other'.[21] We might compare the rise of the *Athenian Mercury* and its stablemates the *Athenian Oracle* and the *Ladies Mercury* with the 'ask Google' queries that are our contemporary shortcut to information, and which offer democratized – if potentially problematic – answers to queries from cancer symptoms to the meaning of love. Like the *Athenian Mercury*, the relative anonymity of querist and respondent means that the user does not need to display knowledge in order to ask for more. And as with the early eighteenth-century print publications, search engines enable participants to ask a bewildering range of questions without fear of ridicule or exposure. In response, they receive clear answers which do not require a high entry-level of expertise to be useful. Google's corporate mission statement, 'to organize the world's information and make it universally accessible and useful', might have been Dunton's.

So far, so straightforward. But we might also ask whether Dunton's periodical was as earnestly educative as it seemed to be. Looking over the lists of queries in the publication – which, as we have seen, range from matters of theological scruple to basic bodily function – we might also wonder whether the *Mercury* exploited ignorance for comic effect. Fictional queries could be used to both showcase accessible knowledge, and, at the same time, to mock the ignorance of those who wondered things like: 'Why do we commonly Fart in Pissing?'[22] The aspirational readers conjured by the periodical were at once its beneficiaries, but also a source of entertainment for their more sophisticated contemporaries. Not for the first time, we see the complex ways in which the tension between knowledge and ignorance, insiders and outsiders, played out in the reading materials of the early eighteenth century.

The *Athenian Mercury* was not primarily a vehicle for literary criticism, although it drew on literary sources in answering its questions. It was, however, a publication which emphasized the utility of knowledge, and which used print media to synthesize a range of sources of authority and repackage them in ways useful to its readers. Crucially, it modelled the deployment of culture for those who had not always possessed it. In this it demonstrated the ways in which the emerging print culture of the period was shaped by the needs and interests of curious and non-expert readers. It was a form of print generated by the gap between the assumed knowledge base of the highly educated and a readership who needed some help to gain access to contemporary cultural forms. In this, it resembled one of the other major publishing successes of the turn of the century: the printed commonplace book, a guide to literary effect and composition.

Edward Bysshe's two volume *The Art of English Poetry* was a vast collection of literary quotations first published in 1702, and running into many editions in following decades.[23] Most of *The Art of English Poetry* was made up of 'A Collection of the most Natural, Agreeable, & Noble *Thoughts* [. . .] that are to be found in the best *English Poets*.'[24] It was a dictionary of alphabetically arranged quotations arranged by theme. The collection enabled readers to flick with ease from poetic illustrations of 'Dissension' to 'Dolphin' to 'Doubt'. It was the sort of book that many owned and used – but not everyone would admit to. Ostensibly designed to aid budding writers in their own compositions, it served a more general purpose as a handbook of poetic effect – a series of quotations that could be lifted and used to enliven other forms of writing. If readers wanted to produce a passionate exclamation on the nature of existence, they could flip to the section on 'Life' and choose, among others, between John Dryden's 'When I consider Life, 'tis all a Cheat; / Yet, fooled with Hope, Men favour the Deceit', Shakespeare's 'Life's but a walking Shadow; A Poor Player', or Thomas Shadwell's 'Life is but Air / That yields a Passage to the whistling Sword'.[25] We know that *The Art of English Poetry* was part of the collections of Alexander Pope, Samuel Richardson, Henry Fielding, Isaac Watts, Samuel Johnson, Oliver Goldsmith, Hugh Walpole, and William Blake.[26] Like Wikipedia in the twenty-first century, it was a fruitful source for many readers and writers who ostensibly disapproved of its scholarly shortcuts. It is now established that

Samuel Richardson must have used it for many of the literary quotations in his masterpiece *Clarissa* (he replicated some of the same errors in transcription or attribution that Bysshe had made), yet it is nowhere acknowledged in the novel, which for centuries of critics and readers gave the impression of Richardson's wide familiarity with the English literary canon.[27]

*The Art of Poetry* was a work expressly designed not for the privacy of a study but for casual consumption. In the dedication, Bysshe states: 'This is a Book that may be taken up and laid down at Pleasure, and would rather choose to lye about in a With-drawing-Room, or a Grove, than be set up in a Closet'.[28] In content and format, this was, Bysshe suggested, a work for 'dip-n-skip', desultory reading. Again, the practical uses of the collection were emphasized – the extracts within would serve a social or recreational purpose. Moreover, despite the fact that in his preface Bysshe claimed that his work was to help poets with their compositions, judging by the kind of advice on offer, the compilation was also aimed at a lower level of literary expertise than this suggested. Bysshe took his readers through the basics of poetic form. He opened by explaining that verse was structured through syllables, which could be long or short. He led the reader carefully through some examples, showing where syllables occurred in blank verse and rhymed verse. It was fairly elementary stuff. He proceeded to explain what an accent was, what a pause was, and other fundamentals of scansion and diction, concluding that if these rules were followed poetry would ensue: 'the observation of them, like that of Right Time in Musick, will produce Harmony; the neglect of them Harshness and Discord; as appears by the following Verses'.

Bysshe attempted to clarify poetic effect: to show his readers how the best bits of English literature were constructed, and how readers might also achieve those effects. Like the *Athenian Mercury*, he selected what seemed to him the prime examples from the present and past, and arranged them for practical use. He reinforced the value of applied knowledge and synthesized information. He also seemed to be suggesting that poetic skill could be learnt through a series of rules, and that readers of this digested form might gain entrance into the sphere of the poetic arts.

But as Bysshe explained the purpose of his selection, he stumbled into the conundrum exposed by his work:

> Having given *Rules for making Verses*, and a *Dictionary of Rhymes*, I consider'd what other human Aid could be offer'd to a Poet, a Genius and Judgment not being ours to give; and I imagin'd he might have both these, and yet sometimes be at a stand for Epithets and Synonymes, with which I have seen Books of this Nature in several Languages plentifully furnish'd.[29]

Bysshe exposes one of the dilemmas present at this opening up of literary culture to a new readership. In his book he had creatively and entrepreneurially set out to supply all the materials essential to poetry – rhymes, rules on scansion and metre, epithets – but there were some elements that he could not teach: 'a Genius and Judgment not being ours to give'. The criteria for entry into the world of literature were at once within the grasp of those who studied the *Art of Poetry*, but also painfully elusive and seemingly innate. This difficulty lies at the heart of much of the discussion of widening participation in eighteenth-century literary culture. As canny publishers and editors sought to create innovative products to capture an aspirational readership keen to acquire cultural *savoir faire*, they faced some of the intractables of their time. Steering a course between ignorance and expertise, accessibility and pedantry, they revealed contradictions in the conception of secular reading in the period. Was literary sensibility innate? Was poetic skill a gift of birth or of the muse, or could it be acquired through instructional manuals? As we shall see, these uncertainties – and their comic potential – were to reverberate throughout the burgeoning print culture of the early eighteenth century.

One of the main features of Bysshe's *Art of Poetry*, like that of popular compilations of 'beauties' of English literature that were to appear later in the century, was that it indexed nuggets of verse and drama by theme, focusing on the topics described in individual passages rather than the wider context. It encouraged its readers to approach imaginative literature as a storehouse of useful or powerful descriptions of the world. In doing so, *The Art of Poetry* was partly reflecting a broader contemporary

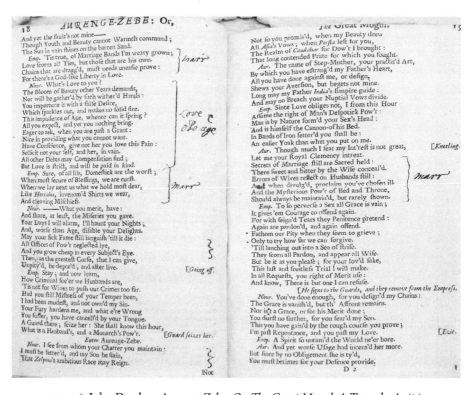

FIGURE 6. John Dryden, *Aurenge-Zebe: Or, The Great Mogul. A Tragedy. As it is Acted by Her Majesty's Servants*, third edition (London: printed for Henry Herringman, 1690), by kind permission of Cardiff University Special Collections and Archives, PR3415.A8.C90, pp. 18–19.

understanding of literature as a source of adages or rhetorical nuggets, a habit derived from Renaissance commonplacing.[30] We can't know for sure how far contemporaries were influenced by *The Art of Poetry* or any other particular publication, but there is evidence to show that as non-expert readers of the early eighteenth century tried their hands at literary appraisal, this thematic indexing was the way in which they too evaluated what they read. Rather than using their notes to record personal observations or evaluations, they noted in margins the topics covered in a work, or the nature of the description it provided. A 1690 copy of John Dryden's heroic tragedy *Aureng-Zebe* in Cardiff University Library (figure 6) shows its owner marking up the text with thematic annotations in the margins, which provide summaries of topics addressed. A dispute between the Emperor and his wife, Nourmahal, has notes indicating that the declamatory passages of the tragedy refer to 'Love & Old Age' and 'Marriage'.[31] A discussion between the Emperor and his captive, Indamora, of the role of force in satisfying desire is marked 'Rape'. [32] This looks like someone who is considering the work with newly acquired literary skills: they have also transcribed on the verso of the title page an extract from Henry Felton's 1713 guide to literary criticism, *A Discussion of Reading the Classics and Forming a Just Style*.[33] The extract offers Felton's views on Dryden, John Oldham, and other Restoration wits, finding them wanting in polite easiness. It's interesting to see the way the owner of this copy of *Aureng-Zebe* is clearly reading the play alongside an introductory work, one which told the would-be critic what made for good literature and who the best exemplars were. There is some irony in the fact that within Felton's essay, there is a condemnation of the act of commonplacing, which is seen as reductive:

> *Common Placing* the Sense of an Author is such a stupid Undertaking, that, if I may be indulged in saying it, they *want Common Sense* that practise it. What Heaps of this Rubbish have I seen! O the Pains and Labour to record what other People have said, that is taken by those, who have Nothing to say themselves![34]

For all this disapproval of commonplacing, the thematic annotation of literary works was clearly at the heart of many early eighteenth-century readers' practice, including that of the reader in the Cardiff copy of *Aureng-Zebe*. When Ben Browne, the yeoman farmer from Troutbeck in Cumbria, took a pen to his eight-volume 1714 edition of Shakespeare's plays, he did three things: correct typos, work out which scene in the play was being depicted in the illustrated plates, and mark up the theme of individual passages.[35] In his copy of *Othello*, his one intervention was to write next to Iago's singing of 'And let me the canakin clink clink' in Act 2:3 the phrase 'Drunken Scene'.[36] In Act 1:2 *King Lear*, he notes next to Gloucester's response to Edmund's counterfeit letter from his brother 'Confusion [?] espoused'.[37] In Act 4, in which Edgar conjures for the sightless Gloucester a vision from the top of the cliffs, Browne has

written 'description of Dover Cliffe' with a hand drawn manicule pointing to the passage.[38] When later on in the same act, Lear reflects on the
ways he has been tricked by false praise, Browne notes 'Flattery, a fine
report of it'.[39] Next to Lear's powerful lines at the end of the scene on
abuses of power ('Thou rascal beadle, hold thy bloody hand!') Browne
notes 'Corruption of Justice'.[40] In *Cymbeline* he notes merely 'Army, de-
feat of one described'.[41] The edition of the plays that Browne was using
was one which came accompanied by an 'Index of the most Beautiful
Thoughts, Descriptions, Speeches, &c in Shakespear's Works'. It's clear
that Browne had read it quite carefully, because he marked corrections
to some of the page numbers across its sheets. Like Bysshe's *Art of Poetry*, this index offered guidance to readers in how to appreciate literature, and which notable features to look out for. And as we can see from
the kinds of markings on the volumes, that instruction came to shape
individual response to the text, encouraging Browne and others to focus
on the indexing of moments over more holistic interpretation of the
work. While it might now seem to us a form of misreading of Shakespeare's plays, in the terms of contemporary advice on how to be a
good general reader, Browne was dealing with the bard in exactly the
right way.

## Talking about Ideas

As Dryden, Dunton, and Bysshe's works illustrate, accessibility was crucially linked to tone. How an author talked to their readers was as
important as what they said. And nowhere was this more evident than
in the hugely influential periodical essays of the *Tatler* and *Spectator*.
Both publications sought to introduce contemporary discussions of
culture, politics, and social mores to new readerships in an accessible
way. Conversationality and affability were key to the series of daily culture and lifestyle essays written and edited in *The Spectator*, primarily by
Joseph Addison and Richard Steele from March 1711 to December 1712.[42]
Supposedly all springing from the pen of 'Mr Spectator', the essays addressed the topics of their day, framing ethical, intellectual, and cultural
debates in terms accessible to non-specialist readers. This was part of a

wider political project: Addison and Steele, both members of the Whig Kit-Cat club, were partly using the essays to develop a Whiggish cultural agenda, one which sought to promote politeness and moral reform in a public sphere outside the court and aristocracy. In enabling the middling sort to participate in contemporary cultural and ethical debates, the periodicals showcased what affable discussion might look like outside elite social groups and their institutions. [43]

The *Spectator* pieces, like the discussions in the *Athenian Mercury*, appeared under the aegis of a social group, in this case an imaginary club which included an old-fashioned country squire, a prosperous City merchant, a young lawyer, a soldier, an elderly man about town, and a serious-minded clergyman. The topics covered in the essays were supposed to stem from the conversations of this little cluster, and often began with a fictional anecdote from daily life which provided the starting point for the discussion, framing their discussion within the everyday. There was no professional critic among the group – Mr Spectator declared himself well-read, but by no means an expert. In a preliminary account of his character and background, he tells us that his schoolmaster said of him 'that my Parts were solid and would wear well'.[44] At university, he tells us, he was strikingly silent. He read his books but did not speak of them: '[I] left the University, with the Character of an odd unaccountable Fellow, that had a great deal of Learning, if I would but show it'.[45] This blend of assurance and invisibility is key to the persona of Mr Spectator, who walks the city largely unknown, watching all that goes on around him and commenting upon it in his papers 'as Standers-by discover Blots, which are apt to escape those who are in the Game'.[46]

The literary essays that appeared in the *Spectator* covered a variety of topics – true and false wit, the qualities of *Paradise Lost*, the pleasures of the imagination, the literary merits of the ballad form – and they shared an emphasis on clarity, accessibility, and good sense. Addison and Steele's choice of subject matter often tended towards an exploration of apparently accepted but often unfathomable terms of literary appreciation. What exactly was wit? How did humour work? Who were the great writers of previous ages and on what terms should one value

them? The tone was carefully judged. Each essay began with an epigraph, usually in Latin, and not translated for the reader. But from this
point in, all the discussion was presented in a way that made it possible
for the reader to gain a sense of historical context, literary allusion, and
critical framework without the feeling of being lectured to or patron-
ized. Here is Mr Spectator introducing the topic of wit:

> Nothing is so much admired and so little understood as Wit. No Au-
> thor that I know of has written professedly upon it; and as for those
> who make any Mention of it, they only treat on the Subject as it has
> accidentally fallen in their Way, and that too in little short Reflec-
> tions, or in general declamatory Flourishes, with-out entering into
> the Bottom of the Matter. [. . .] I shall endeavour to make what I say
> intelligible to ordinary Capacities; but if my Readers meet with any
> Paper that in some Parts of it may be a little out of their Reach,
> I would not have them discouraged, for they may assure themselves
> the next shall be much clearer.[47]

Mr Spectator is both confident and reassuring. He has the effortless
assurance to be able to survey the critical field and find it wanting, and
the intellectual authority to assume the role of the man who will get
to the bottom of what exactly wit is. Yet he combines these forms of
cultural superiority with a commitment to keeping matters clear for his
'ordinary' readers – and if they lose their way, it will be his fault not
theirs, an error he will rectify. He is not there to bamboozle, but to elu-
cidate.[48] What follows is a winning combination of irreverence and as-
sertiveness. Rather than invoke impressive classical authorities to shore
up his opinion on the nature of wit, he shows a scepticism about the
knee-jerk deference to the ancient past that characterized so much traditional literary criticism. He describes false wit through the example
of ancient Greek 'shaped poetry', a kind of verse in which the poem
assumes the shape of the thing described. According to Mr Spectator,
its impenetrability is not the fault of the modern reader, but the original
author, who 'seems to have been more intent upon the Figure of his
Poem, than upon the Sense of it'.[49] Mr Spectator is at pains in this essay

and others to show that clarity and sense are the primary literary virtues – that incomprehension is not a thing to be ashamed of, but a marker of writerly folly.

Mr Spectator was clear from the outset that his notion of readership was a broad one, and that in writing his papers he considered the needs of his audience. Writing of his potential female consumers, he observed that

> As these compose half the World, and are by the just Complaisance and Gallantry of our Nation the more powerful Part of our People, I shall dedicate a considerable Share of these my Speculations to their Service [...] When it is a Woman's Day, in my Works, I shall endeavour at a Stile and Air suitable to their Understanding. When I say this, I must be understood to mean, that I shall not lower but exalt the Subjects I treat upon. Discourse for their Entertainment, is not to be debased but refined. A Man may appear learned, without talking Sentences; as in his ordinary Gesture he discovers he can dance, tho' he does not cut Capers. In a Word, I shall take it for the greatest Glory of my Work, if among reasonable Women this Paper may furnish *Tea-Table Talk*.[50]

The *Spectator's* alertness to, and direct discussion of, the relationship among gender, access, and comprehension was distinctive in positioning the periodical.[51] The care with which Mr Spectator delineates his approach ('not lower but exalt the Subjects I treat upon' in a discourse 'not to be debased but refined') indicates the perceived importance of the papers as a form of mediation of knowledge for those who might have been accustomed to being excluded or talked down to.[52] Addison is also explicit in his discussion of reach: in the tenth paper, he remarks with delight of his circulation figures of three thousand copies every day, at a cost of 1 penny each.[53] With an estimate of twenty readers to each of those issues, he imagines no less than 'threescore thousand Disciples in *London* and *Westminster*'. There was an intellectual and social ambition to the *Spectator* project – Addison hoped that through reading the periodical, his flock of sixty thousand would 'take care to distinguish themselves from the thoughtless Herd of their ignorant and unattentive Brethren' and that the whole effect of this will recover those readers 'out of that desperate State of Vice and Folly into which the Age is fallen'.[54] So within the *Spectator* – a publication dedicated to shifting cultural capital away from a narrow, wholly male social elite – there was still a crucial principle of differentiation. Some people, it is claimed, would still be kept out of the conversation, and inclusion was predicated on exclusion: 'the thoughtless Herd of their ignorant and unattentive Brethren'. Whether we should read this at face value, or see the faux exclusivity as another part of the marketing strategy of the periodical, this aspect of generalist literary criticism is essential to understanding the complexity of cultural literacy at this time. The currency of newly acquired knowledge and understanding would only hold its value if that knowledge were not really accessible to everyone – or, perhaps more importantly, if it was seen as being restricted. There were many reasons why early eighteenth-century literary works were sometimes designed to frustrate readerly comprehension, and this was one of them.

It is also clear, reading the *Spectator* and other contemporary periodicals, that the much-vaunted rhetoric of accessibility could be used to mock or even exclude certain kinds of readers as much as to help them.[55] As we've seen, the *Spectator*, like the *Tatler*, was explicitly aimed at female readers and those without conventional formal university education. The essays seem to open up discussion for those who had previously felt disqualified to enter a world of cultural debate: yet at the same time they also mocked a lack of knowledge or worldly *savoir faire* in readers. So, for example, in *Spectator* no. 568, Mr Spectator considers the phenomenon of political and topical insinuation in contemporary writing, and the use of blanks, asterisks, and initials to blot out names. He describes an encounter in the coffee house with two men, who offer absurd over-readings of a recent issue of the periodical and fall out over what they perceive to be hidden political commentary. Mr Spectator's response here is not an inclusive one. He uses the example of the two men's argument – and the subsequent anecdote of a reader who has marked up his copy of the devotional work, *The Whole Duty of Man*, with the names of the local sinners he knows. His aim is to ridicule inexpert readers and mock their limited faculties of comprehension, which in both cases lead to false applications:

> At my leaving the Coffee-house, I could not forbear reflecting with my self upon that gross Tribe of Fools who may be termed the *Over-wise*, and upon the Difficulty of writing any thing in this censorious Age, which a weak Head may not construe into private Satyr and personal Reflection.[56]

Any notion that Mr Spectator was trying to break down the barricades of literary culture evaporates when we see the ease with which he dismisses his contemporaries as a 'gross Tribe of Fools' or those with a 'weak Head'.

We can see a similar impulse to mock a naïve readership in other periodicals of this period, which occasionally also suggest that the male personae of the *Tatler* and *Spectator* might themselves be laughed at for their potential misunderstandings. The *Female Tatler* no. 81 of 9–11 January 1710 includes a letter to the editors from a female reader:

> *Ladies,*
>
> I Am a Young Gentlewoman that takes great delight in Plays and Operas, and reads the *Tatlers* both *Male* and *Female* as constantly as they come out. I generally understand every thing I read, all but what's *Latin*, and that I skip; but there is one cramp Word, for which Mr *Bickerstaff* has an extraordinary value, that puzzles me abominably; now I am used to it it sounds very well, every body seems pleased with it, and yet I can never meet with it any where else but in the *Squire's* papers. The Word I mean is *Lucubrations*. I read it a hundred times before I could remember it, and for a good while used to call it *Lubrications*, for which I was horridly laugh'd at by a Gentleman of my Acquaintance. Sometimes I have thought that it was Smutty, and blush'd at the hearing of it; but what is really meant I ingenuously confess I don't understand to this Day: I know several of whom I might be informed, but every body having it so

current, I was always asham'd of appearing more Ignorant than others. I wou'd Write to Mr *Bickerstaff* himself about it, but I doubt he is too high to take notice of such Blockheads as my self: Methinks I am satisfy'd it is something very Comical, and yet I perfectly long to know what it is. Wherefore pray *Ladies* Honour me with an explication of it, either by way of Advertisement, or in any other part of your Papers.[57]

This essay, with its accompanying letter, was written by Bernard de Mandeville, an author whose writings elsewhere betray some scepticism about the *Tatler* and *Spectator*'s democratizing rhetoric.[58] In this example, the letter-from-reader format, a genre often used to encourage an open discussion of cultural matters for a general public, is turned into a vehicle for satire. It is used to mock the readership it supposedly embraces, revealing the correspondent's lack of sophistication and imperfect interpretative skills, here centring on the use of the word 'lucubrations' and its potentially comic or bawdy implications. But the essay is also more complex than this. After the letter finishes, the editor of the periodical then proceeds to offer a mock-scholarly definition of the word 'lucubrations' before going on to suggest that perhaps Steele himself did not really know its meaning and was misleading his readers:

having used the Word too often in the beginning before he was aware, as soon as he saw it and found that other did the same, to prevent our thinking that he had been in an Error, he purposely seem'd to grow more fond of it, and endeavored to persuade the World, that he had all a-long design'd it as a Jest.[59]

Who is misunderstanding here? Is it the naïve female reader, or is it the muddle-headed author of the *Tatler* essays, who seems to be seeking to patronize her and her friends? The answer is probably both, reminding us of the complex dynamics of this moment of printed debate. The opening up of cultural debates in this period created space within itself to mock the very readers it was supposed to be bringing in. It gratified the knowingness of some readers by exposing the naivety of others. There is a double-edged quality to the negotiation of imperfect reading in the print culture of the period: ignorance or imperfect understanding created both a commercial educative opportunity and a source of satirical effect within the same text. The periodicals of the early eighteenth century have been widely seen as an exercise – albeit a demanding one – in cultural democratization. The publications discussed above have been variously claimed to show 'the coalescence of the upper and lower reading groups in a unification of interests, and agreement as to literary standards'; they demonstrate the construction of a public sphere in the literary world, and 'are the cultural arm of the making of the English middle class' – or as T.S. Eliot put it less kindly, Addison 'is definitely a writer for a middle class, a bourgeois literary dictator'.[60] Mr Spectator set out to reform and refine his countrymen by providing them with affable dictates on the polite arts. Yet, as we can see here, this exercise was more complex than it seemed because, as with the *Athenian Mercury*, the ignorant or foolish reader was also part of the entertainment offered by the publication.

## Joining the Club

So how did contemporary audiences engage with these seductive, if tricksy, invitations to join the world of polite culture? Part of the papers' appeal was the way they welcomed readers into a select social gathering. Addison and Steele and their fellow editors addressed their followers directly, describing the circumstances in which they read their papers at home or in the coffee house, and presenting the knowledge which they gave as the fruits of sociability—the offerings of a group of polite, informed friends. They encouraged readers to submit letters on certain topics, which were published. In doing so they reflected a pattern evident elsewhere, in which commercial print forms mimicked the coterie circulation that characterized manuscript writing.[61] An emphasis on polite conviviality, which proved so alluring to readers, applied some of the social attributes of coterie manuscript circulation to mass print, encouraging its consumers to believe that they were part of a group sharing values, ideas, and knowledge.[62]

There's an irony here and elsewhere in the literature of the period, in that an increasing accessibility of content was often mediated through

images of a more restricted literary culture. Points of entry and understanding were predicated on membership of a specific social group. The
fiction of the restricted social group is at the heart of the *Athenian Mercury*, which had lured its readers into dialogue with its little society of
experts, with whom the reader could be in direct communication. Peter
Motteux's *Gentleman's Journal* in the 1690s had a subtitle of a 'letter to a
gentleman in the country', emulating the manuscript newsletter, a genre
in which the epistle form had conventionally signalled the reader's membership of a group that was private or for insiders. The *Gentleman's Journal*
is a public, printed collection consisting largely of 'closet' pieces. Although
published for a widespread, anonymous readership, it demanded the participation of the readers as writers for its continuation.[63] It blended manuscript features with the ingredients of print; for example, it had a contents
page alongside all the personally submitted contributions from its middle
class (and often female) amateur correspondents.[64]

  This combination of inclusive rhetoric and readerly interaction seems
to have encouraged eighteenth-century consumers to engage with the
invented personae of early eighteenth-century periodicals as if they
knew them in real life. It's fascinating to see the way readers wrote about
Mr Spectator as if he were a living person. James Boswell declares in his
*London Journal*: 'I felt strong dispositions to be a Mr. Addison [. . .]
Mr. Addison's character in sentiment, mixed with a little of the gaiety of
Sir Richard Steele and the manners of Mr. Digges, were the ideas which
I aimed to realize'.[65] Later, he comments: 'The Spectator mentions his
being seen at Child's, which makes me have an affection for it. I think
myself like him, and am serenely happy there'.[66]

  The fiction of knowability – the reader's conviction that they were
getting access to a real person – is hugely powerful in this period. It
resonates through many contemporary works which negotiate public
and private, real and fictional, manuscript and print, often through a
rhetoric of sociable exchange.[67] Scandal narratives, secret histories,
epistolary fictions and poems, periodicals which mimicked a society of
friends, interactive satires with blanked out names and places, sociable
verse: all of these genres encouraged their readers to engage in fictional
or hidden worlds peopled by figures that they were unlikely to know

directly. (We might compare this with the podcast culture of the early twenty-first century, and the ways in which the genre enables listeners to eavesdrop on conversations between speakers they have never met and to correspond by sending messages.[68]) Why did readers want to feel included in the fictional coffee-house conviviality of the *Spectator* or the parlour tea-table debates of the *Female Spectator*? Why did they buy printed versions of manuscript verse exchanged between social groups that they could and would never know? Why did they puzzle to fill in the gaps in obscure mock-heroic medical satires, published a decade before? The history of reading and misunderstanding in this period is centrally linked to the fact that readers of all sorts wanted to engage with worlds of people very distant from them.

If part of the appeal of the early eighteenth-century periodical project was its fiction of a genuine persona, another key attraction of the papers was as a template for readers' own thought and conduct. The generalist essays authored by Addison, Steele, and their friends seem to have been valuable to contemporaries as a guide for their personal daily practice, showing them how to speak, write, and behave in modern society. The trainee lawyer Dudley Ryder, who lived in London in 1715–1716, finds in Mr Spectator an exemplar for courtship: 'Read some *Spectators* at night. Have resolved to read them over with very great care and attention in order to observe the peculiar thoughts upon gallant subjects such as are proper to entertain the ladies with'.[69] He continued to pore over the papers as part of his self-development: 'Read several *Spectators* from the beginning, having a design to read them all over again to improve my style and manner of thinking'.[70] The *Tatler* informed the way he presented his own observations to the world:

> Came into my closet. Read some of the *Tatlers*. His characters of human life are extremely fine and judicious, his method of raillery very delicate and exact. Intend to read them often to improve my style and accustom myself to his way of thinking and telling a story and manner of observing upon the world and mankind. [71]

Ryder clearly wanted to get to the bottom of what made the periodicals' insights so compelling: 'Read some *Spectators* and observed very carefully the manner of introducing their thoughts and how they lay in the mind of the author'.[72] And he wanted to mimic thoughts not just for his own intellectual growth, but also to impress others. We see here how far the emergent cultural criticism was linked to social performance. It was the way in which Mr Spectator talked about other people that was particularly compelling, and it was a skill worth emulating:

> At least I think it is very useful to be acquainted with books that treat of characters. Nothing fits a man more for conversation. This is indeed what the *Tatlers* and *Spectators* are most of all remarkable for, that you see the different manners of men set in a very clear and distinguishing light.[73]

The shopkeeper Thomas Turner was also a big fan, reading the *Spectator* and *Tatler* at work and in the evenings. He talks of his pleasure in one of the Spectator's *Paradise Lost* papers:

> Read part of *The Spectator*; prodigiously admire the beauties pointed out in the eighth book of Milton's *Paradise Lost* by *The Spectator*'s criticism, wherein is beautifully expressed Adam's conference with the Almighty, and likewise his distress on losing sight of the phantom and his dream, and his joy in finding it a real creature when awake. [74]

Turner's reading of *Spectator* 345 shows his receptiveness to Addison's presentation of Milton: he admires the beauties in the poem as they are shown to him, finds the wonders that the essayist has picked out, and it is hard in the end to work out whether it is Milton or Addison, as his curator, who is the real subject of praise.

An anonymous eighteenth-century reader of *Othello* also registers the impact of periodical criticism on his sense of the literary classics. On the title page of their copy of the play, now in Cardiff University Library, the reader declares: 'best next to Hamlet'. And on the verso of that sheet, they have added:

> In ys play ye favourite of ye audience was[?] under their calamity. Scene in ye 3d Act betwine Jago & Othello has bin alwayes justly

esteemd one of ye best wich was ever represented on ye Theater. vid. Guardian vol. 1er n:37[75]

The note suggests they have been reading the work alongside contemporary generalist literary criticism, in the form of the *Guardian*, the successor to *The Spectator*, which appeared between March and October 1713. The paper mentioned here, issue no. 37, offered the essayist's account of taking his female wards to see *Othello*. Having described his companions' responses, the author goes on to enumerate the beauties of this 'uneven' play, saving his greatest praise for Act 3:3:

> But there is nothing in which the Poet has more shewn his Judgment in this Play, than in the Circumstance of the Handkerchief, which is employ'd as a Confirmation to the Jealousie of *Othello* already raised. What I would here observe is that the very slightness of this Circumstance is the Beauty of it.[76]

As we can see, the owner of the Cardiff copy followed suit, framing his reading of the play and the particular qualities of the third act within the critical evaluation offered by *The Guardian*.

The *Spectator* was a source of great interest to Ben Browne, the yeoman farmer in Troutbeck. His eight-volume 1729 edition of the periodical is peppered with notes, manicules, and summary phrases, indicating a particularly thorough engagement with the essays.[77] As with his reading of Shakespeare and other works in his book collection discussed earlier, Browne's characteristic approach to the essays is to mark them up thematically. At the top of essays, or pages, he writes short descriptions of a key concern. 'Ovid. His description of ye Palace of ffame' appears on *Spectator* 439. 'Authors, for what most to be admired' on no. 355.[78] What's interesting is the topics that take his fancy: not every essay draws a comment. But some areas seem to be a particular focus for curiosity: 'Love, in what manner discover'd' in essay 325; 'thoughts on education' in 313; 'Snuff-taking' in 344; 'the art of growing rich' in 283.[79] What emerges from this series of jottings is a reminder of just what a rich world of expertise was offered to contemporary readers by the periodical. Within the few short pages of an individual essay, they could find useful, genial advice on nearly every area of contemporary life. If Addison and his friends were playing a game of cultural gatekeeping for their less well-educated contemporaries, it was one in which many amateur readers were delighted to take part. There is little sense that the readers discussed here felt that they were being excluded, mocked, or toyed with: they took the generalist, inclusive expertise of Mr Spectator and his companions at face value, and used it within their own lives.

The question of how to be a good literary reader in the Augustan period was far from straightforward. All the works discussed here are preoccupied with knowledge acquisition. They were all, remarkably, written within fifteen years of one another, and, although they function in very different ways, they are all attempting to explain in accessible terms the ways in which one ought to read, judge, and approach literature, and how to remedy a deficit of understanding or formal expertise with new forms of instruction. While they have different emphases, they are predicated on some shared assumptions: that not everyone knew how to understand or evaluate what they read, and that there was a group of readers who wanted more literary knowledge on easier terms. The new literary criticism shaped the way in which keen, non-expert readers approached imaginative works, giving them a framework and vocabulary to describe what they saw. However, at the heart of all these matters was a tension between accessibility and restriction. In apparently enabling new readers to become good readers, they show how vexed the dynamics of access were. Some of these texts exploited the potential comedy of their readerly engagements. What wasn't funny about earnest correspondents asking about farts and fish or the precise meaning of double entendres? And from Bysshe through to Addison and Steele, writers register some kind of unease at the idea that good reading could be taught by rules. It is within the context of these crosscurrents of explication and denial, opening and shutting of literary worlds, that we need to see the print culture and reading history of the early eighteenth century.

# 5

# Mind the Gap: Reading Topically

I can't conjecture ye meaning of this tho' tis capable of sevrl Interpretations.
—BEN BROWNE OF TOWNEND, TROUTBECK COMMENTING
ON JONATHAN SWIFT'S *TALE OF A TUB*

THE LAST THREE CHAPTERS have told a story of innovation and of confusion. From the Bible to the classics to the periodical essay, the Augustan era saw the burgeoning of print forms designed to help new and inexpert readers navigate their culture. But at the same time, those introductory works also reminded their users how easy it was to get things wrong, and how funny it was to miss the point entirely. And to add further complexity, across many disciplines there was a profound and hotly fought contest over what being an expert actually meant and who was capable of becoming one. What we shall see next is what happens when all these debates met real readers and real books, and how a world of misreading and muddle shaped the major and minor literary works of the period. And we begin with some of the most confusing writing of all, the massively popular and hugely evasive topical satires of the period, published in their hundreds and thousands and completely dependent on reader interaction to make their meanings.

The final decades of the seventeenth century and the first ones of the eighteenth are said to be the golden age of English poetic satire. Verse commentary on public affairs was the dominant poetic genre, and collections of topical verse satire were everywhere.[1] But what is not so

often said is that eighteenth-century political satire looks very odd and
is really difficult to read. Before we even begin to think about what
the myriad topical printed works of the era mean, we are faced with
pamphlets, books, and broadsheets whose formats deny us as much
information as they provide. There are hundreds of anonymous works
bearing titles which allude to long-lost controversies: *The Country Parson's Advice to Those Little Scriblers Who Pretend to Write Better Sense
Than Great Secretaries: Or, Mr Stephen's Triumph over the Pillory* (1706);
or *Poor Robins Dream, or the Visions of Hell: with a Dialogue Between the
Two Ghosts of Dr. T. and Capt. B.* (1681).[2] Even in their own time such texts
demanded substantial background knowledge of their readers. They are
not the kind of titles which promise easy entry points for those not already aware of the historical and political context. There are also entic-
ingly mystifying titles which refuse to reveal anything helpful at all
about what lies within their pages: *An Answer to the Great Noise about
Nothing: or, a Noise about something* (1705); *The Litany of The D. of B.*
(c. 1679); *The Dog in the Wheel. A Satyr* (1705); or *Mordecai's Memorial:
or, There's Nothing done for him. Being A Satyr upon Some-body, but I name
No-body* (1716).[3] Once inside the pages of the work, a bewildering range
of typographical play signals the need for readerly interaction and interpretation. Italics, dashes, asterisks, blackletter text, and capitals – and,
of course, blanked-out names, places, and words – were all put to work
to conjure a world of hidden meanings and interpretative puzzles. To
take one example, the title page of *The Plotters*, a 1722 verse satire on the
Jacobite court, has a subtitle which offers the reader further information
about the content, but which also obscures that information by providing initials instead of full names: '*Occasion'd by the Proceedings of the
Earl of Or—y; the Lord B. of R. the Lord N. and G. and Others*'.[4] A further
paragraph introduces more incomplete names and suggestions of intrigue. Within the book itself footnotes and marginal glosses are used
to help the reader decode the content, but these too are elusive: an
opening reference to '*He* who his Freedom cou'd, by Wit command' is
footnoted 'John S—ple', while the line '*Him*, who Ocean might ha' clean
gone o'er' is footnoted 'Capt. K—lly'.[5] Printed notes are supposed to

clarify and amplify meaning, not withhold it, but here, as in many other works, they are part of the game of interpretation. However, elsewhere the text is strangely fulsome in its self-explanation. Later on within *The Plotters*, we find notes explaining the allusions in the poem. In one case, a series of pastiches of contemporary writers such as Waller, Rowe, and Pope has a key to the names of the authors intended.[6] We might wonder why a satire would be presented in this way, so fraught with allusive and teasing references, and yet, at the same time, explaining or half-explaining them in the margins. The format of the book is ruthlessly exploited for its ludic potential, and the paratextual features which we might look to for clarification become part of the guessing game. Given this context, it is ironic that within the text of *The Plotters*, the poet declares his intention to make his writing open and clear for the reader:

> An AUTHOR having thus resolv'd to be,
> I'd let my gentle Readers the Whole see;
> 'Tis fit then we go back to th' Plot's first Spring,
> To th' utmost to describe and paint the Thing.[7]

As this discussion suggests, the interactive forms of textual presentation of eighteenth-century verse satire often made the reader their own textual editor. It was their job to supply the additional information needed to understand the work in front of them. Owners of works like the one described above wrote their explanations in the gaps and margins of the page. Sometimes they created their own footnotes. A copy of Paul Whitehead's satire *The State Dunces* (1733), a response to Pope's *Dunciad Variorum* (1732), shows its owner both neatly filling in missing letters to complete the names of individuals referred to in the text and supplying manuscript footnotes at the base of the page to clarify where necessary.[8] And although this reader has gone to some effort to provide this supplementary information and completion, only the first volume of the work has been marked up. In an era in which, as we have seen, textual scholarship was increasingly becoming the domain of the trained academic expert, it is ironic that the general reader was at the same time encouraged to create their own interpretative apparatus for the works they read. The kinds of materials that we now associate with the learned critic editor – marginal glosses, footnotes, and hand-written keys to allegorical representations – were handwritten on the pages of the books of the period by the non-specialists who pored over them. This chapter asks what we might learn from these puzzles and their puzzlers, and how we might better understand the cross-currents of incomprehension in eighteenth-century topical satire.

## How Did It Work?

Abel Evans's poem *The Apparition* (1710) is a work neither famous nor particularly remarkable. It is certainly not a poem which is accessible to the modern reader. A long verse satire in couplets, *The Apparition* is subtitled from the second edition, a 'Dialogue Betwixt the *Devil* and a *Doctor* Concerning a *Book* Falsly call'd, The *Rights* of the *Christian Church*'.[9] It is an attack on the deist Matthew Tindal, exposing the potential heresies and immorality of his writing. Published in January 1710, *The Apparition* was evidently popular, with four authorized editions in sixteen years and five piracies.[10] The majority of the editions and piracies date from the same year, and the proliferation of copies of the poem across research libraries of the globe suggests that, for a brief moment in eighteenth-century print culture, this pamphlet must have been everywhere.[11] We might now wonder why. From the detail of the religious dispute at its heart, to the referencing of a string of now unknown historical figures, it is fairly rebarbative as a modern reading experience. But for all this, it is also typical of many political or topical poetic satires of its time in depending heavily on reader interaction and completion to make its meaning. As such, it gives us some insight into how densely topical and allusive writings worked for their early readers.

The poem is a satirical response to Matthew Tindal's 1706 *The Rights of the Christian Church Asserted*, a controversial republican argument about the relationship between church and state which had elicited more than thirty contemporary responses.[12] The *Apparition*, like so many texts of the period, uses typography to set up a complex network of allusions, with blanked-out letters and italicized references encoding a host of intellectual and classical authorities, contemporary literary works, and recent political and religious events.

Many of the surviving copies of *The Apparition* have annotations by readers who have completed missing names which are now almost impossible for the modern reader to retrieve (figure 7). What is evident from the first pages of the poem is the tricksiness of the presentation of the text and its guessing games. Its difficulty was acknowledged by early readers, one of whom wrote on the title page 'a most excellent satire, if rightly understood'.[13] The poem recounts Satan's visit to Earth and his encounters with his supporters, depicted as Anglican heretics. But the identification of these figures is far from straightforward. The devil addresses the reader and describes some contemporary figures:

B——ss aloft Harangues the gaping Crowd,
While Witty H——G below *Blasphemes* aloud;
And to each other, tho' so Opposite,
Yet in my *Cause Both* lovingly Unite:
The N——T to my Wish proceeds,
Neglected *Gardens* must be choak'd with *Weeds*.[14]

The occlusions here seem taxing enough for the modern reader, but what makes them even more testing is that they operate with slightly different rules. We can see from the annotations in several annotated copies that readers had supplied 'Burgess' for 'B——ss', finding the letters at the start and end of the name enough to get them to Burgess (in this case Daniel Burgess, a celebrated Presbyterian minister). But the reference in the following line to 'Witty H——G', alluding to the poet and physician Samuel Garth, works in a different way – not only is the name absent, but the order of the letters in it is reversed. This is a poem which is deliberately confusing in its interpretative puzzles, swapping at random over the course of thirty odd pages between different kinds of hiddenness. The third occlusion in the passage above – 'The N——T to my wish proceeds' – is a different logic again; the letters are reversed, but here the reference is not to a person but a political principle, that of 'Toleration'. Some readers managed this shifting mode of encoding, deciphering all three references, while others seem

But hold ———my Time is almoſt quite expir'd;
Beſides, Below my Preſence is requir'd.
——— Rot theſe *Republicans!* I am Betray'd;
That *Tutchin!* has an Inſurrection made
With his Depoſing Doctrines ; but e're Day,
I'le teach that *Dog* ' *Hell's Monarch* to Obey.

Do Thou, then, quickly theſe few Orders take,
And I thy Room, at preſent, will forſake.
' To all thy real and admiring Friends,
' *Satan,* by Thee, his hearty Love commends.
' To T*ol*a*nd*, C*ollins*, St———*ns, A*ſ*g*i-*l*, tell,
' Sir R*obert* H*oward* Greets 'em kindly well;
' And hopes to ſee 'em ſhortly All———in *Hell.*
' From me the *Phœnix Editors* Salute;
' And I've a Letter here for Eſquire S*hit*te.
' *John* D*ryden* n, with his Brethren of the Bays,
' His Love to G*arth*, Blaſpheming G*arth*, conveys;
' And Thanks him for his *Pagan* Funeral Praiſe.
' Hopes W*icherl*y, whoſe Chriſtian Name is *Will,*
' Continues very Witty, Wicked ſtill :
' The like of C*ongre*ve, V*anbrook*, and the Reſt,
' Who Swear, that *all Religion is a Jeſt.*
' Tell Doctor B*urne*t, *Theory* I mean,
' His *Eve* and *Serpent* have our *Tatler* been:
' *Lucian,* the Maſter for that Dialogue Thanks;
' The *Snake,* and *Lady* faith, play———pretty Pranks.
' *Hugh Peters* ſomething ſaid, a Canting Sot,
' About One *Ben*———his Sir-name I've forgot:
' His *Meaſures of Submiſſion,* were Obey'd
' Exactly, by *Wat Tyler,* and *Jack Cade.*
' *George Fox* to *Lacy* had ſome Warnings groan'd,
' But his ſtiff Scribe was no where to be found:
' The Fool himſelf, can neither Write nor Read;
' The Motions of his *Chops* I did not heed.
' Old *Arius* cry'd, O *Lucifer!* I charge ye,
' Thank *Wh*i*ſto*n for his *Moneo* to the Clergy.
' *Oliver's* Porter ſtop'd me at *Hell's* Door,
' And in my Ears this *Propheſy* did roar.

*Hoadly*

C 4

FIGURE 7. Abel Evans, *The Apparition. A Poem. Or, A Dialogue Betwixt the Devil and a Doctor, Concerning the Rights of the Christian Church,* second edition (London, 1710), Bodleian Library, University of Oxford, G.Pamph. 61 (1), p. 22.

to have been foxed by it, completing only the names in which the letters were not reversed.[15]

The remainder of the poem continues in a mixed mode, giving and denying information seemingly at will, with different principles for disguising and revealing. Some names are completed, while others, such as biographical information about the Earl of Dorset are provided in a key. Elsewhere, as above, the letters are reversed. Sometimes the partial names are for specific people, such as 'C——ve' for 'Congreve', and, at other times, for groups of people, such as 'P——t' for Parliament or 'D——s' for Dukes.[16] Although we can find substantial discussion in contemporary political periodicals over the political dangers of such naming strategies, it is also clear that these typographical effects were often used merely to create an appearance of subterfuge. In the case of *The Apparition*, as with many other texts, what is said and not said does not correlate with whether or not the content is particularly libellous or compromising – the presentation seems to fetishize the act of not revealing and to insist on reader interaction, as figure 7 suggests. Because there are several annotated copies of the poem surviving, we can get some sense of how this piece landed, and how historical readers responded to the interpretative challenge.

One of the first things that becomes obvious from surveying a small sample of annotated copies of the poem is that no reader appears able or willing to complete all of the gaps in the text. None of the copies I have seen shows completion of all the hidden names.[17] We also see a variety in the kinds of information that readers supply. One provides a note on the title page about the identity of the author.[18] Another explains the lines on the devil assuming human form ('Like an *Old College-Bedmaker* he bent; / His *Cloven-Foot* he wriggl'd as he went') with an intriguing comment about Dr Tindal's personal life, noting that Tindal had shown 'too great familiarity wth his bedmaker'.[19] For this reader, perhaps someone closer to the Oxford context, the poem gives up its topical satire more fully than for others. The owner of a copy in the Bodleian, the one who wrote on the cover 'an excellent satire if rightly understood' seems not to have rightly understood many of the references in the poem, or at least has only marked in a couple of the blanks at the end.[20] But what they have done is to index the main themes of the poem in a fairly basic way, writing in the margins of the poem 'Churches or the Devil's Doctrine', 'Empire', 'Law', 'Plays', 'Rakes', 'Malice and Scandal'.[21] Another reader, probably a T. Hitchcock of St John's College, Oxford, used the margins of their copy of the work to fill out not just the names of the missing figures in the poem, but to provide a short explanation of who these people were, perhaps suggesting that these annotations might have been shared with others.[22] This is evidently not a poem that worked in the same way for everyone. The evidence of reader engagement demonstrates both an imperfect or partial comprehension of the text, and forms of response that betray different points of engagement.

## Editing Difficulty

Yet when we encounter such poems in their modern editions, we are presented with a reading experience markedly different from the ludic confusion evident in this example or in the thousands of other topical satires published at this time. This is particularly clear if we turn to the magisterial set of collected volumes of *Poems on Affairs of State: Augustan Satirical Verse, 1660–1714* (1963–1975), led by the Yale scholar George DeForest Lord.[23] The Yale *Poems on Affairs of State* was a huge research project, involving a large editorial team over several decades, which drew together hundreds of poems that originally circulated in manuscript and print, and republished them with headnotes and copious annotations. The topics covered the period from the accession of Charles II to the death of Queen Anne, spanning the Dutch Wars, the Exclusion Crisis, the Warming Pan scandal, the Revolution of 1689, and Henry Sacheverell's trial. The volumes' annotation is based on phenomenal archival and historical digging, and the notes retrieve each coded name, each allegory or symbol, and offer us a gloss on their intended meaning.

The edition supplies a comprehensive clarity of explanation that was not available at the time of the poems' initial circulation or publication.[24] These were verses, like *The Apparition*, issued almost wholly without annotation or contextual explication. But this is not evident from the Yale *Poems on Affairs of State*. The editorial treatment of the poems in this collection supplies all the missing words and identities, and offers a dense annotation explaining the background to the poem. For the modern reader, the experience of reading the poem is laborious because of the reliance on annotation. But it is also essentially passive – we are told all the answers, there is no guessing game, and each reader is granted the same level of knowledge and access. The general editor's introduction to the collection claims that 'the particularity which made them popular in their own day helps make them teasing and inscrutable in ours'.[25] Yet in using editorial annotation to remove the teasing inscrutability of these texts – an inscrutability that was always part of the reading experience – this and other modern editions present us with a very different reading experience from that of the poems' first readers.

The implications of this kind of treatment can also be seen in the *Poems on Affairs of State*'s representation of one of the longest and most dense topical satires of the period, Samuel Garth's mock-heroic medical satire, *The Dispensary* (1699). *The Dispensary*, loosely based on Boileau's satire on a clerical spat in *Le Lutrin* (1674), details the dispute between apothecaries and physicians over the building of a medicine dispensary for the poor at the Royal College of Physicians, broadly siding with those in support of the dispensary. Published in six cantos, the poem mocked the main protagonists in the fight, and the original poem contains a bewildering array of blanked-out dashes for names, combined with fictional titles such as 'Camillius', 'Horoscope', or 'Colon'. Even for its enthusiasts it has represented a challenge: 'It must be confessed that *The Dispensary* [...] is somewhat indigestible, though taken in small morsels it has a flavour'.[26] The poem was hugely popular in its own time: there were three editions between May and June of 1699, a fourth in 1700, and a fifth in 1703.[27] In all, ten editions appeared in Garth's lifetime, two of which were pirated.[28] At least three keys to the piece survive.[29] The poem's preface teases readers with the prospect of identification within the work:

If the *Satyr* may appear directed at any particular Person, 'tis as such only as are presum'd to be engag'd in Dishonourable Confederacies for mean and mercenary Ends, against the Dignity of their own Profession. But if there be no such, then these Characters are but imaginary, and by consequence ought to give no body Offence.[30]

Yet the elusive nature of the poem's intended significance is counteracted by the extensive editorial glossing which accompanies the Yale edition. The editors again replace the many blank dashes throughout the poem with names of historical figures – identifications derived from a combination of contemporary keys and historical scholarship. What's more, they also substitute their own interpretations in place of contemporary, authorial explanation. So, for example, when annotating a reference to the figure 'Horoscope', the editors note that Garth, the author of the poem, had identified Horoscope as someone called James Haughton.[31] However, the editors are not convinced Garth was right in this, and they instead suggest that he really meant the royal physician, Francis Bernard. We see here the expert editor's displacement not only of the ignorant early reader, but also the ignorant author.

Even a limited sampling of reader marginalia in surviving copies of Garth's *Dispensary* reveals again both the range of interpretation of specific figures, and, once more, demonstrates that no reader seems to have been able to understand all the references in the poem. So for example, glossing a line in Canto I, 'Why S——rages to survive Desire', the Yale editors remark: 'Since the meaning of this line is not absolutely clear, even contemporary readers made wildly varying guesses at the identity of S——, ranging from John Sheffield, Marquess of Normanby (Chicago University Library copy) to "Southcott A Baud in So-ho" (Royal College of Physicians copy)'.[32] Sir Charles Sedley and Henry Sidney, Earl of Romney, are also listed as contenders. In the end, the Yale editors plump for 'Scarsdale' to fill in their gap in the text, referring to Robert Leke third Earl of Scarsdale. Yet in doing so they betray a false certainty. Copies I have examined add further options on who is referred to here: other contenders for this figure 'S——' are 'Scotnor' and 'Sands'. And the uncertainty of early readers can sometimes be seen in annotation which points not to single identification but to multiple answers: a copy of the sixth edition in Wadham College Library in Oxford offers a reader's opinion on a line which refers to 'Two brothers, named Ascari-des'. The marginal note shows a reader uncertain about who this refers to, offering a note which says 'Bridges or Parrot 2 apothecaries'.[33]

The Yale edition prioritizes storing and showcasing of information above the experience of historical reading. No reader could really hope to be on top of all the references within *The Dispensary*, *The Apparition*, or many other allusive topical works of this period. And the fact that the edition gives the impression that such historical context was accessible creates a further problem if we are seeking to understand how such dense texts really worked in their own time. As Michael McKeon has argued, reading a poem like *The Dispensary* with the help of the enormous historical annotation supplied in the Yale volume is misleading. To presume that these coded and interactive works were readily intelligible to their original readers prevents us from seeing a fundamental part of their appeal because the fact that they did not fully deliver full disclosure was part of the point: the state poems did not simply dispel secrecy by disclosing what had been private to public view. Themselves illicit, they also sustained an aura of 'secrecy' by obscuring not only their own authorship, but also the precise nature of what they themselves were predicating about state affairs.[34] Their impact was dependent on the fact that they were almost impossible to access fully – that each act of reading would likely offer only partial clarity.

## Knowing Readers

The manuscript evidence discussed so far comes from multiple anonymous readers, engaging with the guessing game of decoding topical verse in their own ways, according to their own competencies. The slim traces of ownership on these copies enable us to infer little about the annotators' background and relationship to the topics at issue, contexts which provided a variable starting point for interpretation. We have more information about other owners and collectors of topical satires. The book collector and historian Narcissus Luttrell is an intriguing example of a reader who routinely marked up works in a recognizably consistent manner. Luttrell trained as a lawyer and had two spells as an

MP, but is chiefly known for his extensive book collection and his work as a chronicler of his times; his writings were posthumously published as *A Brief Historical Relation of State Affairs from September 1678 to April 1714* (1857).[35] Luttrell began collecting books in 1675 when he was still a student at Gray's Inn, and over three decades he accumulated a wealth of contemporary publications with a particular interest in political works and poetry, especially topical verse. The pamphlets he assembled have subsequently enabled scholars to piece together the print culture of many of the political and cultural debates of his age. In his *Life of John Dryden* (1800), the scholar and biographer Edmond Malone writes of Luttrell's role in preserving the print hinterland of Dryden's great Exclusion Crisis satires, *Absalom and Achitophel* (1681) and *The Medal* (1682):

> Both these poems accordingly were opposed by numerous Answers, of many of which even the titles would have been lost to posterity but for the care and attention of a gentleman of that time, Mr. Narcissus Luttrell, who [...] continued his Collection by purchasing the principal poetical productions that appeared in his own time, particularly those of a political kind, which he bound up in folio and quarto volumes.[36]

Luttrell clearly had a powerful combination of interest, expertise, and first-hand political experience that fed into his reading of contemporary topical verse. Here we have someone who seems to have been supersaturated in the political, literary, and cultural contexts of the topical verse of the time. So what kind of reader did that make him?[37] Study of Luttrell's written markings of his collection reveals some patterns: he commonly inscribed the date of publication of a work and the price paid for it on its title page, along with an indication of authorship and topic.[38] His title page comments are often a summary: 'Endeavouring to persuade ye Queen to quit the Whigg Interest and stick to ye Church' or 'a tory thing'.[39] The notes sometimes read as though he is not making a formal cataloguing but rather talking to himself, as on the title page of *An Address to the Honorable City of London ... Concerning their Choice of a New Parliament* (1681) where he writes 'Good wholesome advice and touches a little to home'.[40]

Luttrell collected and read hundreds of contemporary pamphlets and satires, and considering both this exposure to print and his political experience, one might expect that his annotations within the works would demonstrate a high level of political interpretation. But what we in fact find is that Luttrell's interventions show a patchy understanding of contemporary references, a delight in completion of scurrilous meanings, and a predilection for adding in largely unnecessary information. So, for example, his copy of *Commendatory Verses on the Author of the Two Arthurs, and the Satyr against Wit* (1700) bears Luttrell's description 'most scandalously abusive on Sr Richard Blackmore, a Physitian' on its title page, along with the date of purchase.[41] The *Commendatory Verses* are a collection of satires and lampoons mostly authored by the group of writers and allies known as the 'Christ church wits', who attacked Blackmore's writings and his political associates. It was an ad hominem literary spat which spilled out into politico-cultural debates of the period. One recent scholar has asserted that 'there must have been fairly widespread knowledge of the literary feud at the time [. . .] and many of the authors were known, or supposed, from the first'.[42] Many modern readings of eighteenth-century satires rest on such claims for reception history. But is that assumption correct? Luttrell was evidently reading other satires in this debate, as we can tell from surviving annotated copies.[43] Yet when we look at the detail of the way he has marked up his pages, we see that he fills in what entertains and is familiar to him – which is by no means all of the blanked-out content. He fills in missing identities that are in no doubt – so he completes Blackmore's name and title throughout the collection. He also completes some of the other occluded identities – for example, the authors Charles Boyle, Samuel Garth, and John Dryden. But there are many others which are left uncompleted, presumably because Luttrell wasn't sure who they referred to: these include the scholar Richard Bentley, the publisher Jacob Tonson, and Christopher Codrington. What he did complete without fail was the scurrilous and abusive content – 'A–rse', 'T–d', and 'Sh–te'.[44] This pattern is common across many of his annotated copies: he repeatedly fills in names which are not in doubt, frequently

fhall lead them fuch a Dance,
re not follow with their (r) *Nants.*

faid, it hap'ned that a Hot-fpur,
on one Heel had got Spur,
chance gaul'd-fide of Beaft,
not how to take a Jeft,
Kick'd about and Fa-y-ted,
he whole Battalion Started;
d at the dreadfull (s) Puff,
hey took the Smell in Snuff,

FIGURE 8. *The Irish Rendezvouz, or a Description
of T——ll's Army of Tories and Bog-Trotters*
(London: printed for Randal Taylor, 1689),
British Library, C.107.k.19, p. 8. Annotated by
Narcissus Luttrell.

leaves identities blank, and completes the scatological and the abusive.[45] A 1681 single-sheet broadside ballad entitled *The Tune of the Devonshire Cant: Or, an Answer to the Parliament Dissolved at Oxford,* bears
the note 'In defence of ye Parliamt', the date of publication, and the
completion of the word 'Fart' in the ninth stanza.[46] Luttrell's copy of the
1689 lampoon *The Irish Rendezvouz, or a Description of T——ll's Army
of Tories and Bog-Trotters* is filled in not only with the names of relevant
figures but also with the completion of blanked-out words such as 'Arse'
and 'Farted' (figure 8).[47]

Luttrell has taken the opportunity to fill in all the missing gaps, even
when their meaning was both obvious and inessential to the topical
intention of the poem. In other cases, he uses his marginal annotation
not to clarify missing identities but to expand on the titles of various
figures mentioned in the poem. In his copy of *Corona Civica* (1706) – a
poem addressed to the Lord Keeper, Baron Somers, and described by
Luttrell on the title page as 'A Fulsome flattering piece, in commendation of him and all ye Whigg party' – Luttrell writes repeatedly through
the work, not further information about the figures alluded to, but

merely the full title of men mentioned by name: Orford corrected to 'Earl of Orford', 'Somers' to 'Ld Somers'. and 'Marlbro' to 'Duke of Marlborough'.[48] A whole page is dedicated to filling in the words 'Duke of' next to the various nobles cited by name only in the text. Filling in the full title of named individuals does not seem to add materially to an understanding of the poem, but perhaps fulfils a need to engage in some way, to show some supplementary information, however inessential. If this is the work of an expert reader, one with access to twenty-four-carat political, literary, and cultural knowledge, what kind of response did such texts find in others?

Collections such as Luttrell's are rare. Mostly we have only scattered examples with little information about ownership. Occasionally libraries reveal an annotated book owned by a well-known author, as is the case with Alexander Pope's marked up volume of satirical verse. His copy of the 1705 collection of *Poems Relating to State Affairs* shows him engaging with the ludic elements of the reading process in much the same way as Luttrell does.[49] Pope is a more active annotator than Luttrell – he adds in more supplementary information to the text, and attempts to attribute authorship to individual items. In a poem entitled 'Dialogue Between two Horses', he notes next to a reference to a copper farthing that the copper farthing has a legend attached to it, and, in the Earl of Mulgrave's *Essay on Satire*, he notes that the poem reflects well on its author, describing it as 'the Author's Compliment to Himself'.[50] In places he seems to want to improve the verse: so, for example, he corrects the text of Sir John Denham's *Directions to a Painter*. Interestingly, nowhere does he register any kind of political or personal disapproval or dissent with the content he comes across, despite the fact that much of the argument must have been offensive to him. Like many other readers of his time, including Luttrell, he read texts that argued against his own viewpoint.[51] It's an interesting counter to the 'filter bubbles' that mark contemporary consumption of political polemic in digital reading.[52] While there are many parallels between the rise of print culture in the early eighteenth century and the advent of online reading in our own time, an appetite for reading content across political divisions does not seem to be one of them.

Pope also seems, like Luttrell, to take pleasure in filling in names and slurs even when unnecessary to the overall meaning. So, for example, in the lampoon 'The History of Insipids', he completes every 'C——' reference, of which there are many, with the name 'Charles', despite the fact that the whole poem is a republican attack on the king. We find him completing the identifications in poems with which he is unlikely to have been in political sympathy such as John Tutchin's *The Foreigners* or Andrew Marvell's *Hodge's Vision*. Pope fills in blanked-out content in the poems within the volume where he can, and many of the texts show a patchy competency in piecing together the references. The lines of William Walsh's 'The Golden Age Restored' are partially covered with attempts at completion, but there are also whole areas of suggestion left blank. In some ways it is not surprising that Pope was unable to complete all of the references in the poems within the volume; not only does the *Collection* represent a very specific set of satires on short-lived controversies, but most of the events covered by the poems date from before his birth. But it was still a book he wanted to take part in. An absence of comprehension does not seem to have limited his pleasure in the readerly games staged by the interactive forms of the poems. He continues happily to fill in poem after poem with what he can, playing the game at the level of knowledge he bears, his interaction undimmed by partial comprehension.[53]

It is significant that for Pope, as for other readers, the appeal of the game of completing the blanks in topical satires was not always diminished by historical distance from the events at the heart of the poems, or his own personal experience of the historical moment. There was, it seems, a pleasure to be had in trying to reconstruct the arguments of an earlier era even when those arguments were no longer in play. And this engagement with the interpretative games of long-past satires runs through to twentieth-century scholar-enthusiasts. The book collector James M. Osborn copied out his friend Maynard Mack's transcription of Pope's annotations of the *Collection of Poems Relating to State Affairs* in a copy of the volume now held in the Beinecke Library.[54] Some copies of Garth's *Dispensary* show a similar retrospective engagement. In a heavily annotated copy of the sixth edition of 1706 in the British Library, a reader has recorded next to the list of subscribers whether or not the figures are alive or dead at the point of writing: Garth, who died in 1719, is dead, but Daniel Coxe, who did not die until 1730, is alive.[55] The notes must have been made sometime in the late 1720s or 1730, almost two decades after the initial publication, yet still the reader is trying to puzzle out the complex world of physicians and apothecaries. And there are much later examples of the appeal of that challenge. Another copy of *The Dispensary*, which has 'RW Nov 30 1793' inscribed on the title page, shows the signs of readerly determination – and uncertainty.[56] Next to the line 'Charms in Lady G-', the reader has filled in 'Grace' but added in a note at the bottom 'Perhaps not Grace but Case the Doctors Wife mentioned p. 39'. Further on he makes suggestions as to the meaning of a reference: 'Seems to mean Golden Lane or Grub Street'.[57]

The kind of time lag between work and reader described here is often hard to pin down with any great accuracy. Few readers date their annotations and the ownership inscription may not belong to the same hand as that marking the pages. Even if they do correlate, the two may be written at very different times in the lifetime of an owner's reading. However, if we can't always determine the temporal gap between the moment of publication and the moment of annotation, marginalia does often give a sense of other kinds of gap – of knowledge, sophistication, or inclusion. I have argued that even 'expert' readers of the early eighteenth century were unable, it seems, to supply all the answers to the ludic satires of their time. Others, whose identities are now unknown to us, show some sense of unevenness in their knowledge. An annotated copy of a prose work by William Wagstaffe called *The Story of the St Alb--ns Ghost, or The Apparition of Mother Haggy* (1712), a satire on the Whig Junto, contains no marginal annotations, but on the verso of the title page is a handwritten key to the identities of the figures featured within it.[58] 'Haggit' is the Duke of Marlborough, 'Clumzy' the Duke of Sunderland, and 'Bacon face' the Earl of Godolphin. While the key shows this user to be competent in mapping fictional identity onto real-world figures, it also suggests some distance from the subjects of the poem, so that 'Jacobo' is identified as the publisher Jacob Tonson, but the author of the key evidently needs to clarify his role in relation to contemporary political life, by adding the supplementary information 'door-holder to ye Kit-Cat-Club'. A reference to

'Jointed-Babies' in the text is glossed with similar suggestion of a lack of sophistication: 'The Figure is intended for ye Procession on Queen Elizabeth's Birthday'.[59] This reader is not, it seems, someone at the heart of contemporary political life.

Elsewhere we can find readers who have mixed competencies in their knowledge, able to gloss with accuracy some kinds of content but not others. Narcissus Luttrell's annotated copy of a verse satire called *The Seditious Insects: Or, the Levellers Assembled in Convocation. A Poem* (1708) – a work Luttrell describes as 'A Scandalous Whiggish poem agt ye Convocaon & in commendation of ye Low Church men by name' – suggests that Luttrell was better able to identify the ecclesiastical and political figures in the poem than the literary ones. He is able, for example, to supply the names of all the bishops alluded to, but not all the poets.[60] By contrast, another contemporary reader, the owner of a copy of Richard Blackmore's *A Satyr against Wit* (a satire against contemporary Tory writers), is far more confident in identifying literary figures in the poem than political ones. [61] This reader is able to identify John Dryden, Joseph Addison, and Robert Boyle, but not very many of the clergymen who are also the subject of the poem. It's worth remembering that the topical satires of the early eighteenth century demanded a lot of their readers: in collapsing political, religious, cultural, and legal worlds to create their satirical fictions, they relied on knowledge across a range of fields – and perhaps, not surprisingly, their readers were not evenly skilled across this wide terrain.

And as we think again about the absence of knowledge foregrounded here, we might consider the literary ramifications of such practices. Readers clearly became used to both their own role as completers of the text and the fact that many works could not be fully solved. This was a fertile basis for the creative exploitation of missing text. The rise of the fragmented or purposefully incomplete literary artefact is often associated with Romantic and proto-Romantic writing, with ideas of the sublime and the ineffability of certain kinds of experience, as for example in Coleridge's 'Kubla Khan' or Keats's *Hyperion*. But we might also, more surprisingly, compare such fragmented works with the satirical forms of the earlier seventeenth and eighteenth centuries, which also use an absence of content for rhetorical effect. Some satirical works were clearly exploiting these textual effects. The anonymous *Manlius or the Brave Adventurer: A Poetical Novel* (1749) is an account of the Jacobite rebellion of 1745 in the form of a narrative poem.[62] It is peppered with blanked out words and opens with an imitation of Virgil's *Aeneid*:

> Arms and the Man renown'd, who last from——
> Attended with his seven steady Friends
> On——'s forbidden Coast did land
> In search of Glory, to retrieve the——[63]

The copy in the British Library shows us a reader who has dutifully filled in numerous missing words, many of which are nouns such as 'King' or 'Crown' or 'Home'. That reader has played their part in making the meaning and making the text whole. Yet the ending of the poem takes this game of absence to its extreme, using the occlusion of the final words of the poem to gesture to the unknown future of the Stuart pretender:

> Yet Fortitude and Virtue did support
> Young MANLIUS amidst Distresses great:
> JEHOVAH, whom he rev'renc'd from his Youth,
> Guided his Steps thro' Labyrinths of Woes,
> Till he at length *************

FINIS.[64]

The poem relies on its reader for its completion, yet the reader cannot provide the ultimate closure, because this political narrative is not yet fully written, its end not yet in sight. If we are to be attentive to the varied ways in which texts landed in their own time, we need to be alert to evidence such as this which pushes us to question what other readers made of what they found, and how far our abundantly annotated and explained modern editions of such works distort the original reading experience. Topical satire thrived in the early eighteenth century as never before, and as print culture burgeoned with polemical exchange and interactive forms, readers made their own meanings of the allusive and libellous confections within them.

# 6

# The Intimacy of Omission

There has been a comical paper about Quadrille describing it in the
terms of a Lewd debauch among four Lady's meetting four Gallants
[...] it was not found out a long time, the Lady's imagining it to be
[a] real thing begann to guess who were of the party. A great Minister
was for Hanging the Author. In short it has made very good sport.

—DOCTOR JOHN ARBUTHNOT TO
JONATHAN SWIFT, 5 NOVEMBER 1726

ARABELLA OR 'BELL' FERMOR, a seventeen-year-old Catholic heiress,
bore some of the most famous ringlets in history. Her hair, by a quirk of
literary fate, transcended its physical embodiment to become a symbol
for England, the new world, female virginity, and much else besides. As
Alexander Pope's Belinda in *The Rape of the Lock*, Fermor was re-
imagined as a beautiful warrior goddess, armed with hairpins and snuff-
boxes against the rapine of the elegant Baron, who had stolen a lock of
her hair. The poem famously takes the mythic proportions of classical
epic and shrinks them to the scale of teacups and hairpins, miniaturizing
literary models to address the dispute. Epic feasts of beefsteak are transformed into lacquerware and the ceremonies of coffee-pouring.

Accounts of Pope's poem have commonly described it as a *jeu d'esprit*,
a piece which in comparing a social incident between two families to
classical forms, flattered its subjects and transformed a social-diplomatic

event into a witty literary joke. The poem is one of the few works of the early eighteenth century that survives into the classroom syllabus of the early twenty-first century.[1] Its playful juxtaposition of the excesses of polite society with the rituals of classical epic has long made it a fine exemplar with which to introduce ideas of neoclassicism, politeness, satirical form, and the creative arts of imitation. But it is also a challenge to teach – I would not be the first whose students have met the poem with bewilderment.[2] Puzzled, sometimes fascinated, sometimes frustrated modern readers wonder what on earth Pope was getting at – is it just a joke about two rich families? Does it celebrate a modish world of card games and social spats, or does it suggest the emptiness of the culture that centred around such trivia? Does it represent female identity as empty and vain, or does it defend it? What, in short, is the point of the poem?

These questions about meaning are not merely the product of late twentieth- and early twenty-first-century critical uncertainties. A debate about purpose reverberates through the poem's reception history, and it is hardwired into the poem from its origins, in part because of the way *The Rape of the Lock* simultaneously references and denies biographical application. 'It must mean something, but what, exactly?' is a refrain which has characterized responses to the poem over three centuries. Pope frustrated his readers' desire to secure lucid interpretation, and the poem was, in turn, met with confusion. Because of this, *The Rape of the Lock* is an interesting place to begin looking at some of the ways in which a culture of imperfect comprehension operated in less overtly political contexts, in the occasional verse and coterie writing of the period. As we have seen in the previous chapter, political verse of the period set up games with its readers, creating forms of engagement and confusion through the withholding of full disclosure. What we begin to discern through the example of *The Rape of the Lock* and other forms of sociable verse is the degree to which similar forms of referentiality were used to encourage readers' engagement with friendship groups and specific social worlds, creating problems of interpretation and application. This particular dynamic of sociable verse – as it tantalizes with the revelation of intimate elite gatherings – offers striking evidence of the mixed competencies, imperfect readings, and interpretative uncertainty generated by the literature of the period.

## A History of Uncertainty

Pope's poem seems to have had an early and widespread appeal, which, according to John Gay, ran the length of the social spectrum from the literary elite to 'Pleas'd Sempstresses'.[3] Yet contemporary critics were foxed by the wider purpose of the poem, remarking on the mismatch between the heroic style and its slight subject matter. Charles Gildon, author of *A New Rehearsal* (1714), a satirical play, accused Pope of promoting novelty for novelty's sake, noting that the poet chose 'some odd out of the way Subject, some Trifle or other that wou'd surprise the Common Reader that any thing cou'd be written upon it, as a *Fan*, a *Lock of Hair*, or the like'.[4] Faced with the trifling subject matter, early critical readers nosed out hidden offence in Pope's lines, with their bawdy jokes about maids and bottles and pubic hair. At the heart of these charges lay a doubt about whether the poem really could just be about hair snipping and social faux pas. Eighteenth- and nineteenth-century critics were also not clear on its purpose. Romantic and Victorian readers criticized an indulgent want of design in Pope's satire – for William Hazlitt 'It is made of gauze and silver spangles [. . .] You hardly know whether to laugh or weep. It is the triumph of insignificance, the apotheosis of foppery and folly'.[5]

While this view continued to hold sway for much of the nineteenth century, during the twentieth century readers began to emphasize a new seriousness in its apparently slight subject matter. Although Pope's major biographer, Maynard Mack, describes the piece as 'a happy poem for a happy interlude', other critics emphasized the darker and more challenging resonances.[6] Yet the problem of meaning remained: even if it was serious, in what way was it serious? In the early 1960s, Aubrey Williams explored the relationship between the material fragility of china and the theme of sexual violence and chastity in the poem, arguing that 'amidst all the glitter and gaiety and irony, amidst all the shimmering brightness and lightness and sheer fun of the poem, there are insistent reminders of the shades just beneath and beyond the pale of paint and light'.[7] As this suggests, twentieth-century readings of *The Rape of the Lock* were often concerned with 'dangerous powerful motifs – sex and religion'.[8] For post-colonial critics, the poem is about the exploitation of empire, political economy, and the denigration of the fruits of slavery to a place on an Augustan dressing table.[9] Or it frames the objectification of women and replays traditions of misogynistic satire.[10] Some of these debates around the seriousness of the poem can be seen as a reflection of their own critical moment – a Romantic and Victorian emphasis on moral purpose in the late eighteenth and nineteenth centuries, while late twentieth-century interpretations were shaped by third-wave feminism and the material turn. But beyond the tides of critical fashion, the question of *what on earth the poem means* seems to have been a recurring feature of the *Rape of the Lock*.

The uncertainties described above touch on many different elements of the poem: its seeming silliness, its attitude towards its heroine, its moral propriety. These are different from the kinds of gaps and lack of knowledge found in the satires of the previous chapter. But in their demonstration of readerly uncertainty, they are an encouragement to go back and look at how the poem was built on unsettling meaning-making in the first place. In its contradictory signalling of its own referentiality, *The Rape of the Lock* was not unlike much of the occasional verse of the eighteenth century, playing with the sense of a knowable subject which often could not be fully identified by contemporary or later readers.

The origin myth of the poem is well known. At an unidentified social gathering in the summer of 1711, Lord Robert Petre, the son of a prominent recusant family, snipped off a lock of hair from the society beauty Arabella Fermor. Fermor and her relations were furious, and the incident prompted a substantial dispute between the two sets of landowners.[11] The action in itself was apparently trivial, but its social ramifications were not. In an attempt to pacify the warring factions, John Caryll, who had been staying at Petre's family seat in Essex around the time of the event, asked his friend Alexander Pope to write a poem about it, which might, he thought, 'laugh them together again'.[12] Pope himself was not a member of this social group – his family was not one of the established elite dynasties of Catholic families, and he had probably not met either side in the debate. He seems to have begun drafting the poem in the summer of 1711, and lines which later appeared in the published poem are included in letters to friends from that period.[13] Pope was writing coterie verse for a coterie of which he was not himself a member.

The verses first circulated in manuscript. Arabella Fermor handed them about to her friends, who knew the basis of the story and enjoyed its neoclassical metamorphosis – she seems to have been so pleased with the fictionalization that she later had her portrait painted by Sir Peter Lely wearing the cross Pope describes. The poem then moved into print, as a two-canto *The Rape of the Locke* (1712). According to Pope, he did not intend the poem to appear in this way, but was forced to publish because of the threat of a pirated edition: 'Copies of it got about, and 'twas like to be printed, on which I published the first draught of it'.[14] At this point, no link was made in the text between the figure of Belinda and Arabella Fermor as the biographical source of the story. Those at the heart of the affair might have recognized that Arabella Fermor was given the poetic code-name Belinda, Robert Petre was the Baron, and Sir George Browne, a cousin of Fermor's mother, was Sir Plume. But the poem mixes generic identities with these specific figures – so for example, Belinda's accomplice Clarissa does not seem to reference any single individual.

Although Pope's anonymous publication of the first version of the poem in May 1712 apparently had Fermor's agreement, Fermor subsequently seems to have had some misgivings post-publication: Pope writes that 'the celebrated lady herself is offended, and, which is stranger, not at herself but me'.[15] There is some sense among later commentators that the subject of the poem was foolish not to have understood her own representation in the poem. The author of a satire entitled *The Plotters* (1722) writes:

I laugh'd, like * *Ale*, when ** *Belinda*'s Breast
Approv'd the Picture, nor the Painting guest;

Or like the *Lady*, when her easy Eye
Smil'd at the *Lock*, nor knew it grew so nigh.[16]

[*Mr Alexander Po---e.
**Mrs. Ara. Far---r.]

The suggestion is that Arabella Fermor was an imperfect reader of
her own poem, not able to see what was intended by the *Rape* or the
potential dangers of the application. And at this point Robert Petre, the
lock snipper himself, was also less pleased about what he saw – perhaps
because he realized, reading more carefully, that the foppish Baron was
not an entirely flattering depiction, or perhaps because it was one thing
to be gently mocked among a group of friends, but quite another to
expose a private joke to an anonymous public. Others who similarly
identified rather unflattering portraits of themselves also seem to have
complained. On 8 November 1712, Pope wrote to Caryll 'Sir Plume blus-
ters, I hear', referring to Arabella Fermor's cousin, Sir George Browne,
who had cavilled at the harsh but apparently accurate depiction of him
as the vain Sir Plume 'of *Amber-Snuff-box* justly vain, / And the nice
Conduct of a *clouded Cane*' (II, 41).[17] Pope himself felt burnt by the
reception of the poem by its subjects:

> The best way I know of overcoming calumny and misconstruction is
> by a vigorous perseverance in every thing we know to be right, and a
> total neglect of all that ensue from it. 'Tis partly from this maxim that
> I depend on all times upon your friendship, because I believe it will
> do justice to my *intentions* in every thing; and give me leave to tell you
> that as the world goes this is no small assurance I repose in you.[18]

Pope claims that his poem has been misread and sees his friend
Caryll's intervention as the only option for setting this right. (It was, it
has to be said, a little bit disingenuous to talk of calumny and misconstruction given the mixed signals the poet was giving about the poem's
referentiality.) The fact of publication seems to have put more pressure
on its first readers, those at the heart of the Fermor-Petre circle, to identify themselves within the poem and examine how they might appear
to others outside their group. Already we can see that the 'meaning' of

Pope's poem was altered by a sense of who the wider readership might be. While it had circulated in manuscript among a group of intimate friends, 'with the air of a Secret', the figures lying behind the poem seem to have accepted the slipperiness of the fictional representation. After print publication, the poem was opened up to a range of potentially less sympathetic readings, and the friends were less happy about its significance.

This shifting sense of reference and meaning did not end here. Robert Petre died unexpectedly of smallpox in 1713, but the poem in which he was memorialized continued to evolve. In 1714, Pope published a significantly expanded, five-book version accompanied by six engravings and a preface dedicated to Arabella Fermor. The first two-book version had sold poorly, but the second, expanded version, published by Bernard Lintot on 4 March 1714, was an enormous success: a second edition was issued within days, and a third appeared in July. On 12 March 1714, Pope wrote to Caryll that the first issue had 'in four days time sold to the number [of] three thousand, and is already reprinted tho' not in so fair a manner as the first Impression'.[19] New printings were issued in 1715, 1717 (including further revisions), and 1723. Its reach extended far beyond the small social clique at the heart of the story, and as it circulated ever more widely within contemporary print culture, its resonance and its sense of topicality undoubtedly changed. This second edition may have been intended in part to soothe those who had been displeased by their satirical representation in the poem. Pope explained to Caryll in December 1713 that he was revising the poem and dedicating it to Fermor 'as a piece of justice in return to the wrong interpretations she has suffered under on the score of that piece'.[20] Within his dedication, Pope addressed the move from private to public circulation:

it was intended only to divert a few young Ladies, who have good Sense and good Humour enough, to laugh not only at their Sex's little unguarded Follies, but at their own. But as it was communicated with the Air of a Secret, it soon found its Way into the World. An imperfect

Copy having been offered to a Bookseller, You had the Good-Nature for my Sake to consent to the Publication of one more correct.[21]

While the first two-canto edition of *The Rape of the Locke* appeared without prefatory comments or mention of the source of the story, the second, expanded edition of the poem reinforced its origins in a specific coterie through its preface to Fermor and suggestion both of the 'air of a secret' and of the social origins of the incident 'intended only to divert a few young Ladies'.

In a letter to Caryll, Pope explained his thinking behind the concealment of identity in the poem:

> As to the *Rape of the Lock*, I believe I have managed the dedication so nicely that it can neither hurt the lady, nor the author. I writ it very lately, and upon great deliberation; the young lady approves of it; and the best advice in the kingdom, of the men of sense has been made use of in it, even to the Treasurer's [Robert Harley, Earl of Oxford and Mortimer]. A preface which salved the lady's honour, without affixing her name, was also prepared, but by herself superseded in favour of the dedication. Not but that, after all, fools will talk, and fools will hear 'em.[22]

Pope claims here that his partial identification of Fermor was an attempt to try to manage the exposure of the figures within the poem, to protect them and also himself. By revealing more, he paradoxically protected his subjects. But it is also the case that the dimly lit exposure of individuals in the poem, who were visible through initials, blanks, and fictional names, continued to tease readers with tantalizingly partial access to this world. In both the first and second editions of the poem Caryll was referred to only by initial 'This Verse to C---, Muse is due', and the name did not appear in full until the posthumous Warburton edition of 1751. In a letter of February 1714, Pope told Caryll that he thought of putting the name in 'at length' in the enlarged second edition, but 'I remembered your desire you formerly expressed to the contrary'.[23] In mixing fictional and biographical characterization, both revealing and concealing its origins in a Catholic coterie from which Pope would be increasingly concerned to distance himself, *The Rape of the Lock* played with its readers' desire to know more about the actual social world that it transfigured, or, as J. Paul Hunter puts it, 'to invade the privacy of those involved, to have knowledge of their private lives, to ogle them and eavesdrop on their lives'.[24]

The evidence of marked-up copies of the poem shows the way in which readers, presumably at some distance from the subjects, clearly thought it important to decode the poem by noting the identities of figures within it. A copy of the 1714 second edition with the ownership inscription 'Phill. Musgrave' provides the name 'Caryll' in the blank at the opening of Canto 1: 'I sing—This Verse to C---l, Muse! Is due'.[25] No other names are supplied on the text, but Musgrave has underlined and made marginal notes next to phrases and couplets that he seems to have found particularly striking, from 'Mighty Hearts are held in slender Chains' to 'Beauty draws us with a single Hair'. Another copy, in the Bodleian Library in Oxford, seems to show a reader who misidentifies Belinda as someone by the name of 'R Stewart'. On the seventh page, beneath the description of Belinda waking to her billet doux, is written 'R Steuart' at the bottom of the page, and the name is repeated under Louis du Guernier's engraving of Belinda at court before the start of Canto 3.[26] Recent unpublished work by Valerie Rumbold has traced the way in which the character of Thalestris, unidentified in the lifetime editions of Pope's poem, gradually became attached in late eighteenth- and nineteenth-century editions to a Mrs Morley. Assertions about the putative relation of this original to Sir George Browne (original of Sir Plume) and other Morleys have been contradictory, largely unevidenced, and sometimes plainly erroneous – but also remarkably persistent.[27] The mid-nineteenth-century editor Robert Carruthers seems to have spoken for many when he opined that 'Of the characters introduced we know less than most readers would desire'; for it is clear that commentators have cared far more about telling readers the names of people behind the poem's characters than Pope himself ever did.[28] What all this suggests is that *The Rape of the Lock* was a poem that seemed to demand some forms of specific identification, yet denied many of its readers a confident sense of interpretative closure. Like so much social verse of the time, its playful evocation of a hidden private joke is dependent on its readers' inability to pin down all its reference points: perhaps a good reader of *The Rape of the Lock*, as with many other works of the period, is one who knows they don't know the answers.

## Making It Up

One of the changes between the two-canto version and the five-canto version was the inclusion of a preface in which Pope emphasized the role of his artistic imagination, stressing that the events and creatures of the poem were the products of his fancy. He said that the cantos were:

> as Fabulous, as the Vision at the Beginning, or the Transformation at the End [ . . . ] The Human Persons are as Fictitious as the Airy ones; and the Character of *Belinda*, as it is now manag'd, resembles You in nothing but in Beauty.[29]

With these words on the imagination, Pope moves out of biographical specificity, and, importantly, into a world of poetic imagining that is more clearly his creation and less indebted to the Fermor circle for approval or interpretation.[30] It is an extraordinary sleight of hand within a few lines both to inform readers of a tantalizing real-world source of the poem's visions of polite excess and conflict, and at the same time to claim the entire poem as a work of the imagination. In an essay on teaching the poem to contemporary students, Arlene Wilner notes that she begins a classroom discussion of *The Rape of the Lock* by 'reviewing the historical occasion for the poem and making sure students understand "the plot".'[31] But as we see here, the relationship between the historical occasion and the historical subjects is not in itself straightforward. Its author signals that the poem both is and isn't about a specific group of individuals in a specific moment. *The Rape of the Lock* is both a piece originating in a little friendship group, and, at the same time, an imaginative vision that has nothing to do with that world. We see how some of the fault lines of the poem's critical reception might stem from Pope's original Janus-facing orientation of his work. No wonder readers have been confused. As we shall see, this combination of specific and non-specific reference was central to much of the sociable verse of the period.

This staging of interpretative challenge is also present in Pope's use of his sources for the poem. He writes in his dedication to Fermor:

> I know how disagreeable it is to make use of hard Words before a Lady; but 'tis so much the Concern of a Poet to have his Works understood, and particularly by your Sex, that You must give me leave to explain two or three difficult Terms.[32]

By 'difficult Terms' Pope here means his earlier reference to the mythic machinery of the poem, which he had described as based on 'the Rosicrucian Doctrine of Spirits'. Although the main problems of readerly 'understanding' of Pope's poem did not and do not primarily seem to lie in the matter of Rosicrucian doctrine, the explanation that Pope went on to give of this intellectual background offers further insights into the complex web of reference with which he is muddling his readers. In order to help them understand the *Rape*, Pope directs his reader to *Le Comte de Gabalis* (1670) by Abbé Villars, a book which, in describing a kind of sprite, was a model for *The Rape of the Lock's* otherworldly sylphs. However, *Le Comte de Gabalis* was more than a source of airy visions, being in itself a work notoriously difficult to interpret and widely misread. *Gabalis* had been read as both a satire on and a defence of occult beliefs. It was a work which secured no interpretative consensus. Joseph Warton's later account of *Le Comte de Gabalis* describes a work whose fate chimes uncannily with that of Pope's poem:

> The five dialogues of which it consists, are the result of those gay conversations, in which the Abbe was engaged [. . .] with a set of men, of fine wit and humour, like himself. When this book first appeared, it was universally read, as innocent and amusing. But at length, it's consequences were perceived, and reckoned dangerous, at a time when this sort of curiosities began to gain credit. Our devout preacher was denied the chair, and his book forbidden to be read. It was not clear whether the author intended to be ironical, or spoke all seriously.[33]

*Le Comte de Gabalis* was a work that framed questions about the stability of irony and parody in this period; it was a piece which began as a light-hearted joke among a small group of friends and was later taken to be dangerously heretical. In *The Rape of the Lock*, Pope drew attention to and used as a primary source for his mock-heroic poem a work that was already fraught with interpretative uncertainty.

The evolution of *The Rape of the Lock* offers us a fascinating insight into interpretation and misreading in Augustan print culture. The poem began as a private joke that circulated in manuscript form and ended up with widespread print dissemination. It started life as a response to a very specific topical incident, but once it met wider circulation, its author disavowed this specific frame of reference. Its subjects were happy to be figured as fictional figures until they realized that their portraits weren't quite so flattering. What and whom the poem referred to kept changing. We can discern how the restriction of access to the identities of specific figures could help increase the allure of a poem framed as emerging from a glamorous coterie but at the same time create a very uneven reception. One might say that *The Rape of the Lock* models the challenges of referentiality within eighteenth-century verse. As with much of the topical writing of the period, it is a poem which both exploits and frustrates the problem-solving interactivity that so much eighteenth-century literature seems to invite.

## Unlocking the Lock

As we have seen, from its first publication *The Rape of the Lock* garnered critical confusion over its true meaning. Critics attacked the poem for its indecency: applying the deadening hand of sexual morality to the erudite froth of Pope's poem, they read his hints and allusions to the female body and female sexuality as profanity. In *A New Rehearsal*, Gildon suggested that Pope had made 'the Ladies speak Bawdy, no matter whether they are Women of Honour or not', while in his satirical ballad, *The Catholick Poet* (1716), John Oldmixon accused Pope of bawdry: 'Growing warmer, and warmer, / He *Ravish'd a Lock* from the pretty *Bell. Fermor*, / And thought with vile *Smut* to have charmed, the *Charmer*.'[34]

The subtext of much of this criticism appeared to be that what may look like a harmless jest must be dangerously immoral in its tendencies. The confusing nature of the *Rape of the Lock*'s relationship to the world it came from made it ripe both for suspicious interpretation and for parody of those suspicions. As we have seen, a confusion over the scope of the poem's satire was inbuilt by Pope himself, who positioned and repositioned the poem in contradictory ways. And his gaming of his readers continued with his 1715 publication of *A Key to the Lock*, a pamphlet which purported to be a definitive guide to the secret subtexts of the fashionable but elusive poem. *A Key* was published a year after the five-canto version, under the pseudonym Esdras Barnivelt. Its subtitle mocks the outraged tones of so many of Pope's detractors: 'A Treatise proving, beyond all Contradiction, the dangerous Tendency of a late Poem, entituled, *The Rape of the Lock*, To Government and Religion'.[35] *The Rape of the Lock* had been attacked for many things – its indecency, the nature of its classical borrowings, its whimsicality – but never, until now, its politics or religion.[36] They were topics that appeared frequently in other pamphlet attacks on Pope and his works, many of which invoked Pope's Catholicism and purported Jacobitism as grounds for their critique.[37] *The Key to the Lock* shows us Pope poking fun at the habits of over reading and application which he had himself encouraged in the presentation of his poem:

> Since this unhappy Division of our Nation into Parties, it is not to be imagined how many Artifices have been made use of by Writers to obscure the Truth, and cover Designs, which may be detrimental to the Publick; in particular, it has been their Custom of late to vent their Political Spleen in Allegory and Fable.[38]

In the *Key to the Lock*, Pope embraced the questions of significance and meaning that had plagued, and continue to plague, his poem. He took the idea of political conspiracy, the one way in which *no one* had interpreted his poem, and applied this theory, painstakingly and line by line, to the verse. The *Key to the Lock* was a festival of overdetermined misinterpretation. Barnivelt announces triumphantly, at the start, that Belinda represents no less than Great Britain, the giveaway lines being 'on her white breast a sparkling cross she bore', which, he reveals, alludes to 'the antient Name of Albion, from her white Cliffs, and to the Cross, which is the Ensign of England' (11). The lock of hair was the barrier treaty which had concluded the war of the Spanish succession. The lap dog, Shock, was the Anglican clergyman Dr Sacheverell, and the game of ombre was the war of the Spanish Succession itself. If one were actually to apply all these readings to the poem, the allegory would not stack up – not least because Barnivelt assigns multiple historical identities to the same characters, so that Belinda is at once Queen Anne, England, and the Catholic Church.[39] Like many conspiracy theories, it attempts to combine a series of discrete suspicions into an overarching thesis, which cannot be sustained by the weight of the evidence.[40]

In assembling such a nonsensical series of interpretations, Pope mocked the ways in which his contemporaries distorted what they read as they tried to pin historical and political specificity onto a work of the imagination. But there is more to the *Key* than this reader-teasing. There was an irony in Pope's rebuttal of specific application, because at some level he was actually using his *Key* to address biographical difficulties lying behind the satire. One of the purposes of the pamphlet was to defuse the offence caused to Sir George Browne, who had objected to his portrayal as Sir Plume. In the *Key*, Pope suggested that there were multiple claimants for the person of the foppish and vain knight:

> Upon the Day that this Poem was published, it was my Fortune to step into the *Cocoa Tree*, where a certain Gentleman was railing very liberally at the Author, with a Passion extremely well counterfeited, for having (as he said) reflected upon him in the Character of *Sir Plume*. Upon his going out, I enquired who he was, and they told me, *a Roman Catholick Knight*.
>
> I was the same Evening at *Will's*, and saw a Circle round another Gentleman, who was railing in like manner, and shewing his Snuffbox and Cane to prove he was satyrized in the same Character. I asked this Gentleman's Name, and was told, he was a *Roman Catholick Lord*.[41]

By suggesting that at least two separate Catholic men claimed to be the original of Sir Plume, Pope probably aimed to blunt some of the force of the poem's earlier hostile reception from Browne, who had apparently threatened violence when he read the poem. There is also a suggestion that the *Key* enabled Pope to update his satire and give it more topical relevance: Swift wrote to Pope shortly after the publication of the pamphlet: 'I saw the Key to the Lock but yesterday: I think you have changed it a good deal, to adapt it to the present times'.[42] From Swift's point of view, far from downplaying the topical significance of the original poem, the *Key to the Lock* enabled Pope to refresh its contemporary political relevance.

The *Key* shows us a writer disavowing the specificity of his work while simultaneously trying to manage the outcomes of its intended application. It reveals the complex relationships between topical social satire and its reception in a wider world, and the degree to which the process of dissemination created uncertainty among readers. The *Key to the Lock* purported to clarify the intended meaning of the poem, but of course, all it actually did was to parody habits of over-interpretation. And unsurprisingly, it produced new uncertainties in its readers. On 29 May 1728, Mather Byles wrote to Alexander Pope: 'Forgive me Impertinance if I beg leave to give you one Trouble more, and ask, who was the [Au]thor of the *Key* to the *Rape of the Lock*? and what was the true design of that satirical performance, The *Key*?'[43] For Byles, reading the *Key* some fifteen years later, it was not at all clear what the purpose of the key was – he relies on Pope's authority to tell him. Yet as we have seen, Pope seems to have changed his mind over what exactly that meaning was as the poem and its reception evolved. We see the hall-of-mirrors world of Pope's poem, in which understanding is ever deferred – a poem whose meaning and frame of reference is unclear, whose author wrote a satirical key to point to the dangers of overreading, a key which was also not understood by readers. Mather's question, like the *Key* itself, touches on contemporary perceptions of the relationship between a text and the person who wrote it. Was the author the key to its meaning? In a culture of mass publication, and often, anonymous authorship, the notion that a reader might better understand a work by knowing more about the personality, intention, or biography of its author was becoming increasingly untenable. Yet the author and their story were still something that readers looked for to clarify meaning.[44]

## Sociable and Occasional Verse

The example of *The Rape of the Lock* shows how a literary work could move out of the initial circumstances of its composition, and in circulating more widely raise questions of intention and significance. In doing so, it exposes the complex role of social circulation in the creation of meaning. It also illuminates the challenges posed by the transition from small group to wider public dissemination. Although Pope clearly invited early readers to see his poem as a coterie piece, he also denied those readers full access to that exclusive world. *The Rape of the Lock* is a poem which plays with the dynamic of inclusion and exclusion which is at the heart of so much early eighteenth-century literature – a dynamic particularly evident in occasional verse, described by J. Paul Hunter as 'by far the most ubiquitous and popular class of poetry in eighteenth-century England'.[45] There are hundreds of poems of this period and later which use particular events and social specificity to offer a teasing inclusion to the worlds they describe. Many address a named or specific audience: 'Impromptu to a Young Lady Singing'; 'Written at Bath to a Young Lady who had just before given me a short answer'; 'An Epistle to Flavia, on the Sight of Two Pindarick Odes on the Spleen and Vanity, written by a Lady her Friend'. Other forms – such as dialogues, verse epistles, addresses to specific friends, and occasional pieces, written by both men and women – allude to individuals through concealed identities or locate events within specific local settings. These popular but often overlooked modes of 'sociable verse' or private occasional verse seem to gesture to known, limited audiences yet were bought and read by groups far beyond the single or small group readerships imagined in their titles or prefatory materials. By exploring some of this overlooked material we can see how a readerly information deficit was often key to the genre of occasional writing.

## Group-Think

Not all occasions are equal, and within occasional verse the trope of the familiar exchange worked very differently from one publication to another. Some works must have circulated in print within a fairly restricted reading group. So, for example, a poem called *The Celebrated Beauties: Being an Heroick Poem, Made on the Colledge Green and Queen's Square Ladies* was published in Bristol by Joseph Penn in 1720.[46] There was only one edition. Its title page bears the Ovidian epigram, '*meritas celebrare / Puellas dos mea*' ('it is my gift to celebrate deserving girls'). It is a light-hearted celebration of a group of women from the West Country city: 'Each Sov'reign Beauty I'll to you rehearse, / You view them, as they Crown my flowing Verse' (3). The poem paints contemporary Bristol as a pastoral idyll, the whispering breezes and shady delights of the 'verdant plain' of the college green, and sets up a guessing game for its readers by giving the real-world figures it describes neoclassical names:

> Ye Sons of *Mars*, now Guide my wandring Pen,
> You best can tell, how *Delia*'s Charms do Reign,
> Your Rhetorick can best describe her Mein,
> But not to you alone she seems Divine;
> Though Soldiers lay aside their heavy Arms,
> and are enthrall'd by her endearing Charms,
> Yet all their vain Efforts can't pierce her Heart,
> An *Æsculapius* best can play his Part.[47]

There are only two surviving copies of the poem. One is a clean copy in the British Library, and the other, in the Beinecke Library, is annotated by a contemporary who filled in the fictional names of nearly all of the women mentioned in the poem, though they were not quite able to identify all of the men.[48] In the passage quoted above, the book's owner or reader has glossed Delia as 'Mrs Winter' and 'Aesculapius' as 'Mr Winter' but other names proved more taxing: the real-world figures behind 'Priscus', 'Celsus', 'Godolphus', and 'Marcus' all resisted decoding by this particular reader.

The limited number of surviving copies of *Celebrated Beauties* suggests that it was a provincial publication without extensive circulation, aimed at a smallish social group who would enjoy the pastoral transformation of their world and its friendships. There are many such local productions, and they often play with their accessibility to those outside the circle they describe. The inventor and poet Richard Poekrich's *The*

*Temple-Oge Ballad* (1730) is a poem centred on a village in southern County Dublin, and it claims to be published nearby 'at the Cherry Tree' in the town of Rathfarnham (although it was almost certainly published in Dublin).[49] It only appears in one edition and is a false imprint of the Dublin publisher George Faulkner.[50] The title page has an epigraph from *The Rape of Lock*, but the poem itself is concerned with matters much closer to home, offering a satire on local figures and their social lives, amours, and writings. Like the political satires of the period, the poem plays with the paraphernalia of explanation – the footnotes to fictional figures offer us blanked-out names and only suggestive descriptions of those involved. A line declaring that 'The RIVAL QUEENS, with equal Charms, / Attract the Standers Eyes', has a footnote attached which takes us to 'Miss *Pen—f—er* and Miss *Ve—y*, two Lady's equally Amiable'.[51] The lines 'I speak to *B—y—le* and *H—pson* to, / You shou'd your Parts with warmth pursue' is footnoted: 'These are two young Gentlemen every way agreeable and have very good Sense, but are liable, by the Company they keep, to Degenerate; this is a Friendly Admonition, and I hope they will be sensible of it'.[52] The marked-up copy in the British Library shows a reader filling in these blanks fairly assiduously – the pleasure of knowing enough to do this sits alongside the tease of the footnotes which prompt as many questions as they answer.[53] Once again, the paratextual apparatus which was supposed to clarify meaning was used to further entangle it.

It seems likely given the limited publication history and survival of this poem that it had a currency for those familiar with this local scene but not for those far beyond it. However, other collections, many of which are presented as the fruit of university or male clubs, were consumed by readers at some distance from their point of origin. Elijah Fenton's 1708 collection of *Oxford and Cambridge Miscellany Poems* contains works by authors from across several decades, and it includes pieces which are anonymous but refer to specific events (such as, 'To a Lady, who in the late Storm just left her Chamber before a Chimney fell on the Bed where she lay') and others which seem to replicate specific exchanges between friends (such as, 'An Epistle from Mr. *W—n* to Dr. *C—* of *Queen's* College, Oxon. when he had the Gout' or 'An Epistle from Mr. *W—n* to Dr. *C—* upon his refusing to take the Oaths').[54] It offers light, witty pieces with a local referentiality alongside translations and pastorals of a more general nature, and it seems to have been popular in its time: it only appeared in one edition, but it survives in a large number of copies in libraries across the world.[55]

A similar collection of 1719 entitled *Musapædia or Miscellany Poems*, 'never before printed', is said on its title page to be 'By several Members of the Oxford Poetical Club, late of Eton and Westminster'.[56] The presentation of the works within it foregrounded the group nature of much of the content. We find pieces entitled 'A *Song* by *E---S---*, On Mrs. *S---T---*', 'Written Under Mrs. *A---H---n's Picture*. Drawn by Mr. *Verells*', and 'On Mrs. *M---t*, Extempore'. The spread and survival rate suggests it is more than a limited coterie publication, and, like the *Oxford and Cambridge Miscellany*, it poses a question about how social group verse worked in its printed forms.[57] There is very little in the content of these pieces that would enable readers to identify the figures involved, but they must have had an appeal to consumers beyond the social group that the compilation claims to be its point of origin.[58] The poems frequently blend a specificity of address with generic content and compliment. Here is 'To Mrs *A---H---n*, Translated from Buchanan':

> Happy's the Man, whose Eyes can ev'ry Grace
> Behold, and smiling wanton in your Face:
> He's happier yet, who, like *Arion's* Throng,
> But hears your Voice and dwells upon your Tongue;
> But he's a Demi-God, who all those Charms,
> Does Kissing hold within his circ'ling Arms;
> Among the Gods, a perfect One is He,
> Who does those Limbs enjoy, as well as see.[59]

It is not essential to know the identity of *A---H---* to appreciate the piece, which is, after all, a translation of an earlier poem by George Buchanan. The compliment and the conceit of the lover as demi-god stand on their own, merely given added piquancy by the suggestion that they might have a real-world referent. Part of the appeal of such loosely personalized forms must have been that they offered the allure of intimate verse exchange with few interpretative hurdles. But other collections of university material pushed much harder into the realms of the genuinely inaccessible. *News from both Universities. Containing* [. . .] *Mr Cobb's Tripos Speech at Cambridge, with a complete Key inserted* (1714) is largely made up of a poem mocking figures in the University. It was published ten years after the occasion of Cobb's tripos, on his death in 1714, by which point its extreme topicality must have become even less accessible to an external reader.[60] As a concession to the inward-looking nature of its jokes about university life, the publication boasts a 'key' in the form of footnotes at the bottom of the page which appear to clarify references in the text. But on closer inspection these notes either duplicate information in the main text or offer completely redundant amplification. There is a bizarre pointlessness to the explanations on offer. So, for example, the lines 'A Man by his Regalians known / For Timber measuring and Stone' is glossed as 'He was very much given to the Study of Architecture' (8). An unnamed figure, described as 'One who's in constant motion, always ambling', is footnoted as 'A Fellow who is continually loitering about the Town' (12). A man described as 'Knight-Errant of the shaking Head' gains the unhelpful annotation: 'One that always shakes his Head about from one Shoulder to the other' (15). This is an almost entirely futile key, with a circular logic, referring only back to the work it purports to clarify. As with Pope's *Key to the Lock*, the tools of clarification are themselves mocked for their failure to supply understanding.

While the collections discussed above have their origins in male university groups, compilations of coterie verse were also an important form of dissemination for women writers of the period. The toggling between private and public worlds enabled by occasional, sociable verse had a particular resonance in an era in which female self-display, in the form of performance or of publication, was often seen as morally and socially damaging. Sociable verse could be a way of demonstrating a skill in writing and in forging connections with others without attracting censure or opprobrium.[61] Women wrote poems addressed to their friends, celebrating or lamenting or merely commenting upon matters of local concern, a mode which enabled elite and middling women to display an easy, conversational style, to demonstrate their social networks, and to gain access to print while maintaining the guise of the polite amateur.[62]

Jane Brereton's collection of verse, discussed in the introduction, is typical of this mode: *Poems on Several Occasions* (1744) is a collection of occasional verses said to be 'written for the Amusement of the Author, and three or four select Friends'.[63] The compilation declares its origins in Brereton's local Wrexham social circle, and the content is heavily autobiographical. According to the preface, the poems were not designed for publication 'only a few can be said to be prepared for Publication, as they were to make their Appearance in a feigned Name'. And the contents of the volume both grant the reader access to the genteel friendship group and withhold it. There are poems such as 'Epistle to Mrs *Anne Griffiths*', 'On seeing Mrs *Eliz. Owen*, now Lady *Longueville*, in an embroider'd Suit, all her own Work', and 'On Mrs *Sybil Egerton*'s singing an Anthem in *Wrexham* Church' which clearly allude to episodes from the local life of the author. It was common, as here, for prefatory pages of collections of women's verse to state that the verses within were written for a select group of friends, rather than to engage at large with a bigger public. Modern scholars of women's poetry have sometimes taken this language of intimate exchange, coupled with the occasional nature of the work, and inferred from it a limited exclusivity: Paula R. Backscheider notes, for example, that some of Brereton's works 'elude full interpretation and remind us that friendship poems were indeed often private communications between intimate friends'.[64] But rather than seeing the seemingly private exchanges of female poets as a retreat from public statement or engagement, we might instead read them as part of the wider culture of staged and limited revelation that we find elsewhere in the verse of the period. It is clear that a wide range of historical readers bought and read verse collections without access to the friendships and events underlying them. And the same was true for the growing output of sociable verse produced by women writers. Those readers probably did not know who Miss Smith was, or what happened at Bath, or Tunbridge, or what befell the author or her friend in their sickness, but they were nonetheless able to enjoy works that they were not fully able to interpret, but which gained them the illusion of access to a particular social network.

We know little about how sociable collections were understood by their readers, beyond the marginal completions of elided names. Rare examples of marked-up copies show that the pleasures of the text were varied. A surviving annotated copy of Elijah Fenton's *Musapædia* shows how it was handled by one reader, Thomas Turner. Turner wrote an ownership note on the inside cover of the volume indicating his sense of the importance of understanding what lay within: 'Thomas Turner His Book God Give him Grace not to Look But Understand for Learning is Better than House or Land'. But the kind of understanding evidenced in Thomas Turner's annotations is general rather than topical. When he comes to 'The Character of an Happy Life. A Relique of Sir Philip Sidney', he marks and copies out the lines 'Whose Soul is still prepar'd for Death' and 'And having *Nothing*, HE has *All*'. Alongside 'To Two Gentlemen, reputed Authors of Timely Advice, &c'. he writes out the statements 'Woman best' and 'Man a Brute'.[65] Nowhere in the collection has he used his notes to supply the missing names that many of the pieces within seem to demand for complete comprehension. As with so much of the evidence of historical readers, we cannot know from the unmarked text what he made of the volume – was he puzzled by it, uninterested, accepting? Maybe he knew all the answers and didn't write them in. What we can see is that Thomas Turner was a reader who actively engaged with his copy of *Musapædia*, but he was not able, or did not want, to do this by filling in missing information or names – for him, the poems had meaning for their extractable and quotable aphorisms.

All the examples discussed above force us to think harder about how far eighteenth-century readers expected to get the intended meanings of the literary works they consumed, or what they took the primary meaning to be. For some, to grasp the poem will have meant the truffle hunting of personal familiar allusion; for others, it will have been the application of commonplaces to their own lives and reading. For yet others, the fact of not knowing and then finding out was a form of social connection. It's worth noting that pleasures of this kind of sociable reading seem comparable to other forms of leisure activity popular in the period – the culture of riddling and puzzle-solving. The cloaked identification or typographical conventions invited in poems such as this one invited completion on the part of readers. Much the same can be said for the compilations of acrostics, rebuses, and puzzling quips that appeared in abundance in both print and manuscript throughout this period, often as part of a jestbook collection, in titles such as *De-lights for Young Men and Maids: Containing Near an Hundred Riddles with Pictures and a Key to Each* (1725) or *Wit Newly Reviv'd: Being a Book of Riddles. Set forth for the Trial of Wit and Diversion of all Persons of Either Sex, to create Mirth and Merriment* (1711). Archives of personal corre-spondence demonstrate that friends regularly exchanged riddling and word games in letters, challenging one another to 'smoak' or guess the intended name or reference. The young bluestocking Margaret Portland habitually circulated such material among a wider group: 'I have found out your Riddle & have Dazzled a good Many People with it, I have sent you one in return that you may send to the Wit'.[66] Jonathan Swift writes to his friend Knightley Chetwode (Saturday, 28 December 1715): 'I do not understand the Rebus. I would apply it to myself, but then what means *"narrow in flight"*?'[67] Friendships were sustained by shared enter-tainment – offering puzzles, answering them, asking for help in solution – and all these practices were also evident in the print and manuscript cultures of sociable verse. As with other forms of writing in the period, the fact of not knowing formed a sociable bond between one reader and another.

Critical accounts of the literature of the period have rightly empha-sized the game-playing nature of many Augustan texts, the ways in which they toyed with readerly engagement, creating satires, allegories, and verses which needed to be 'solved' or completed by the reader. It has been easy to view these textual strategies as an ingenious form of cultural politics, a mode of gatekeeping that shored up authorial status and rewarded the cleverness of those who could penetrate the mystery within the pages. But as so many of the examples across this chapter and book show, the nature of that engagement varied considerably from reader to reader. There weren't good readers and bad readers, experts and non-experts. Instead, the evidence of individual readers' responses shows a wide range of interaction, which cannot so easily be pinned down to class, gender, or geography. While the literature of the period often seemed to demand a fixed solution, it is important to recognize that it also offered pleasures for those unwilling or unable to provide this.

## Fictional Occasions

Collections of occasional verse evidently had an appeal which extended far beyond their original social grouping. But not all such verse began in a real-world community, and sometimes it is hard to tell the difference between fictional and actual referentiality. Writers and publishers might create invented coterie content, using the alluring promise of access to a hidden world of friendship to mask content which was generic and generalized. Thus the guessing games of occasional verse multiplied: not only was the reader uncertain how to map cloaked identity onto specific figures and places, but they might also wonder whether those figures and events existed at all. *The Diverting Muse, or the Universal Medly. Written by a Society of Merry Gentlemen, for the Entertainment of the Town* (1707) uses the idea of a 'society of merry gentleman' to market the sociable appeal of the collection. The pieces inside are predominantly comic verse – jocular and satirical – apparently largely written by Edward Ward. The illusion that they were produced by 'a collection of merry gentlemen' vanishes when we see the advertisement asking readers to submit their own offerings for what was to become a short-lived monthly miscellany:

> any Song, Poem, Epigram, Epitaph, Elegy, Epithalamium, Satyr &c, provided that the Subject be no ways offensive to the State, or tending to the Scandal of any particular Person. If they please to communicate their Instructions to the Persons concern'd in this Miscellany, which will be continued Monthly, by a society of merry Gentleman, they shall have it done gratis, and inserted herein.[68]

This collection wasn't the fruit of a particular social group, and was in fact open to entries from interested readers – but in branding itself as the work of a group of merry gentlemen, it acquired an interest and coherence it might otherwise lack. When the bookseller Edmund Curll opened a shop in the fashionable spa town of Tunbridge Wells, he published a collection entitled *The Tunbridge Miscellany*, which was sub-titled *Poems &c Written at Tunbridge-Wells this Summer by Several Hands*. The title of the compilation aimed to give the impression that the works were the legacy of a recent season of sociable fun in elite society, but the reality was that most of the contents were assembled rather randomly from existing stock, unrelated to the location.[69] Curll was to continue the series as a vehicle for older material with follow-on miscellanies in 1713 and 1714.[70] As authors and booksellers began to market the aura of the coterie, offering their readers the voyeuristic pleasure of accessing the poetry of a restricted network of writers, readers, friends, or the experience of a writer in a particular geographical setting, they created the impression of worlds within worlds of co-creating literary friend-ships. Yet some of these were clearly invented to appease market de-mand or add a gloss of exclusivity to generic content.

However, it was not always so easy to differentiate between stock content and genuinely individualized reference. Some works played with the tension between specific and unspecific application. Mary Chandler's frequently republished poem *A Description of Bath* (1733, eight editions by 1767) is an encomium to the spa resort, its location and visitor attractions. It came accompanied by footnotes at the base of the page which clarified some specific references. We are told that 'this fair Pavilion' refers to 'Harrison's *Banquetting-House*' and that 'the Moun-tain's Rocky Sides' refers to the local quarries.[71] Mary Chandler names James Leake's the bookseller, Lindsey's new assembly room, and the royal baths.[72] The poem used its reference points to create a sense of lived intimacy with the town; a familiarity which no doubt secured the poem's popularity for a middling sort of readership keen to acquaint themselves with the pleasures of the fashionable resort. There are a few mentions of well-known historical figures such as John Dryden, Beau Nash, and William III, and these sit alongside elusive and apparently generic references. Towards the end of the poem, Chandler imagines an estate set just outside the town in which:

Here could the Muse for ever spend her Days,
And chant, in humble Rhymes, the Owner's Praise,
how by his Art, young MYRA* shall no more
Her STREPHON's Letter lost, with Sighs deplore,
Unjustly jealous of her faithful Swain.[73]

We might have hoped the asterisked 'Myra' might indicate the identity of this figure but instead Chandler's notes offer information on the
development of the local postal service. The poem both does and
doesn't allow the reader to try to apply its content to local knowledge.
It is impossible to tell here whether Chandler invokes a specific estate
and landowner, whether Myra suggests a particular woman or is merely
a generic neoclassical type.[74] This takes us to the crux of the problem in
reading occasional verse of the eighteenth century. Poems based in a
precise location and friendship group deployed generic vocabularies of
pastoral, amatory, or religious discourse, rendering the individual instance or reference both accessible and conventional. And conversely,
stock pieces or generic verse were given a new allure by being repackaged
as emergent from a particular social group or location. In this context, it
is almost impossible to parse correctly the appropriate level of decoding
and application demanded by such forms.

   We can start to see how complex the rhetoric of accessibility was in
the occasional and social verse of this period. At a distance of several
centuries, we assume that much of the particularity of verse compilations of the period alludes to a closed world of social connections at
which we can only guess. But in this case of the *Tunbridge Miscellany*
and many other collections, that appearance of exclusivity was a carefully contrived illusion. All these kinds of publication create a puzzle in
terms of thinking about ideas of readerly comprehension in eighteenth-
century literary culture. At one level they create an inclusive model:
they invite the reader into an intimate world of shared experience and
local detail; they celebrate and cement friendships and social networks.
And at another they clearly exclude those readers who were unable to
map the scenes and individuals described onto their own lived experience. To read the sociable verse of the period could mean to enjoy the

literary reflection and consolidation of a familiar social group; it could enable a voyeuristic sense of participation in more elite circles; it could create a sense of baffled exclusion. Or it could offer a form of enjoyment completely divorced from the question of fixing meaning and intention. A poem like *The Rape of the Lock* seems to be playing with all these modes of engagement. By adjusting our lens on that most famous of coterie productions, we can get new insights into the web of interpretative games and challenges that were so characteristic of the early eighteenth-century reading experience.

# 7

# Unlocking the Past

I've just got a bunch of Keys to ye Atlantis & find upon ye Inspection
some of em so unfit yt I must have a farther recourse to ye Learned in
ye art of deciphering all invidious Refflections

—ANNE BYNN TO SIR WILLIAM
TRUMBULL, 27 MARCH 1710

IT COULD BE SAID that early eighteenth-century verse staged a game
of revelation by omission. Authors created an impression of names that
were unsayable, compelling arguments that could not be made in the
light of day, and social groups which invited the reader in but also left
them guessing. Texts teased with acts of semi-revelation, showing and
not showing. These features were not unique to the verse of the period.
The numerous secret histories and scandal narratives of the early eighteenth century also depended on their readers' ability to unlock their
hidden meaning through romans à clef and other forms of allegory. In
these prose works, the uncovering of secrets played out at a thematic as
well as a textual level, suggesting that little was as it seemed, and that the
truth frequently hid beyond layers of fiction. The act of interpretation
both made the reader complicit in the political critique and encouraged
hermeneutic suspicion. Yet such readerly decoding inevitably raised
levels of textual proliferation and uncertainty. And there was the question of legal challenge: if meaning was effectively made by the reader,
where did responsibility for seditious content lie?

The secret history, a prose genre that aimed to foment conspiracy theories and discredit official versions of recent history by exposing the seamier side of past events, was a fusion of existing forms.[1] It combined the publishing of 'secret' political correspondence with the sexual intrigues of the prose narratives of early modern romance to form a heady blend of political and personal exposé. While the first use of the phrase 'secret history' itself only emerged in the titles of English publications in the late 1600s, the form dates back to the sixth century, when the Byzantine historian, Procopius of Caesarea produced a history of the Emperor Justinian's reign, entitled the *Anekdota*, 'unpublished [things]'. The rise of party politics – as well as public awareness of a series of high profile plots and plotters towards the end of the century – fed the emergence of the form we now recognize as the secret history.[2] Between 1690 and 1750 over eighty different works mentioning 'Secret History' in their titles appeared, and many more publications used the phrase in their subtitles.[3] Claiming their authority from sources inside the closets and cabinets of those in power, the secret histories of the early eighteenth century exposed the clandestine intimacies of the Stuart monarchs or mounted conspiracy theories about a range of scandalous possibilities, from unspeakable leagues between England and France, to the wicked machinations of the Whig oligarchy, to the corruptions of court life.[4]

Contemporary history supplied ample material to support this theme. The Popish plot of 1679 (focusing on an alleged Jesuit conspiracy to assassinate Charles II and put his Catholic brother on the throne) was a thesis with potentially endless extension, and it fed public fascination with dark rumours of political scheming. It created a framework of suspicion upon which any wisp of Catholic sedition might rest, and it was soon followed by other conspiracies, including the Rye House plot of 1683, a scheme to murder both Charles II and his brother, James; the warming pan scandal of 1688, in which a baby boy was said to have been smuggled into the birthing room of the Queen in a warming pan to create the future James III; and the Jacobite Assassination plot of 1696, the final attempt to remove William III and replace him with the Stuart

James II. In the context of the widespread fascination with these events, it must have seemed utterly plausible to many contemporary readers that further schemes had been and were afoot. Alarmist versions of history proliferated, extending to never-realized fears of a full Jacobite invasion.[5]

In encouraging their readers to believe that courts and all those who dwelt in them were hotbeds of intrigue, the scandal narratives spun out during these years – from *The Secret History of Whitehall* (1697), to Eliza Haywood's *The British Recluse; or Secret History of Cleomira, Suppos'd Dead* (1722), to Daniel Defoe's *Secret History of the White Staff* (1714) – offered a form of revisionist history. They enabled their audience to reread the events of recent years and to discern within them hitherto undisclosed patterns.[6] Eliza Haywood's *Female Spectator* parodied contemporary readers' appetites for intrigue in a contribution from a dissatisfied reader, 'Curioso Politico', who complains that he has been palmed off with 'Home-Amours' and 'Reflections on Human Nature' instead of the meaty revelations promised:

> Every body imagined you [*The Female Spectator*] had a Key to unlock the Cabinet of Princes, – a Clue to guide you through the most intricate Labyrinths of State, – and that the secret Springs of Ambition, Avarice and Revenge, which make such dreadful Havock, would have been all laid open to our View. – Yet the eternal Fund of Intelligence you vaunted of, has given us not a Word of all this.[7]

Mr Politico doesn't want straight news or domestic content – he wants the alluring revelations typified by the secret history, which will decode the latent machinations and motivations of the great.[8] Haywood, in the guise of the Female Spectator, responded by acknowledging that she had claimed to be able to 'penetrate into the mysteries of the *alcove*, the cabinet, or *field*', but that it might not be entirely safe to reveal all:

> IF Princes have a Mind to play at *Bo-peep* with each other, or with their respective Subjects, who shall dare to draw the Curtain, and call the Rabble in to be Witness of what they do! – We little People may

hear and see, but must say nothing. – There are some sort of Secrets which prove fatal if explored, and like massive Buildings erected by Enchantment, will not endure too near Approach, but fall at once, and crush the bold Inspector with their Weight.[9]

The Female Spectator's response reinforces a gap between ignorant 'little people' and the unseeable machinations of the great – a gap which Haywood's own secret history fictions exploited. The exchange above again hinges on the gap between those who are in the know and those who are not. Not only did the stories themselves demand unlocking, but they also framed hiddenness as a theme of their fictions. Haywood's stories turn on problems of knowledge and access to truth, with story-lines featuring trespass, keyholes, eavesdropping, intrusive curiosity, and invisibility.[10] The reader repeatedly learns that surface appearances are profoundly unreliable:

> *Gigantilla* had so exactly counterfeited Artemia's Hand in this horrid Aspersion on her Honour, that it was impossible for it to be known for any thing but what it represented; and the fair Incendiary observing, with her utmost penetration, the Duke's Countenance while he was reading, perceiv'd to her very great Satisfaction only such Changes as were occasion'd by his Surprize, and nothing that look'd like a suspicion of the Truth.[11]

Such prose is crammed full of deception and counterfeit, with power and its abuse often hidden behind veils of subterfuge which must be penetrated by protagonist and reader. In this textual marketplace of revelation, secret histories almost invariably advertised their unique veracity and authenticity: '*the whole consists chiefly of* Original Manuscripts, *never Published till now* [. . .] *there are such* Secret Memoirs in this Work *as are not to be found else where*'; 'Faithfully Translated from the *Italian* Copy now lodg'd in the *Vatican* at *Rome* and never before Printed in any Language'.[12] In reality, many works recycled similar material, re-packaging older plot lines and insinuations in new ways. While each one claimed to know the specifics of individual intrigues, they had in common a fascination with the personal motivation behind the affairs of public life. The contemporary French historian René Rapin conceded that:

> nothing is more divertive in a Narration, than the decyphering of what is secret and of importance, in the designs and intentions of those whose Action it divulges [...] For nothing does more excite the Curiosity of men, than when they have discover'd to them what is most conceal'd in the Heart of man, that is to say, the secret Springs and Resorts, which make him act in the Enterprizes, which are ordinary to him.[13]

Rapin's emphasis on the pleasures of unlocking what cannot normally be seen echoes the delight we know so many readers found in allegories, riddles, and what some called 'mystery mongering'. In the case of secret histories, the key to the puzzle was human nature, the psychological flaws that drove the great to act as they did.

There was, however, a paradox at the heart of the secret history. The genre relied on a series of manuscript or oral devices – the unofficial accounts of first-hand observers, secret meetings, private thoughts, intimate conversations, and backstairs gossip – to discredit the official printed records of public life. The preface to Eliza Haywood's *The British Recluse* (1722) is typical: 'the following little History [...] I can affirm for Truth, having it from the Mouths of those chiefly concern'd in it'.[14] Their prefaces and title pages were dotted with references to secret personal papers and manuscript documents on which they were based: 'The Popish Damnable Plot against our Religion and Liberties Fairly laid open and discover'd in the Breviats of Threescore and Four Letters and Papers of Intelligence past'; 'A Secret Collection of the Affairs of Spain During the Negotiations Between the Courts of England and Madrid [...] With several curious and valuable pieces under their own Hands, to be found no where extant, but in this Book'.[15] But once they were published, the stories began to derive their credibility and authority from the very fact of being printed – being made public and semi-official. Like the sociable verse of the period, they were works that sat at the crux of the personal and the private, selling personal revelation for an anonymous reading public keen to gain access to the intimacies and failings of those they could not know.[16] And in marketing restricted information for a wider readership, they opened themselves up to diverse modes of interpretation and engagement.

## Unlocking the *Atalantis*

One of the most celebrated secret histories of the era was the Tory journalist Delariviere Manley's *The New Atalantis* (its full title was *Secret Memoirs and Manners of Several Persons of Quality, of both Sexes, From the New Atalantis, an Island in the Mediterranean*), which appeared in its first volume in May 1709, with a second volume in October of the same year. The work was so popular that 'Atalantis' became shorthand for the whole genre of secret history.[17] It has been described as 'a defining moment in the political and cultural life of early eighteenth-century England'.[18] Like other works by Manley, *The New Atalantis* was a roman à clef. It offered a series of narratives of seduction and betrayal involving notorious Whig grandees told to Astrea, an allegorical figure of justice, who comes to earth and meets her mother, Virtue, who believes herself to have been abandoned by most mortals. The narratives, which in many ways echoed the motifs of contemporary prose romances, were largely told by female characters, who included an allegorical depiction of 'Intelligence' and a midwife. The appeal of the work lay in its combination of gossipy, coded insinuation and titillating narrative detail. We hear the story of the seduction of Louisa, a young orphan virgin, by the scheming and married Hernando who is her guardian. Hernando's assault on her virtue is a calculated triumph:

> Oh that you would but permit me to give you only a Taste of what I feel! that you would once but admit of so much Curiosity in my Favour, to prove but a glimmering of that Delight, that mutual Lovers bestow upon one another. Here he sought her Lips, and prest 'em so tenderly, and so respectively, that he could not fail of insinuating, by that dangerous Contract, something new and tender into the Breast of the unexperienc'd Virgin; he pursued her so artfully, that she consented he should stay there 'till Morning.[19]

One of the distinctions between Augustan scandal stories and our own modern equivalents is that, on the whole, the sex scandals that formed the main part of the story were not in themselves what discredited a ruler. Rather, it was what such personal duplicity said about the likely public morality of the man or woman that was important.[20] So in this case, it was less the fact that William Earl Cowper (Hernando) had had an affair with Elizabeth Culling (Louisa) that was the sensation, but the abuse of his position of responsibility and power. And in an era in which government was both highly personalized and court-centred, it was particularly likely that the affairs of the private chamber would translate into a public arena. This was well-explained by the author Ferrand Spence in a 1686 introduction to a translation of *The Secret History of the House of Medicis*. Spence declared that secret histories showed that 'Irresolution and Passion prevail equally in the Great, as in the Vulgar' and so it was that 'often a little Cabinet-pique, or Bed-Chamber Quarrel, occasions a rumbling World, and is the source of the greatest Transactions'.[21]

While the ostensible purpose of *The New Atalantis* and other scandal narratives was to expose the ethical and political corruption of the ruling elite, there will have been readers who bought and read such works mainly for their sexualized content, and the precise referentiality of the genre will have been of little or no interest to those for whom the erotic narrative was paramount.[22] And sometimes there was no real-world political basis to the tale. A work such as *Palace Amours: or, The Genuine History of Alexis* (1733) claimed to offer its readers access to information about the misdemeanours of the court, with a title page promising 'An Exact Account of his Amorous ADVENTURES among Ladies of Quality, and Fair Ones of inferior Rank. Diversified with Original LETTERS, POEMS, and very curious Discoveries in the BEAU MONDE'.[23] Yet the description then seems to veer into self-parody, with the additional description: 'To which is Annexed, Something about SOMEBODY'S second RECKONING, with some shrewd Guesses WHEN IT WILL BE OUT'. Toying with the notion of real-world application, this text sells itself on the promise of topical revelation. What follows is a series of loosely connected acts of sexual seduction by 'Prince Alexis' unlinked to any wider political narrative. Prince Alexis thrives on sexual violence and the ruination of young virgins: 'in Cases of this Nature, the greater Pains that is taken, and the greater Ruin that it is suppos'd to bring, the Pleasure is still the greater'.[24] The story stretches far beyond the bounds of credulity – we hear that he is so keen for conquest that in the absence of available women he tries to make love to a laurel tree.[25] It is another reminder that the notion of referentiality in early eighteenth-century literature was an evasive one – in some cases, readers were encouraged to hunt down meanings and subtexts that might not be there.

The kind of sexual self-interest driving the narrative of *Palace Amours* is put to more explicitly partisan purpose in Manley's fiction. In these narratives, erotic immorality is often combined with political corruption to attack the powerful. At the same time, the misdeeds of Manley's subjects are hidden with false identities granted by their pseudonyms, the characters themselves continuously dissembling and hiding information, disguising themselves or borrowing false identities. Like other examples of the genre, *The New Atalantis* was dependent on its readers' ability to connect up the fragmented narrative form through their understanding of the subplot of self-interest and corruption that linked the anecdotes within.[26] So, for example, the novel offered multiple allegories of the corruption of the Duke and Duchess of Marlborough. Both figures are given a plethora of fictional identities: the Duke is Hippolito, Count Fortunatus, the Marquis of Caria, or 'the Shining Favourite', and the Duchess is seen as 'young Jeanatin', Marchioness of Caria, and the 'Now great lady'. It was for the reader to piece all these sub-stories together to form an overall critique. But the task was not designed to be easy. Sending a copy of the *Atalantis* to Robert Harley, the Lord Treasurer, a man at the epicentre of contemporary public life, Manley offered to help him unpack the allegorical meaning of the work:

[I] have attempted some faint Representations of some imperfect pieces of painting of the heads of that party who have mislead Thousands. If any thing Sir moves yr Curiosity, I will explain what you desire, if you send but a note without a name directed to me, and under cover, to Mrs Markham at the Bell and Dragon in Paternostre-row.[27]

The history clearly demanded much of its readers, even those close to the events described. Many narratives included an explicit discussion of what kind of readerly competence was necessary. A preface to *The court-Spy* (1744) noted:

> Some *Country* Readers, indeed, may be at a loss to explain the *Characters*, introduc'd in the Place of those *Names* that were in the Original; which, for certain very *important* Reasons, he did not chuse to publish; conceiving, that they were not so exceedingly necessary for illustrating this little *Piece*. Where, even from the bare *Relation* of the *Facts*, those of the meanest Capacity may soon arrive at the *Intelligence* of the *Persons* concern'd.[28]

*The court-Spy* uses a differentiation between different kinds of readers – town and country, sophisticated and those 'of the meanest Capacity' – to talk about how to unpick or decode the text within. Colley Cibber's *The Secret History of Arlus and Odolphus, Ministers of State to the Empress of Grandinsula* (1710) offered an allegorical account of Queen Anne's change of ministry. Its preface offers 'A word to the Reader':

> *if upon the Perusal of the Title-page you find your self in the dark, whisper the first Honest Gentleman you meet (whom you will now easily distinguish by a certain new Life in his Looks) and you will be set right in a moment: But, if this Book's in your Hand, don't enquire at* St James's Coffee-house, *lest you should meet with a surly Answer.*[29]

Cibber suggests both that the meaning of the work is evident to any 'honest gentleman' and that a deficit in understanding can be rectified by social exchange. As elsewhere, the finding of the answers was a bonding process which, in this case, forged a common political perspective between puzzled reader and honest gentleman. An oriental erotic fable by William Hatchett was advertised on 19 March 1740:

> This Day is publish'd, Price 2S. (Very proper for all curious Inspectors into Nature) | The SECOND EDITION, of CHAM YAM, with her Leg upon a Table. A Chinese Tale. Printed for J Cooper in

Fleet-Street, and sold at all the Booksellers and Pamphlet-Shops.
N. B. There is no Occasion for a Key to decypher who is meant under
the Character of Cham Tam, it is needless to the gay Part of the
World, and those who are otherwise, and curious, may soon be
inform'd at any of the Coffee-houses about St James's.[30]

Like Addison's references in his *Spectator* essays to 'ignorant and inat-
tentive brethren', such introductory comments foregrounded questions
of reading and comprehension. They created the impression that class
or geography were the key factors determining incomprehension –
when as we have seen, readers of all kinds were unsure about meaning.
And in reinforcing an impression of those 'in the know' they created a
sense of inclusion for those who read the book, even as those same readers struggled to penetrate the strategies designed to limit their
access.[31]

## Keys to Meaning

One of the consequences of this dual strategy of concealment and revelation was that from Procopius onwards, the secret history was often
published with, or shortly followed by, an accompanying interpretative
key. As we have seen, the notion of books as keys flourished in this period,
and it has been estimated that roughly eight hundred publications calling themselves keys were published between 1650 and 1800.[32] Numerous printed works purported to unlock for the reader a particular skill
or form of understanding. Instructional and self-educational, they enabled those who bought them to access the appropriate information
about architecture, classical texts, brewing beer, or book-keeping.[33] The
interpretive keys attached to secret histories and scandal narratives are
a slightly different thing.[34]

The format of the key to secret histories was commonly a double
column listing fictional names alongside corresponding real ones.
Sometimes it took the form of numbered footnotes at the base of the
page or, occasionally, an appendix to a work. The 1709 printed *Key to
Atalantis* is typical of many in that it carries no explanation of what it is

or how it works, offering merely two columns of names with page numbers on the left-hand side. The first version was swiftly followed by 'Part II' published in the same year, which offered an additional set of names.[35] The presumption implicit within the two-column presentation was that the extraction of meaning lay in a one-to-one correspondence between fictional name and real-world exemplar, and that by substituting the real name for the fictional one, all would become clear. The key presented a straightforward correspondence between fictional and real-world identity, yet at the same time it often refused to supply the external referent it was supposed to give. The key to *Memoirs of the Court of Europe*, the 'third volume' of *The New Atalantis*, contains names which are partial, such as 'B of E—' or 'Ld S—d—d'.[36] The text is only partially unlocked. And beyond this, the scandal narrative itself frequently bore a host of ancillary meanings and needed different kinds of decoding in order to unlock its satirical or critical message.[37] Even within the column format of the key the kinds of information deemed necessary for understanding could vary quite a lot. A manuscript key transcribed inside a copy of the anonymous anti-Whig scandal novel *The Secret History of Mama Oello* (1733) offers names of persons and places, so 'Mama Oello' is Anne, the Princess Royal, and 'America' is a term for Europe.[38] But it also translates concepts: a reference to 'projecting a scheme' is explained as 'the Excise in Tobacco'. As the eye travels down the list, the key is used not just to explain references but also to make corrections to factual inaccuracies within the narrative. The word 'arrived', referring to the Prince of Orange is given the gloss: 'He did not arrive in England until the 17th Novr following'. Keys purported to offer transparent explanations of allegorical names and places within the narrative, but, as this example suggests, their role was not straightforward. Explanation slid into intervention, interpretation into evaluative commentary. It was a form of mediation that was seldom neutral.

For all this complexity, there is substantial evidence that contemporary readers wanted and needed keys to appreciate fully the secret histories that they encountered. Lady Mary Wortley Montagu wrote to her friend Frances Hewet: 'I am very glad you have the second part of the New Atalantis; if you have read it, will you be so good as to send it

me, and in return I promise to get you the key to it. I know I can'.[39]
A series of letters between the elderly lawyer and government official
Sir William Trumbull and his nephew, Ralph Bridges, reveals Trumbull's repeated requests for keys from his family: Bridges first notes the
ask from his uncle on 31 October 1709.[40] Less than two weeks later,
Trumbull is clearly still on the case, and Bridges writes in response to
his questions about who Manley was and how she knew such secrets:

> The author of ye New Atlantis is one Mrs Manley, that has bin a Play-
> wright, of an ordinary rank & hardly ever talk't of til upon this occa-
> sion. She has bin what ye wicked world call a Town Lady, that has
> liv'd separate from her husband a Parliamt man for a considerable
> time & having bin a retainer of ye Court & especially of the Lewd
> part of it, has bin admitted into ye Secret Intreagues of it. She was ye
> beginning of last week sent for by my Ld. Sunderland & own'd her
> self the Author & was committed to Custody but immediately had
> bail. I will as soon as I see my Brothr get his Key & send it to you.[41]

Less than a week later, he writes to reassure that 'Br [brother] Bridges
sends you the Key of Atlantis 1st part next time he writes'.[42] And three
weeks later he returns to the subject again:

> For yr further diversion, I hope you have 'ere this had ye Key to ye
> New Atlantis of my Brothr; whom I've seen but once since my Journy
> from Ashwell. He undertooke to furnish you himself; for otherwise
> I had transcrib'd it. But as I then learn't it was only of ye first Part.[43]

Not content with this supply of information, Trumbull also took up
the matter of keys with his sister, Anne Bynn, early the following year.
Bynn replies to her brother's request for more explication: 'I did not
doubt but to have satisfied your Curiosity by another Key to ye Atlantis
but have not got it yet as soon as I have it I'll send it'.[44] Two weeks
later, she announces that 'I've just got a bunch of Keys to ye Atlantis'.[45]
Readers, even very well-connected readers, obviously felt they needed
keys. But how far did those texts really unlock the work? As we have
seen, secret histories depended on a reader establishing the correlation between a fictional name and a real one, and on their stitching

together a series of discrete incidents to form a coherent narrative. The columns of identifications seem to fix and prescribe meaning in a more narrow way than the rest of the text did. But the presence of the key also illuminated the difficulty of meaning-making in political texts. Keys were not wholly clarificatory: they often continued to draw on the rhetoric of secrecy around the matters they sought to illuminate. For example, *A Complete Key to the Four Parts of Law is a Bottomless-Pit* (1712), one of several keys to John Arbuthnot's anti-war allegorical pamphlet *Law is a Bottomless Pit. Exemplified in the case of the Lord Strutt, John Bull, Nicholas Frog, and Lewis Baboon* (1712) maintained dashes to hide the identity of key figures such as the 'K—g of Sp—n' or the Earl of Ox—d'.[46] Readers took it upon themselves to fill in these blanks, even when their meaning could not have been in doubt.[47] Although keys usually took similar textual forms to one another, they might bear very different relationships to the original. Some keys seem to have been written with the help of the author themselves, some by other writers.[48] It is clear that some readers were suspicious of the quality of their intel. Anne Bynn writes with concern to her brother of the assortment of keys to *The New Atalantis* that she has recently received:

> I've just got a bunch of Keys to ye Atlantis & find upon ye Inspection some of em so unfit yt I must have a farther recourse to ye Learned in ye art of deciphering all invidious Refflections for my own part I'me somewhat scrupulous to fix any of my own Conjectures least I shou'd wrong ye innocent so must deferr satisfying your curiosity till ye next Opportunity.[49]

With such a proliferation of explanation available to her, Bynn fears the possibility of incorrect interpretation might leave her vulnerable to misreading. We know that keys survived in multiple versions, in print and manuscript, each one offering additional insight. In this way, we might say that keys marketized readerly uncertainty, withholding information to generate additional publications. Arbuthnot's *Law is a Bottomless Pit* must have been a particularly fruitful text for explication, with four editions of its key appearing in the first year of its publication. One of them boasted itself as '*With above a Hundred more Explanations than in any former Edition'.* As with biblical commentary or ancillary materials, misunderstanding or readerly incomprehension was generative of print. A key both was a commercial opportunity in itself and could help to sustain or extend sales of the work it explained. Different booksellers could sell the puzzle and the answer, and the 'answer' might correct, confirm, or amplify the reader's initial apprehension of the meaning.

Keys were most commonly printed in London. There is little evidence to suggest, as one might anticipate, that they were provincial publications aimed to introduce readers distanced from metropolitan or elite political debates. Analysis of the publication statistics for keys across the late seventeenth and early eighteenth century shows how closely tied the key was to the moment and place of the initial publication of the work it purported to explain. A few publications included a key from the start, but the majority of keys appeared separately.[50] Most keys were published by a different bookseller to the producer of the original work and seem to have been an attempt to capitalize on the market appeal of the earlier publication. While the majority appeared within one or two years of their original text, sometimes they were an attempt to refresh the satirical bite of works whose currency had diminished through time. So they acted both as a cross-generational translation and a sales pitch for the original work and its spin-offs. For instance, a 1710 edition of George Buckingham's *The Rehearsal*, with accompanying key, was intended to supply knowledge about the author's motivations and aims in his burlesque play 'nothing of this nature having appear'd these *Two* and Thirty Years; (for so long has this *Farce* flourished in Print)'.[51]

Advertisements suggest that the key was often designed to be bound with the original text by the purchaser:

> This day is published, A compleat Key to the Tale of a Tub; with some Account of the Authors; the Occasion and Design of Writing it, and Mr. Wotton's Remarks examined. Printed in the same size that it may be fix'd into any Gentleman's Book. Price 6d. [. . .] sold by E. Curll, at the Bible and Dial against St Dunstan's Church, Fleet street.[52]

Surviving copies of secret histories and satirical works are testament to this practice and are often bound with their keys alongside them. We cannot know how those who collected these items and paid for their binding understood the relationship between text and key – was the relationship one of historical interest, genuine explication, or utility? Like other forms of early modern collecting and binding practice, the conjoined material afterlife of these works has shaped the nature of the text we encounter, in this case, forcing the literary work to be read alongside the key to which it may have been more questionably attached.[53]

While readers bought keys, the evidence of surviving copies of secret histories suggests that their reading was informed by multiple sources.[54] In the case of *The New Atalantis*, the printed keys which were not authored by Manley and published separately do not agree among themselves on the identifications of the pseudonyms within the two volumes.[55] This phenomenon of multiple readings emerges clearly in surviving manuscript annotations to copies of the *Atalantis*. An examination of copies of the first volume, all in the Bodleian Library in Oxford, shows rather different patterns of identification. One copy, the first volume of the first edition of 1709, has the name 'George [?] L'estrange' on its title page.[56] The annotator has written in the identities of historical figures next to the pseudonyms printed on the page, so, for example, the 'old Seignior' mentioned on page twelve is 'Lord Torrington', while the 'richest widow in all Atalantis' is Mrs Cooke, and Count Orgueil is the Duke of Buckingham. The identities given correspond very closely with the solutions provided in the first printed key to the *Atalantis* published in 1709. This reader probably relied on the authority of the printed key to gloss by hand the meaning of the work they had acquired. However, a second annotated copy, also in the Bodleian, shows a different approach to explaining the text.[57] This copy, which bears no ownership inscription, has many more annotations in it than the version described above. It has notes which do not agree with those of the earlier annotator, nor with the printed key. These interventions seem to point to a reader who supplemented their text with information derived from personal sources. One of the notes, glossing the identity of a 'thin raw-boned priest', says, 'Dr Everton parson of Woodstock his wife my friend who dedicated some poems to Ld Halifax'.[58] Keys to other works similarly reveal readers who believed that they had a superior understanding of the text to that of the key-maker. A copy of Anthony Hamilton's 1715 *A Key to Count Grammont's Memoirs* in the British Library is covered in handwritten corrections and comments made by a reader who is keen to show that they know best, to prove that the key is mistaken or incomplete in its interpretation.[59] They correct 'Mrs Blake' to 'Blague', clarify that a 'Miss Denham' was 'formerly Miss Brooks', amend 'Mrs Willis, a she player' to 'Mrs Margrt Hughes', and redesignate a reference to 'handsom Sidney' to 'Robert, brother of Algernon Sidney'.[60] A Harvard copy of a key to *The New Atalantis* features marginal notes also showing disagreement with the attributions provided in the key.[61] While the format and content of the key present interpretation as certain and singular, instances of individual reading practice suggest that reading and using a key was a more interactive, more contentious process than the form suggests. We can also see that readerly knowledge varied according to individual circumstance. Which was most likely to be right: the printed key, or the manuscript annotations produced by someone socially connected with the subject of the history?

## The Engaged Reader

Keys provided one form of correspondence between fictional tale and real-world equivalence. Other readers answered the brief of the locked text by writing their own commentary in the margins and endpapers. As seen above, such markings often confirm a divergence on the identity of particular fictional figures and the discrepancy between printed keys and reader knowledge. But they also illuminate some of the very different attitudes towards the kinds of knowledge or explanation needed to understand or appreciate a work. At one end of the scale are copies of secret histories owned by the customs officer and antiquary William Musgrave. Musgrave was an indexer and list-maker at work and at play. His carefully compiled catalogues of portrait prints and obituaries have become reference works in their own right. And his preoccupation with

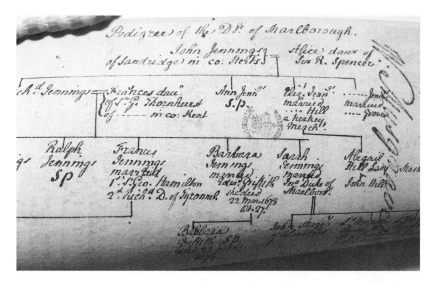

FIGURE 9. Joseph Browne, *The Secret History of Queen Zarah, from Her Birth to the Conclusion of her Reign*, fourth edition (London: J. Wilford, 1745), British Library, 1419.c.48, verso of the title page. Annotated by William Musgrave.

biographical information inevitably shaped his response to the fictional political narratives of the early eighteenth century. Looking at Musgrave's copy of Joseph Browne's *The Secret History of Queen Zarah* (1705, 4th edition 1745), we can see the way Musgrave has added to the volume what most interests him.[62] Musgrave must have been reading *Queen Zarah*, an allegorical attack on the ambitions and political manoeuvrings of Sarah Churchill, Duchess of Marlborough, a half-century or more after its first publication. The book itself details seductions and manipulations of identifiable figures at court all within the fiction of the tyrannous Queen Zarah and her followers. Musgrave's response to this text was not just to note the identities of those mentioned within the book. What he decided to do was to explain the work by way of his specialist skills and extensive biographical research. Written on the verso of the title page is a carefully constructed pedigree of Sarah Churchill showing the lineal descent of the Jennings family (figure 9).

It is a piece of apparatus of almost no use in grasping what happens in *Queen Zarah*, nor how it relates to contemporary politics, but it reflects Musgrave's interest in understanding literature through the lens of biography and genealogy. Similar instincts show themselves in his copy of Manley's *The Adventures of Rivella* (1714), a romanticized account of the novelist's life and writing.[63] Again, Musgrave's response is to supplement the text with ample, or over-ample, biographical detail. The detail he adds does not materially change the meaning of the text, but it provides a layer of anecdotal afterlife to figures who appear often only glancingly within the story. So, for example, he chases down extraneous information relating to minor family relatives in Ireland, identifies a briefly mentioned figure as a pastry cook, and fills in birth and death dates for the Earl of Clarendon. All of this is slightly pointless information – it shows us what additional things Musgrave knows about this political scene which occurred several decades before his birth, but it doesn't materially add to an interpretation of the work. Musgrave's antiquarian zeal for filling in facts might be seen as its own kind of misreading of the text. Why does he do this? Was he, like so many readers of his time, overwriting the things he didn't know with the things he did? Or did biography genuinely seem the most productive lens through which to understand what was, by the point he was writing, an historical curiosity?

Other readers showed similar predilections in their markings. A copy of Eliza Haywood's *The Perplex'd Dutchess* (1727), a satire on George I, contains notes on the title page and endpapers, but none within the text itself.[64] The title page has a short key written in at the top of the page linking fictional names to their real-world referents, and the end papers are densely inscribed with a long account of all George and George II's mistresses, cross-referenced with contemporary sources describing the king as 'a most avaricious sordid Person' and detailing his financial irregularities. Both the initial key and these notes are attributed to 'Dr Barret, fellow of TCD'. Again, these notes far exceed what the text demands by way of explanation, and once more seem to show us someone whose interest lies in showing his own access to supplementary information and the social connections that have enabled him that access. Different again is a reader of *Palace Amours*.[65] As discussed earlier, *Palace Amours* is a work that purports to tell all about the intrigues of the *beau monde* Prince Alexis, but it is entirely fictional, using the notion of its feigned real-world authenticity as a selling point. It consists of a series of seductions in which Prince Alexis succeeds in entrapping vulnerable young women, often aided by their avaricious parents. It is a work which exists to titillate – yet the unknown annotator of a copy in the British Library responds to this content with editorial zeal. Instead of reflecting on the fiction or its appeal, the annotator corrects grammar and comments on narrative discontinuities. Next to a rather chilling description of a young woman who has been presented to Alexis as a virgin on which 'he fed as heartily upon the Meat that had been roasted, cut, and warm'd over again, as if it was a fresh Joint', the annotator has taken the opportunity to cross out 'was' and replace with the more grammatically correct 'were'.[66] Further on in the book there is a longer comment on the placement of a letter concerning an intrigue, and here our reader takes issue with the placing of the letter, noting that it would have been 'more regularly' inserted earlier on in the text.[67] It is surely a response very different to that envisaged by author and publisher. Secret history looks like a genre designed for fairly straightforward allegorical unpicking, but, as these examples show, readers responded variously and surprisingly, often manifesting their own forms of creative misreading.

## Interpretative Responsibility and the Law

Given the proliferating interpretation fostered by Manley's *New Atalantis* and other secret histories, what then was the legal perspective on the potentially libellous claims framed in such narratives? If the reader had to supply their own interpretation to fit the contemporary scene, who was responsible for seditious allegations? The post-publication history of *The New Atalantis* gives some insight into these questions which applied to many satirical and political works across the period. *The New Atalantis* was published anonymously, with only the names of the trade publishers on its title page. It claimed to be a translation of a work originally written in translation, then translated into French, and then finally into English by the present author. The events described were supposed to be set on 'an island in the Mediterranean'. The work is narrated by various allegorical figures, and only hints at the real-life identities of the characters it depicts though their overtly fictional names: 'Prince Adario' for the Duke of Portland, 'Prince of Sira' for the Duke of Somerset, and 'Duchess de l'Inconstant' for the Duchess of Cleveland. Through this variety of distancing techniques, the scenarios described were kept at several arms' length from their intended subjects. But, as we have seen, these strategies were also part of the tease of the book, forcing readers to become complicit in making its meanings.

Other secret histories deployed almost random blanking out of their texts to generate interest in readers. The author or publisher of *Queen Zarah and the Zarazians* had inserted dashes without actually obscuring anything worth hiding: the narrator alluding knowingly to 'his L—ds—p' or the 'Q—n going to C—t'. Such effects created a veneer of intrigue before they had ever spilled any political beans. This world of self-important occlusions was in itself highly mockable: one later publication of 1742 is entitled *A Key to Some Late Important Transactions: in Several Letters from a Certain Great Man, No Body Knows Where, Wrote No body Knows When and Directed to No Body Knows Who* (1742).

In the case of *The New Atalantis*, the potential dangers of publication were genuine, and no number of defensive print manoeuvres could forestall legal action. In October 1709, shortly after the publication of the second volume, Manley was arrested for seditious libel. She was held without bail for a little less than a week and appeared in Westminster Hall several times. The authorities were evidently threatened by her fictional and personalized attack on the government. There is evidence that Manley's works were discussed at the highest levels, and, in a letter to Queen Anne, Sarah Churchill, the queen's favourite, invoked *The New Atalantis* as a work which had spread gossip about the queen 'among all sorts of people'.[68] In the end, Manley was released without further punishment, but her arrest and her account of her trial highlight the complex relationship among authorship, invention, and meaning. Contemporaries discussed the issues surrounding the author and her personal responsibility. Lady Mary Wortley Montagu wrote to Frances Hewet in November 1719:

> But do you know what has happened to the unfortunate authoress? People are offended at the liberty she uses in her memoirs, and she is taken into custody. Miserable is the fate of writers; if they are agreeable, they are offensive; and if dull, they starve. I lament the loss of the other parts which we should have had; and have five hundred arguments at my fingers' ends to prove the ridiculousness of those creatures that think it worth while to take notice of what is only designed for diversion.[69]

Montagu's defence of Manley rests on the notion that the scandal narrative was but a slight thing, entertainment 'only designed for diversion'. It was a line that Manley herself also pursued. In the semi-autobiographical fictional prose work, *The Adventures of Rivella*, Manley offered an account of the prosecution of her writing:

> They us'd several Arguments to make her discover who were the Persons concern'd with her in writing her Books; or at least from whom she had receiv'd Information of some special Facts, which they thought were above her own Intelligence: Her Defence was with much Humility and Sorrow, for having offended, at the same Time denying that any Persons were concern'd with her, or that she had a farther Design than writing for her own Amusement and Diversion in the Country; without intending particular Reflections or Characters: When this was not believ'd, and the contrary urg'd very home to her by several Circumstances and Likenesses; she said then it must be *Inspiration*, because knowing her own Innocence she could acount for it no other Way.[70]

She also pondered, in retrospect, why she had gotten off so lightly:

> Whether the Persons in Power were ashamed to bring a Woman to her Trial for writing a few amorous Trifles for her own Amusement, or that our Laws were defective, as most Persons conceiv'd, because she had serv'd her self with Romantick Names, and a feign'd Scene of Action?[71]

Manley deflected the charge of political sedition by emphasizing her work's fictionality, arguing that the scenes depicted were products of her own imagination, mere 'amorous trifles'. If readers drew inferences from her writing that she had not intended, that was not her responsibility. Like Pope in his *Rape of the Lock*, her representation of her work teeters around on the tightrope between satirical application and fictional invention. The idea of literary creativity was a useful defence against controversial intent. Manley also drew attention to the deficiencies of the law, which she claimed was unable to find a way of accounting for the kind of material she had produced. She was right – English law was in flux at this point, caught between a body of legislation developed to prosecute within an oral culture of seditious activity but increasingly facing challenges from printed texts proliferating faster than they could be pursued or their implications considered. Libel law as it stood was inadequate to address a newly critical and expanding print industry unafraid to take on the government.[72] As one critic has observed, 'the question driving the litigation and statutory activity around libel law during this period involved the future of authorship and the nation in the coming age of mass media'.[73]

The legal status of libel and seditious writing was intimately linked to the role of the author in relation to their work and the question of whose responsibility it was to forge the meanings of an individual text. In the years immediately before and after the publication of *The New Atalantis*, the discussion around defamatory speech and its potential manifestations began to encompass forms of writing previously considered immune to prosecution.[74] Functional ambiguity, whether through allegory, irony, or hidden meaning, was newly open to prosecution. In a landmark case of 1706, John Holt, Lord Chief Justice of the Court of the King's Bench, determined that irony was libellous if the court decided it was or if the defendant was unable to refute an underlying charge of 'ill intent'. He was considering the case of Joseph Browne's *The Country Parson's Honest Advice* (1706), a poem which worked on the basis of simple reversal, in which Whig grandees were praised effusively for virtues that they conspicuously lacked. He concluded that 'an information will lie for speaking ironically'.[75] Doubleness of meaning or irony was no protection against prosecution: 'such Scandal as is expressed in a scoffing and ironical Manner make a Writing as properly a Libel, as that which is expressed in direct Terms'.[76] Similarly, thinking about the use of partial names was changing. In 1700, the Attorney General agreed that the Whig satirist John Tutchin's poem *The Foreigners* was immune from prosecution because Tutchin had only identified those involved with pseudonyms. But by 1713, in a similar case, the Court of King's Bench would rule that:

> a Defamatory Writing expressing only one or two Letters of a Name, in such a Manner, that from what goes before and follows after, it must needs be understood to signify such a particular Person, in the plain, obvious and natural Construction of the whole, and would be perfect Nonsense if strained to any other Meaning, is as properly a Libel, as if it had expressed the Name at large [. . .] And it is a ridiculous Absurdity to say, That a Writing which is understood by every [one] in the meanest Capacity, cannot possibly be understood by a Judge and Jury.[77]

It's a fascinating insight into the way in which many of the works discussed in this book were understood in a legal context. The passage above presents interpretation as something which was obvious to all. But, as this book shows, the 'plain, obvious and natural Construction of the whole' was by no means a given in the reading culture of the period. Readers were frequently uncertain or at odds in their deciphering of coded texts. And despite the claim that 'every [one] in the meanest Capacity' would understand political insinuation, few of the works of the period that positioned themselves as universally accessible were entirely understood. The relationship among meaning-making, interpretation, and responsibility was evolving fast, and, as we can see from this judgement, literary matters of typography, interpretation, and readerly competence were at the heart of legal debates about libel.

The insistence that there was no difference between cloaked and explicit political critique repositioned the norms of contemporary satire. Manley and others tried to defend themselves by saying that their works were fictional or by using incomplete names, but those ruses were no longer working. Contemporaries certainly feared that Manley's prose-cution would mark the end of satire:

> After this, who will dare to give the history of Angella? I was in hopes her faint essay would have provoked some better pen to give more elegant and secret memoirs; but now she will serve as a scarecrow to frighten people from attempting any thing but heavy panegyric; and we shall be teized with nothing but heroic poems, with names at length, and false characters, so daubed with flattery, that they are the severest kind of lampoons, for they both scandalise the writer and the subject, like that vile paper the Tatler. I believe, madam, you will think I have dwelt too long on this business; but I am in a violent passion about it.[78]

The debates summarized here assumed that readers were able to read cloaked meanings, and that authors were responsible for their readers' interpretations. If 'everyone' got the hidden agenda in an apparently fictional work, then why shouldn't a judge and jury? Yet, as we have seen, not everyone did get the meaning of a work, not every work had a clear meaning, and not every meaning was agreed upon. The complex questions of access, interpretation, and misreading that reverberate through early eighteenth-century print culture had clear legal ramifica-tions. The definitions of defamation, libel, and sedition were becoming increasingly focused on the legibility of political insinuation. Yet the evidence of individual reading practices and the diversity of interpreta-tive approaches on display here suggest that such legibility was a fiction. The role of readerly understanding was central to contemporary debates about political agency and responsibility, and, as we shall see, imperfect reading could be easily weaponized.

# 8

# Out of Control

Shall I Own to you That the Greatest Concern I have Upon me is
That the Govornment, whom I Profess I Did not foresee would be
Displeas'd, Should Resent This Matter. I had it not in my Thoughts
that the Ministers of State would Construe That as Pointing at
Them . . .

—DANIEL DEFOE TO WILLIAM PATERSON, APRIL 1703

THIS CHAPTER TURNS for a while from readers to authors, to explore
the issue of control, and the lack of it: it looks at what happens when a
writer loses purchase of the reception of their work, sometimes with
disastrous personal consequences. We have seen the way in which many
early eighteenth-century authors played with readerly uncertainty,
which could be used in opportunistic and creative ways. They offered
guides to how to understand a book or keys which elucidated or
mocked recent works, created texts which both could and could not be
accessed by the reader, teased with the fantasy of social inclusion. Writers professed themselves misunderstood: Alexander Pope, Delariviere
Manley, and others lamented the misconstruction of their works, and
they often did so disingenuously, as a defence against criticism or prosecution. However, sometimes books went genuinely wrong. This is a period
which sees the wholesale misunderstanding of political or satirical
writings: readers not merely unable to identify topical figures or events

but unclear about the basic intention: 'You should have given me a key
to the Invisible Spy, particularly to the Catalogue of Books in it; I know
not whether the Conjugal Happiness of the D[uke] of B. is intended as
a Compliment or an Irony'.[1] 'Have you met with the novel called The
Marriage Act? They say it is a satire against the Chancellor. I don't understand it as far as I have gone; it seems a general satire'.[2] At other times
people inferred an overall meaning that was the opposite of that intended: 'I took the Author for a Friend to our Faction [...] but it seems
I mistook the whole Matter, and apply'd all I had read to a couple of
Persons, who were not at that time in the Writers Thoughts'.[3] For all the
knowing play of the blanks, codes, and omissions of much eighteenth-
century literature, authors couldn't necessarily anticipate the wider interpretation of their words, particularly when those works deployed
irony as way of communicating with their readers. Irony is, as we've seen
in discussions of the Bible, a form of misreading in its own right – based
on the principle that the intended meaning is not that which appears on
the surface, and is in fact often the direct opposite. It depends on readers
performing acts of reversal in order to unlock content and meaning, and
is highly generative of confusion: an anonymous pamphleteer writing
in 1705 described 'these ironies' as 'the confoundedest things in the
World, and of pernicious Consequences some Times'.[4] Henry Fielding
said in 1748 'there was no kind of Humour so liable to be mistaken'.[5]
Irony is at the heart of the strange story of Daniel Defoe, his pamphlets,
and his readers. What did a writer do when his work was wholly and
disastrously misread? What is the role of deliberate, as opposed to accidental, misreading? And how does all this happen? As we follow this
story, we can see just how badly misunderstanding could play out
in the print culture of the period, and what this might tell us about
the vexed relationship between reading, interpretation, and authorial
responsibility.

## The Shortest-Way

On the 14 January 1703, *The London Gazette* ran the following
advertisement:

*Whereas* Daniel de Foe *alias* De Fooe *is charged with writing a Scandalous and Seditious Pamphlet. Entituled,* [The Shortest-Way with the Dissenters.] *Whoever shall discover the said* Daniel de Foe *alias de* Fooe *to one of her Majesty's Principal Secretaries of State, or any of Her Majesty's Justices of the Peace, so as he may be apprehended, shall have a Reward of* 50.l. *which Her Majesty has ordered immediately to be paid upon such Discovery:*

*He is a middle Sized-Spare Man, about 40 years old, of a brown Complexion, and dark brown coloured Hair, but wears a Wig, a hooked Nose, a sharp Chin, grey Eyes, and a large Mould near his Mouth, was born in London, and for many years was a Hose Factor in Freeman's-yard, in Cornhill, and now is Owner of the Brick and Pantile Works near* Tilbury-Fort *in* Essex.[6]

This advertisement is the best description we have of the physical appearance of the tradesman, pamphleteer, spy, historian, journalist, and novelist Daniel Defoe. It is also evidence of what happens when writers lose control of the meaning of their works. The seditious pamphlet which formed the basis for Defoe's arrest, *The Shortest-Way with the Dissenters or Proposals for the Establishment of the Church* (1702), was Defoe's explosive intervention in contemporary debate over religious practice, and, in particular, the question of the relationship between religious Dissenters and the mainstream Anglican church. It marks a high-water mark of unintended misreading in this period. The origins of the debate about religious inclusion are particular and stretch back to the seventeenth century: following the Test Act of 1673, every person who held office – a role in the civil, military, or royal administration – had to swear the oath of allegiance and take communion in the Church of England within three months of taking office. Through this legislation, which set a pretty low bar for participation in Anglican worship, the Dissenting community were able to retain their own faith, and, at the same time, assume professional positions within the various branches of national administration. It was not universally popular within the nonconformist community. Defoe was himself a Dissenter, educated at Charles Morton's dissenting academy in Newington Green.[7]

Like others, he bridled at what he saw as the hypocrisy behind the practice of occasional conformity, the idea that some members of his religious community took communion for the sake of personal advancement.

The political context of these conversations about religious inclusion changed dramatically following the sudden death of William III in 1702 and the accession of Queen Anne. Anne had replaced many Whig ministers with Tories, and she gave signals that her alliances might lie with the high-flying end of the Anglican church rather than the broad-based inclusion of all Protestant groups. By the time Parliament returned at the end of the summer of 1702, Anglican expectations of the new Queen seemed to have been confirmed. The Commons was presented with a new bill against Occasional Conformity, designed to protect the monopoly on local and national offices held by conforming members of the Church of England and to reduce the religious toleration which had prevailed under William III. The bill would effectively stop all Dissenters from holding offices in cities, boroughs, corporations, and crown offices.[8]

Defoe was in a difficult position. He continued to oppose the practice of occasional conformity, but, at the same time, suspected that behind the bill there was a profound desire to suppress the Dissenting community. He made his intervention with an anonymous thirty-page pamphlet, *The Shortest-Way with the Dissenters*, published in December 1702. Issued without any indication of its author, printer, or distributor, the piece did not engage with the specifics of the bill. Instead, it set out to expose the mindset behind the proposal, illuminating the motivations and deeper intentions of its supporters. Defoe employed rhetorical ventriloquism, mimicking the voice and language of an intolerant and prejudiced onlooker, one who was eager to seize the political moment and stamp out nonconformity in the most extreme way. Through the mouthpiece of this fictional zealot, he aimed to discredit the moral and political platform upon which his opponents stood.[9] He appropriated the language of extremism, exploiting a polemical vocabulary found in many other contemporary pamphlets in which Dissenters were represented as subhuman, vermin, or diseased, a noxious and insidious threat to the status quo.[10] Defoe's pamphlet argued that the established church had mistakenly 'nourish'd the viperous Brood, till they hiss and fly in the Face of the Mother that cherish'd them'. Dissenters were described as a 'Contagion', a 'heretical Weed of Sedition', as 'Serpents, Toads, Vipers [. . .] noxious to the Body, and poison the sensitive Life', and 'a Race of poison'd Spirits'.[11] The speaker rehearsed other long-standing tenets of anti-Dissenting propaganda and summed up the present time as a watershed moment in which to save the Church of England. How would later observers judge a nation which left such a poisonous brood unpunished? As this account suggests, the fictional speaker of *The Shortest-Way* ignored the nuts and bolts of the proposed legislation and instead confected an emotive crisis point which called for severe intervention: 'How many Millions of future Souls we save from Infection and Delusion, if the present Race of poison'd Spirits were purg'd from the Face of the Land?'[12] His proposal was a simple one – Dissenters would quickly drop their religious practices if faced with the death penalty:

> 'Tis vain to trifle in this matter, the light foolish handling of them by Mulcts, Fines &c. 'tis their Glory and their Advantage; if the Gallows instead of the Counter, and the Gallies instead of the Fines, were the Reward of going to a Conventicle, to preach or to hear, there would not be so many Sufferers, the Spirit of Martyrdom is over; they that will go to Church to be chosen Sheriffs and Mayors, would go to forty Churches rather than be Hang'd.[13]

Defoe's pamphlet argued the exact opposite of what he believed and did so in the most sensational way. The piece worked through a rhetorical pairing of mercy and murder, kindness and cruelty. His fictional speaker argued that too much lenience towards nonconformists had created a savage breed of disloyal republicans who would only respond to the harshest treatment. Mercy and toleration would be an act of cruelty to future generations of Anglicans. In deploying the language of intemperance, the speaker's proposed solution – suppression of all

Dissent through the threat of death – was an appropriate and just response to an urgent situation. Defoe pushed the logic of intolerance to
its natural conclusion – extermination and expulsion.

It was a rhetorical hand grenade lobbed into an already overheated
political arena, and the results were instant. Defoe had imitated the
voice of his high church opponents too well – with the consequences
that the pamphlet was explosively misread. Rather than being seen as
an ironic exposure of the rhetoric of extremism, it was taken for the
genuine article, a proposal put forward in all seriousness by an unidentified member of the Anglican church who really wanted to start execut-
ing Dissenters. It prompted concern, approval, and outrage in different
measures.[14] In some quarters it went down – temporarily – like a storm.[15]
But many moderate Anglicans and Dissenters, equally unaware of the
ironic intention, were alarmed by the pamphlet and the tenor of its
propositions. The Whig John Tutchin opined in *The Observator* that the
*Shortest-Way* seemed to be the work of an Anglican clergyman. Ponder-
ing the question of authorship, he wrote:

> I rationally conclude him to be one of the Inferiour Clergy [. . .]
> Whatever the Author be, 'tis no great matter, but the Book is a System
> of the *High Flyers Divinity* and *Politicks*, and I am glad those People
> have at length given the World a Sample of their Morals and good
> Nature: I would not recommend a Villanous Book to Publick View;
> but herein those People are drawn to the Life, and those who know
> their Marks and Character will the better know how to avoid 'em.[16]

The low-church author of *The Safest-Way with the Dissenters* (1703)
also took the posturing at face value and considered seriously the advice
to exterminate Dissenting ministers, concluding that the persecution
advised in Defoe's pamphlet was ill-advised and 'no Safe-Way for any
Government to Hang up so many of its Subjects'.[17]

It seems that Defoe had not anticipated these responses. He con-
veyed his surprise at the dissenting response in a contemporary letter:
'I Confess it makes me Reflect on the wholl body of the Dissenters with
Something of Contempt More Than Usuall, and gives me the More
Regrett That I Suffer for Such a People'.[18] But his greatest dismay was

that the government should have taken offence and the personal consequences this entailed: ·

> Shall I Own to you That the Greatest Concern I have Upon me is That
> the Govornment, whom I Profess I Did not foresee would be Displeas'd,
> Should Resent This Matter. I had it not in my Thoughts that the Minis-
> ters of State would Construe That as Pointing at Them, Which I Levell'd
> Onely at Dr Sachavrell, Dr Stubbs, and Such People, my More Direct
> Antagonists; Thus like Old Tyrell who shot at a Stag and Killd the King,
> I Engag'd a Party and Embroild my Self with the Govornmt.[19]

His attack on the high church extremists, typified by Henry Sacheverell, had been wrongly taken as an attack on the whole government.
'Old Tyrell' was a twelfth-century nobleman who had gone on a hunting
trip with William II and accidentally killed the king while aiming at a
stag. Defoe's arrow was keenly felt by the Tory leaders of his day. On
3 January 1703, the Secretary of State Daniel Finch, the second earl of
Nottingham, issued a warrant for Defoe's arrest on the basis that the
pamphlet was seditious libel. Defoe eluded the messenger sent to find
him, went into hiding, and sent his wife to plead his case with Nottingham.[20] He was eventually arrested and indicted for libel in the Old Bailey on 24 February; the following day the Commons lodged a formal
complaint against *The Shortest-Way*. Neither of the two charges made
against Defoe and his pamphlet acknowledged that the work was a
parody, or that it was intended to be ironic. The Old Bailey charge was
that Defoe had been scheming to deny Dissenters religious toleration,
while the Commons claimed that Defoe had failed to treat Parliament
with respect, 'tending to promote sedition':

> de Foe . . . being a Seditious man and of a disordered mind, and a
> person of bad name, reputation and Conversation, by a disgraceful
> felony perfidiously, mischievously and seditiously contriving, prac-
> ticing and purposing to make and Cause discord between . . . the
> Queen and her . . . Subjects . . . [21]

*The Shortest-Way* was ordered to be burnt by the common hangman
in New Palace Yard in Westminster. Defoe was imprisoned in Newgate

until 5 June, and then at his trial in early July, he was sentenced to pay a fine of 200 marks, to stand in the pillory three times, and to remain in prison until he could find a sum of money to vouch for his good behaviour for the next seven years. When he came to take his place in the pillory, he was stationed in Cornhill by the Royal Exchange on 29 July, a position in the heart of the neighbourhood he'd grown up in. For the following two days he stood in bad weather in different public spaces in the busiest parts of London, and then spent the next four months in Newgate, until his release and pardon were arranged by the Lord Treasurer, Sidney Godolphin, and the speaker of the house, Robert Harley. Defoe's prosecution was one of the most expensive in Queen Anne's reign, and each aspect of his punishment was more severe than that handed out to other journalists during this period.[22] So what went wrong? How in this great age of satire, irony, and parody did Defoe manage to write a piece that misfired to the degree that he ended up paying for it with his financial security and reputation?

## Sedition and Meaning

One answer to the severity of Defoe's fate lay in the nature of the legal process. As we have seen, the law around seditious libel was changing fast in response to the burgeoning market in cheap print, the polemical turmoil of the contemporary political scene, and the inventiveness of authors and publishers seeking to evade prosecution for their interventions in the rage of party.[23] It was no longer possible to claim innocence on the ground of blanked-out names, ironic meaning, and unspoken allegations. The case of *The Shortest-Way* demonstrated that seditious libel could be interpreted as the publication of writing that didn't necessarily scandalize an individual – for none was named – but did reflect badly on the institution of government.[24] The role of the jury in the trial of *The Shortest-Way* was not to determine whether or not the pamphlet was libellous – that was the place of the judge – but merely to confirm whether the accused, in this case Defoe, was the author. The trial pivoted on the need to fix a name to the publication, not to work out what the author was using it to say. The fact that Defoe had written one thing, when in fact he meant another, was irrelevant in the legal context of his prosecution. In legal terms, the core of this case was authorship rather than intention. Irony in itself would not become litigable until several years later in 1706, and the trial of Dr Joseph Browne, whose lampoon, *The Country Parson's Honest Advice to My Lord Keeper*, with its ironic praise of Whig grandees was, as we have seen, the subject of a crucial ruling. The judge's decision on that case, that 'information will lie for speaking ironically' ensured that it was then the jury's role to decide the intent of the author, rather than merely determining the obvious meaning of the words on the page.[25]

While the legal conversation around *The Shortest-Way* did not stray into the niceties of productive ambiguity, in the printed exchanges surrounding the pamphlet we witness a debate about the role of irony and the relationship between reading and misreading. Shortly after his arrest, Defoe hurried out a defence of his work, called *A Brief Explanation of a Late Pamphlet Entituled The Shortest-Way with the Dissenters* (1703). In it, we can hear his disbelief at the outcome of his work, declaring that when he wrote the book, he thought 'he shou'd never need to come to an Explication'. But given the contemporary response to the work, he thought best to offer the world the 'Native Genuine Meaning and Design of the Paper, which he hopes may allay the Anger of the Government, or at least satisfie the minds of such as imagine a design to Enflame and Divide us'.[26] He explained that the origin of *The Shortest-Way* was a desire to respond to genuinely intemperate attacks on Dissenters and 'the Virulent Spirits of some Men who have thought fit to express themselves to the same Effect' and that 'by an *Irony not Unusual*' his pamphlet would expose the dangerous motives behind such publications.[27] Acknowledging that readers had mistaken his ironic intent, Defoe went on to discuss ideas of clarity and hidden meaning. His original pamphlet was effectively a coded reprimand to his opponents not to go too far and an indirect warning to Dissenters to beware the real agenda behind the Anglican assault on occasional conformity. Yet in his *Vindication* he argued that *The Shortest-Way* was a model of clarity:

this Book stands fair to let those Gentlemen know that what they design can no farther take with mankind than as their real meaning stands disguis'd by Artifice of words; but that when the Persecution and Destruction of the *Dissenters, the very thing they drive at*, is put into plain *English*, the whole Nation will start at the Notion, and Condemn the Author to be Hang'd for his Impudence.[28]

According to Defoe, *The Shortest-Way* was, in fact, 'plain *English* without Design', and it exposed the true intentions of high church Anglicans and their 'Plain Design in Duller and Darker *English*'.[29] Defoe played here with the notion of what was plain and what was obscure – from his perspective, the cloaked objectives of the Anglicans were the truly hidden meaning, rather than his entirely straightforward pamphlet. Concepts which might seem to us to be straightforward – the difference between truth and fiction, plain language and obfuscation, metaphor and literalism – were here profoundly confused.

It is interesting to see then how the pamphlet was read even after the court case and after Defoe had expressed his true intentions. Some at the extreme end of the high church quoted it approvingly, but then turned on Defoe when his authorship and true intention were revealed. One poetic response explained this logic:

> The Church already has been scandaliz'd,
> Unknowing your vile *Pamphlet* patroniz'd:
> But when discover'd did such ways pursue,
> That justly paid you, what might be your *due*.[30]

Other contemporary pamphlets reveal sympathy with the arguments articulated in *The Shortest-Way*, even while they criticized its deception.[31] And there were readers who followed the legal proceedings and knew of Defoe's self-defence but chose to believe that the pamphlet was part of a more complex murky conspiracy rather than a straightforward use of irony to expose Anglican extremism. As one critic has argued, Defoe's contemporaries 'were largely agreed on how to describe *The Shortest-Way*: most appear to have been convinced that it was a conspiracy; they just disagreed on what the end of that conspiracy was'.[32] Others continued to read the text quite earnestly as a serious intervention in arguments about church and state. A heavily marked-up copy of the pamphlet in the British Library gives us some insight into such a response and the ways in which readers might effectively choose to misread the pages before them.[33] The annotator has written on the verso of the title page their own account of the publication:

> At the sessions in the old Bayly 7 8 & 9 July 1703 Daniell De Foe a supposed Dissenter sometimes a Hosyer [...] pleaded Guilty to a Punishment for the writing & publishing of this seditious libell.[34]

From the evidence of the annotations, the owner of the pamphlet seems to be a Dissenter – or sympathizer to Dissent – who continued to contest the logic of the arguments made in the work even after its author had proclaimed his ironic intention (figure 10). They write at the end of the pamphlet that Defoe ' hereof Pilloryed for this service [...] is a great Champion for the moderate Church of England in opposition to Jacobite & non Juror & the high Church men of passive obedience.'[35] Yet while recognizing that Defoe was hoping to defend Dissent, many of the annotations in this copy of *The Shortest-Way* are cross references to acts of parliament and recent history – they verify the dates and titles of particular pieces of legislation or add substance or clarity to historical references.

As such, the comments show us a writer attempting to engage with Defoe's fictional arguments and counter claims by rooting them in genuine political history, rather than recognizing them as part of the satirical exercise that was intended.[36] At times the marginalia engage more explicitly with the confected outrage of the piece. Midway through the pamphlet, Defoe's extremist speaker imagines and dismisses potential challenge to his radical views: 'BUT, says another Hot and Cold Objector, this is renewing Fire and Faggot [...] This will be cruelty in its Nature, and Barbarous to all in the World'.[37] The annotator chimes in here in support, noting that such an act 'would be otherwise esteemed in Any Government that for the sake of Any one persuasion will destroy all likewise'.[38] What we see here is a person who continues to misread the text, despite Defoe's clear indication of his intention. Rather than accepting that all the arguments made in the pamphlet were ironic, they were unable to resist the urge to engage with *The Shortest-Way* as an

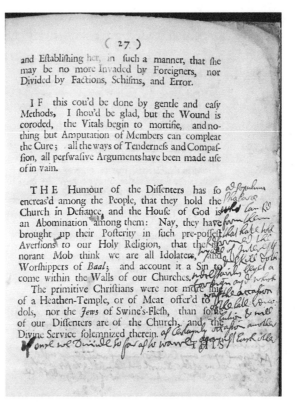

( 27 )

and Establishing her, in such a manner, that she may be no more Invaded by Foreigners, nor Divided by Factions, Schisms, and Error.

I F this cou'd be done by gentle and easy Methods, I shou'd be glad, but the Wound is coroded, the Vitals begin to mortifie, and nothing but Amputation of Members can compleat the Cure; all the ways of Tenderness and Compassion, all perswasive Arguments have been made use of in vain.

THE Humour of the Dissenters has so encreas'd among the People, that they hold the Church in Defiance, and the House of God is an Abomination among them: Nay, they have brought up their Posterity in such pre-possess Aversions to our Holy Religion, that the ignorant Mob think we are all Idolaters, and Worshippers of Baal; and account it a Sin to come within the Walls of our Churches.

The primitive Christians were not more shie of a Heathen-Temple, or of Meat offer'd to Idols, nor the Jews of Swine's-Flesh, than some of our Dissenters are of the Church, and the Divine Service solemnized therein.

FIGURE 10. Daniel Defoe, *The Shortest-Way with the Dissenters: or Proposals for the Establishment of the Church* (London, 1702), British Library, 110.f.27, p. 27.

earnest political debate. Perhaps they preferred the more offensive version, which gave them an outlet for their outrage and the chance to perform what they would have said to the fictional speaker of the piece. They certainly seem to have chosen to read the pamphlet in the wrong way, and in doing so, they offer a reminder of the very varied responses of the historical reader.

The case of *The Shortest-Way* framed a debate about meaning and intention. Was it more honest to make others' thoughts speak through a fictional figure, in order to illuminate the dark core of political extremism, or to speak in one's own voice without the doublethink of irony? Many of Defoe's opponents took the latter view. The author of *The Fox with his Fire-brand Unkennell'd and Insnar'd: Or, a Short Answer to Mr Daniel Foe's Shortest-Way with the Dissenters* (1703) mocked Defoe's protestations of his intention, suggesting that his lack of sophistication gave the *Shortest-Way* only a 'barbarous Irony':

> such *Ironical Figures* as are not to be found in the *Tropes* of our Modern Rhetorick, but a barbarous *Irony* that was much practised by the Old *Romans* on the Primitive Christians, the better to bring their Dogs to worry them.[39]

The author of *The Fox with his Fire-brand* suggested that it was the author who was responsible for making the meanings his readers had found. Defoe would have been better able to control his book had he had more formal education:

> And, if our Author had been bred a Scholar instead of a Hosier, he would have found another kind of Figure *for making other Peoples Thoughts speak in his words.* But, after all, his *Brief Explanation* falls very short of clearing him from *Seditious Designs;* for, all the while, not a Syllable of all that Satyr or *Sarcasm*, Virulency or Malice, or persecuting Spirit is to be seen in those Sermons and Pamphlets upon which he would so *Ironically* sham it.[40]

As this suggests, responses to Defoe's pamphlet extended beyond the specifics of the topical debate and edged into related arguments about interpretation and its vexed relationship with class and education. And as so often in the period, claims based on social status were used as a weapon in an argument about good and bad reading, even when religious or political identity were the main causes of difference.

*The Shortest-Way* has prompted considerable critical debate about Defoe's purpose. It used to be that historians and literary critics assumed that the work was a failure because Defoe ended up alienating both Dissenters and Anglicans.[41] The publication was a misfire, an attempt that went wrong. More recent accounts have complicated this view by identifying the inconsistency in Defoe's own account of his publication and arguing that the pamphlet was a satirical imitation of an extremist work, rather than a sustained piece of irony.[42] They have suggested that Defoe cleverly constructed an ironized extremist whose arguments undermined themselves even as he set them out on paper.[43] What none of this discussion really does is to relate what happened to Defoe to the wider culture of misreading and its exploitation in this era, and to see historical readers' responses as part of a pattern of confusion or uncertainty or deliberate misinterpretation.

Defoe certainly changed his tune on what his pamphlet represented and whether it worked. Although, as we have seen, the *Vindication* (published shortly after *The Shortest-Way*) emphasized the author's surprise at the reception of the pamphlet, by the time he was writing an allegorical account of the whole saga in *The Consolidator* (1705), he depicted *The Shortest-Way* as a triumph:

> The *Crolians* [Dissenters] themselves were surpriz'd at it, and so closely had the Author couch'd his Design, that they never saw the *Irony of the Stile*, but began to look about them, to see which way they should fly to save themselves.
>
> The *Men of Zeal* we talk'd of, were so blinded with the Notion which *suited so exactly with their real Design*, that they hugg'd the Book, *applauded the unknown Author*, and plac'd the Book next their *Oracular Writings*, or Laws of Religion. The Author was all this while conceal'd, and the Paper had all the effect he wish'd for.[44]

According to this version, although the Dissenters failed to see the irony in *The Shortest-Way*, the fact that the high church 'hugg'd the book', cherishing its extremity, meant that it was a success because it enabled everyone, and particularly Anglican moderates, to see the truly persecutory attitudes the high-flyers had cloaked with more moderate language.[45] Perhaps Defoe achieved what he wanted – and he intended his pamphlet to shock both Dissenters and Anglicans, to warn them of the potential consequences against which they should be on their guard. It's hard at this distance to know which version is right – whether the satire failed because its irony was not recognized, or whether it was a success because in passing as genuine outrage it was designed to tease out extremity in those who approved of its radical conclusions. But what is absolutely clear is that by situating the publication and its aftermath in the broader culture of reading we can see that rather than being a one-off, Defoe's fate might better be understood as part of a complex, creative, and potentially unstable world of misreading and interpretative confusion.

## Interpretation and Anonymity

In the case of *The Shortest-Way*, readerly confusion was linked to the conditions of anonymous publication. Without any name or suggestion of identity on the title page, the pamphlet left readers unable to navigate on the basis of recognizable authorial intention. Anonymity was widespread in eighteenth-century publication, used for a range of purposes, and it is key to the culture of textual misunderstanding within which so many eighteenth-century works sit.[46] The proportion of texts published without an authorial identifier is high. For prose fiction, approximately 50 per cent of works from 1660–1750 list no author on the title page, while an additional 20 per cent are effectively anonymous, using only a pseudonym or initial. Nearly 25 per cent of texts listed in the English Short Title Catalogue were published anonymously.[47] There were many reasons to publish without authorial identification: fear of litigation; class or gender; the desire to test the water for future named publications.[48] In the case of Defoe's *Shortest-Way*, anonymous publication was designed to protect the author from the potential legal backlash to politically contentious content. But how did it work for readers?

Anonymity made interpretation even more difficult, providing no identifier on which to hang coded or allusive or ironic works.[49] Although it is clear that anonymous texts sold well, and that in some ways anonymity added to the appeal of apparently controversial, salacious, or private content, the material evidence of annotated books shows that many eighteenth-century readers also wanted to fix a name to the works they read. Title pages are littered with readers' manuscript attributions, made by owners keen to fill in the information that was not provided at first publication. Accounts of markings in books in this period repeatedly cite the commonness of authorial attribution.[50] The habits of annotation of readers in this period show that they wanted to make sense of the work in their hands by filling in its context – and the author was a large part of that background. As David Brewer has argued, this assigning of names was less about linking those texts to a biographical story than about using the name as 'a set of tacit instructions as to what should be done with that text [. . .] or a sign of where that text or reader or writer should be located, literarily, socially, geographically'.[51] Such tension between anonymous publication and readerly desire for attribution underlies the culture of misreading of the early eighteenth century. Without an identifiable author-figure, contemporaries were unable to gauge the significance of a work, unable to measure the gap between author and word, and in this case, unable to see that Defoe must have been channelling the voice of a very different kind of thinker.

Defoe's own habits of anonymous publication have proved particularly challenging for his critical afterlife, and the attribution and de-attribution of fictional and non-fictional works to his name has been a subject of scholarly debate. Defoe anticipated the way in which so many anonymous works would become assigned to him, and he mocked his contemporaries' urge to fix a name to what they read, complaining in 1705 that he ended up as the assumed author of the majority of contentious works, which 'must be the Devil or De Foe'.[52] He also suggested that the habit of attribution reflected more on those who did it than on the authors themselves: 'they [his antagonists] need not ask me for a name . . . for they give it themselves, and I hate to be always telling people their own names'.[53] Many of the political, economic, and historical works which came to acquire his authorship post-publication have since been de-assigned on the grounds of internal evidence.[54] But beyond the fate of individual works, there is a question about why modern readers feel the need to assign authorship at all. Some critics have argued that the process of attribution is related to critical investment in an author's canon, and that the act of attaching names to texts places the coherent body of works above the singularity of the text and its context.[55] We put names on things because that is how we conceptualize literary value and status. Linking to an author name allows us to identify an oeuvre and a book's place within it: without that, perhaps we have to work harder to interpret it through its time and place. Moreover, uncertainty about authorship has probably led to some texts' exclusion from traditional literary histories. But once again, in assigning information to a page that is supplementary to the original publication, we distort the historical reading experience.

An absence of authorial identification is particularly problematic in considering the use of irony. As critics and linguists have long shown, ironic speech and writing are underpinned by social relationships, built on an implicit understanding between speaker and audience. Irony signals a complicity between speaker and audience, generally based on a set of agreed values or understanding. The complicity at the heart of irony inevitably excludes other groups from 'getting' the joke. Henry Fowler's 1965 *Dictionary of Modern English Usage* is no longer very modern, but its definition of irony is helpful in this context:

> Irony is a form of utterance that postulates a double audience, consisting of one party that hearing shall hear and shall not understand, and another party that, when more is meant than meets the ear, is aware both of that more and of the outsiders' incomprehension. [It] may be defined as the use of words intended to convey one meaning to the uninitiated part of the audience and another to the initiated, the delight of it lying in the secret intimacy set up between the latter and the speaker.[56]

The notion that some readers were initiated, while others were not, was, as we have seen, a common dynamic in early eighteenth-century literature, which so often played with the inclusion and exclusion of its readers. In the case of Defoe's pamphlet, as in other texts discussed here, the problem was that the various parties listening to Defoe's utterance did not know who was initiated and who wasn't. The semantic challenges of the ironic text were compounded by anonymity: if readers did not know who the real speaker was, because they could not perceive a difference between the person speaking and what they were saying, they were unable to appreciate the purposeful dissonance on which the satire was built. Recent cognitive accounts of the use of irony have drawn attention to the role of 'pretence theory', the idea that the ironized speaker is effectively pretending to be someone else, usually someone uninformed or injudicious.[57] There are potentially two victims of the ironic joke: the type of person represented by the 'pretended' voice, and then the listener who doesn't realize that the voice is a pretence and accepts its absurd or illogical hypotheses. But these models are dependent upon an accepted and understood delineation between the initiated and the uninitiated, between authors and readers who knew where they stood in relation to one another and how they aligned. And as we know, these distinctions were far from clear in the print culture of the early eighteenth century. The rapid expansion of printed publication, the prevalence of anonymous print, and the replacement of systems of social manuscript transmission by the more amorphous and unknowable circulation of print, all contributed to a culture of potential muddle and uncertainty. Defoe's critics charged him with being unable to master the reins of his irony because he wasn't trained in the classical rhetorical forms that he was trying to use. It is certainly clear that whether we deem *The Shortest-Way* a polemical success or failure, Defoe lost control of his pamphlet: he could not determine the way it was received partly because it was not predicated on a securely understood and accepted set of relationships between the author and those he spoke to.

There are intriguing parallels here with the emergent digital culture of the twenty-first century and the role of the internet in mediating opinion and argument among a largely anonymous global readership. In this modern context, we find the same uncertainty of relationship between speaker and listener, writer and reader, that characterized early eighteenth-century print. And it plays out with similar consequences. 'Poe's law', an informal principle of internet culture, rests on the thesis that without a clear indication of the author's intention, it is impossible to create a parody of extreme views so obviously exaggerated that it cannot be mistaken by some readers or viewers as a sincere expression of the parodied views. So, for example, a parodic expression of the most extreme creationist account of natural history or human development will find an audience somewhere who accepts and endorses that account as a sincere expression of a valid viewpoint. Poe's law has often been applied in the context of various expressions of extremism or fundamentalism. It is seen as a product of digital communication since public conversations online offer their observers fewer opportunities to consider paralinguistic signals alongside a particular statement. Viewers rarely have access to the full relational content of a given interaction.[58] But the surfeit of anonymous print and broadening readership of the beginning of the eighteenth century created similar conditions. Defoe's *Shortest-Way* is Poe's law in action. The performance of online identity is hard to parse, and so was the anonymous display of political identity in Defoe's time. The contemporary parallel both shows that the challenges of digital communication have a prehistory in print and highlights some of the long-standing questions about control, irony, and misreading raised by the exposure of extremist rhetoric and ideology.

A recent study of the role of play, irony, and confused meaning in an online environment has highlighted the difficulty in gauging the appropriate response to seemingly racist or fascist speech or images. If a Nazi symbol is claimed to be used ironically, does that make it acceptable?

> The social and the anti-social are [. . .] always nipping at each other's heels online; what could be one thing one second, with one audience, could shift into the other with a simple retweet, unbeknownst to the original poster. As a result, the rejoinder that 'I was just joking' or just as frequently, 'I was just trolling' becomes an even tougher sell. Even when both teller and listener are on the same basic page, the idea that one shouldn't be held accountable for one's own offensive speech and behavior and, furthermore, that if someone is offended it's the person's problem – for being oversensitive, for not knowing how to take a joke – is a highly self-involved, myopic, framing.[59]

Our current discomfort with these questions gives some insight into the ways in which Defoe's contemporaries questioned his performance of extremist rhetoric, and the ways in which they too sometimes felt that irony was not a valid defence. Contemporary debates over online offence and satire have a prehistory in the print conditions of the early eighteenth century and help us to understand why and how Defoe was misread. If, under normal circumstances, satire involves a community of readers recognizing and being in on the joke, then in other, more volatile situations it can involve just the opposite: instead of cementing a consensus of insiders it produces debate, conflict, and fragmentation. It becomes unstable and even unrecognizable, and the question of whether or not something is satirical might be not just difficult but undecidable.

## Wilful Misreading: Defoe's Succession Crisis

*The Shortest-Way* exemplifies how far texts could be read in ways utterly antithetical to their authors' intentions: there were some readers who were genuinely confused by the satirical strategies within the piece, and who failed to recognize the ironic deployment in the communication of a particular message. But there were also those who deliberately misread ironic intention in political commentary as a way of discrediting or damaging the author. Misreading was a potential liability for the eighteenth-century author, and it could also provide a source of attack for their opponents. These issues played out very clearly in Daniel Defoe's later foray into ironic political commentary: a series of pamphlets addressing the threat of Jacobitism and the prospect of the death of Queen Anne.

As Queen Anne's reign wore on, her health declined and the prospect of an heir vanished; attention on the future governance of Great Britain came increasingly to focus on the Protestant succession. Under the Act of Succession of 1701, should Anne die childless, the throne would pass to the Electress Sophia of Hanover and her Protestant heirs. This was designed to remove uncertainty over the continuation of a Protestant succession and to prevent the Jacobite claim to the throne by the exiled James III. Defoe, like many Protestant subjects, was fervently opposed to the Jacobite challenge, but also mindful that a mere piece of legislation might not be bulwark enough against the combined forces of a French and/or Jacobite intervention. In the spring of 1713, he published a set of three pamphlets concerning the succession, in which he presented arguments in favour of the Jacobite succession that – once again – were the exact *reverse* of what he actually believed. They were a kind of thought experiment, in which he imagined for his readers the likely outcomes of a French king, the loss of democratic process, and the imposition of Catholicism as the national religion.

The trio of pamphlets – *Reasons Against the Succession of the House of Hanover* (February 1713), *And What if the Pretender Should Come?* (March 1713), and *An Answer to a Question that No Body Thinks of, viz, But What if the Queen Should Die?* (April 1713) – were published in swift order, and they all employed reverse psychology to emphasize the dangers of allowing the nation to sleepwalk towards a contested succession. The pamphlets offered imagined scenarios of absolutist government, the loss of liberty, and the accession of the French king as the real power behind or even on the throne as a way of testing out the consequences of such events. In *What if the Pretender Should Come?* Defoe suggested that political liberty – the value that he and so many of his contemporaries held most dear – might be overrated. Maybe life was better under an absolutist regime. It might not be so bad to exist as the disempowered and poor French people did:

> they are as Industrious in Trade, as Vigorous in Pursuit of their Affairs, go on with as much Courage [. . .] and as they plant Vines, and plow Lands, that the King and his Great Men may eat the Fruit thereof, they think it as great a Felicity as if they Eat it themselves. The Badge of their Poverty, which we make such a Noise of, and Insult them about so much, (*viz.*) their Wooden Shoes, their Peasants make nothing of it; they say they are as happy in their Wooden Shoes, as our People are with their Luxury and Drunkenness.[60]

Defoe flipped the conventions of anti-French polemic to suggest that all the horrors of poverty and servitude associated with the rule of Louis XIV were in fact benefits. He listed further ridiculous positives of life under an unbridled autocrat: no need to travel or make complicated arrangements to participate in political elections. Under absolute monarchy there would be no vexing rage of party or endless political debate as in present-day England. The speaker pretended to offer a reasoned exploration of the realities of a French invasion but in doing so exposed all that was most fearful to the majority of contemporary readers. In *Reasons Against the Succession*, he offered a further thought experiment, in which he suggested that accepting the Pretender and the imposition of Catholicism might be a kind of necessary purgative: 'let us take a *French* Vomit first, and make us Sick, that we may be well'.[61] And in *But what if the Queen Should Die*? he deployed the running refrain 'and what if the queen should die?' without ever answering the question or suggesting that there was any real reassurance of a good outcome: he concluded that 'the Design of this Tract is rather to put the Question into your Thought, than to put an Answer into your Mouths'.[62] In repeatedly framing the question without offering a single solution the piece articulated all the fears of a Catholic future that his contemporaries could not assuage merely by putting their heads in the sand.

In these pamphlets Defoe was again toying with the sayable and the unsayable. As an outlawed and potentially treasonous political ideology, genuine Jacobite sentiment was typically couched in allusive forms – particular symbols, social codes, or cultural allegiances.[63] Defoe's strategy was to take these hitherto unsayable aspirations of Jacobite sympathizers, and, by exposing them and their imagined consequences to the cold light of public attention, to show what the genuine dangers were for the political future. He was explicit about his intention behind the pamphlets. In an article in the Whig periodical *The Review* of April 1713 he explained quite clearly that what he was trying to do in publishing these pieces was to expose 'the foolish senseless Advantages which some alledge shall accrue to us by the admitting the Pretender'.[64] And in *The Review* of 16 April 1713 he said, 'The Books I have written are as plain a Satyr upon the Pretender and his Friends, as can be written, if they are view'd Impartially; but being written Ironically, all the first Part, if taken asunder from the last Part, will read, *as in all Ironical speaking must be*, just contrary'.[65]

The Succession pamphlets presented palpably ridiculous arguments with the intention of exposing very genuine fears about Jacobite invasion and French tyranny. They were not confusable with genuine polemic in the way that *The Shortest-Way* had been. But even though the true intention of these works seems and must have seemed glaringly obvious to readers, there was still room for deliberate misinterpretation. And that was what happened. Three of Defoe's Whig rivals decided not to see the obvious irony or sarcasm in the pamphlets, and instead to use the potential for confusion to score points against him. A minor Whig writer, William Benson, along with two other Whigs, Thomas Burnet and George Ridpath, filed a complaint against Defoe before the chief justice, accusing him, once again, of seditious libel. They did so partly to distract from or mitigate their own legal challenges. All three were themselves under prosecution for their contentious political pamphlets, and, unlike Defoe, they had no special protection from Harley's ministry. They succeeded in stirring up a fight. There was gleeful coverage in the contemporary pamphlet and periodical press, which immediately announced details of his arrest and custody, and claimed that he had published works 'too tedious, too barefac'd, and too disloyal to be exposed to uncorrupted Minds'.[66]

On 11 April a warrant was issued for Defoe's arrest, and when he appeared in court, the indictment accused him of being a Jacobite intent on 'subverting' the Protestant succession. Lord Chief Justice Parker, supporting the prosecution of Defoe, argued that the idea of irony was no defence: 'There is in some parts a Mixture of what They call banter – which seems design'd to screen the rest, and to make way for a pretence of an innocent intention, To which I shall say no more at present than that these are no Subjects to be play'd with'.[67] Defoe was not a Jacobite, as all these men well knew, but the legal definition of seditious libel meant that irony was not a valid defence. The meaning inhered not in authorial intention but in the text itself, even if it was designed as an exact reversal of what it ostensibly said. New genres and new voices in the marketplace, combined with the rage of party, had driven an understanding of authorial responsibility to an inflexible insistence on the author's liability for the most wrongheaded interpretation of their text. In this particular case, Defoe's opponents exploited this inflexibility to settle personal or professional scores. And in doing so, they illustrate the potential power of wilful misreading.

Rather extraordinarily, Defoe's response to this situation was to go straight to the top and write to the monarch herself. He crafted a petition to the now rather frail Queen Anne, in which he defended himself and his publications by offering her a short lesson on the art of irony and indirection. He explains that what he was really trying to do was to expose the threat of Jacobite plotting despite the fact that

> The Titles Seemed to look as if written in Favour of the Pretender and Sundry Expressions, as in all Ironicall Writeing it must be, may be Wrested Against the True Design of the whole, and turned to a Meaning quite different From yᵉ Intencion of the Author.[68]

It seems extraordinary now that a writer's personal fate should rest on his ability to teach the basics of literary rhetoric to his monarch, let alone that such matters could seem pertinent to affairs of state. But they were. What we also see is the way in which Defoe's defence rested on the premise that enlisting his readers through irony made his argument more powerful. This also comes through in his correspondence with Robert Harley, in which he explains that his intention was only ever to teach his readers how better to interpret a current political situation: 'a Reason for the Manner of writeing in all these books, the Necessity There has been to give a Turn in all I Wrot, which should gratifye Some of the Weaknesses of those poor people, to Detect the Rest'.[69]

There is a profound paradox here. Defoe wrote all these political pamphlets to try to enable his contemporaries to 'detect' better, to be better able to read between the lines of contemporary political culture and see what the genuine threats and issues of the day were. He used irony and satiric reversal to try to expose what to him seemed obvious. But whether by chance or design, each one of these texts ended up being misinterpreted itself, taken to be a serious endorsement of the very position it was intended to parody. Defoe was legally responsible for those misreadings even though they were texts which put responsibility on the reader to decode their real meaning. He aimed to deploy forms of misreading in order to achieve a polemical end, but ended up being victim to his readers' ability to interpret texts in ways he had not anticipated or desired. The history of misreading in Augustan England is a story of opportunity, play, and also danger.

# 9

# Messing with Readers

A man that *can* write in this age, *may*; but he really will find that he writes to fools: and it is now a most unreasonable demand to cry *qui legit, intelligat*.

—ALEXANDER POPE TO JOHN CARYLL

As to the *Dunciad*, it is greatly admired [...] The Metaphysicians' part is to me the worst; and here and there a few ill-expressed lines, and some hardly intelligible.

—THOMAS GRAY TO RICHARD WEST
[JUNIOR], C. 1 APRIL 1742

LIKE SO MANY of his writings, Alexander Pope's 1733 lines to his friend John Caryll offer dogmatic assertion as a form of self-defence. [1] As far as Pope is concerned, readerly incomprehension is a product of his age, and being misunderstood is inevitable in a debased culture in which authors can no longer expect that '*qui legit, intelligat*', that he who reads, should understand. His suspicion of the mistaken or ignorant reader, and the changing expectation of their knowledge, is nowhere more powerfully articulated than in his *Dunciad*s, a series of poems that both showcase acts of misinterpretation and in themselves present challenges to all but the most erudite. In his 1943 preface to the Twickenham edition of the poem, the critic and literary historian James

Sutherland described the kind of reader for whom the poem was intended:

> The reader whom Pope had in view was one who possessed the intellectual background of a well-read amateur man of letters in the early eighteenth century. This ideal reader would have a lively recollection of at least the more familiar classical authors, and would therefore be quick to respond to the classic phrase in a modern context, the deliberate echo, the epic turn, the *double entendre*; he would have an intimate acquaintance with the London life of his day, and more particularly with the leisured world of wits and beaux and men of letters; and he would be easily familiar with the political and domestic history of the period.[2]

The skillset imagined by James Sutherland is formidable and suggests something of the range of reference demanded by the poem. It also assumes the male and metropolitan identity of the ideal reader. We know that there were many eighteenth-century readers who would not have been able to bring all this knowledge or these characteristics to the poem, a reality of which Pope must also have been aware. The gap between this 'ideal' reader and the realities of the eighteenth-century consumer, let alone a modern one, is key to understanding *The Dunciad*'s relationship with the art of misreading.

Published in four versions, over fifteen years, with two different heroes, *The Dunciad* offers a mock-heroic account of the triumph of the goddess of Dulness and her team of hack writers, or dunces, over contemporary culture.[3] Over the course of three, and then four, books, Pope describes the energetic activities of the dunces and the worlds of folly they inhabit, ending with the annihilation of all culture in darkness. It is an attack on contemporary authorship, print culture, scholarship, and science, coupled with a parallel and linked assault on the Hanoverian establishment and the forms of art and culture it chose to patronize. As a printed poem, *The Dunciad* evolved over a decade and a half in response to the moving targets of Pope's attack, as the poet attempted to skewer everyone, and everything, that had provoked his ire: he is intent on presenting the poem as an up-to-the-minute dissection of modernity.

Pope opens his account of the apocalyptic condition of modern culture in *The Dunciad Variorum* with the assertion that 'This happened in
the Year 1725, and continued to the Year 1728'.[4] The contemporary specificity of his cultural critique becomes even more heightened in the
revised four-book version of 1743.[5] And the poem also expanded as Pope,
and latterly his friends, added to it layer upon layer of mock-scholarly
appendices, glosses, and prefatory remarks. At times it feels as though
Pope and his collaborators have exercised the lack of writerly restraint
that the poem mocks in the dunces. One visual element of the mockery
of contemporary scholarship was the presentation of the poem as if it
were one of Richard Bentley's classical editions. At times the lines of
verse are, like Bentley's Horace, almost dwarfed by the commentary
upon them. As that commentary evolved, it played with the identification
of characters within the poem and the classical reference points. Like
other satirical works of the time, it used the apparatus of explanation to
further muddy the process of meaning-making.

Although *The Dunciad* was presented as an acutely topical diagnosis
of the ills of contemporary society, there was a strangely old-fashioned
quality to Pope's intellectual and cultural loyalties.[6] The poem was not
written in the heat of the Battle of the Books debate – by the time it was
published, numerous participants in that particular fight were dead, and
Richard Bentley and his new scholarship were beginning to attain more
credibility. Moreover, while Pope claims to be performing a dissection
of his own precise historical moment, he had also plotted his analysis of
duncehood onto a pre-existing tradition of bad writing:

> She saw old Pryn in restless Daniel shine,
> And Eusden eke out Blackmore's endless line;
> She saw slow Philips creep like Tate's poor page,
> And all the Mighty Mad in Dennis rage.[7]

William Prynne and Nahum Tate are not the Scriblerian dunces: they're
the writers that were the targets of Restoration satirists such as John
Dryden. More than half of the people who appear in Pope's poem were not
even contemporary with Pope.[8] The 'dual perspective' of a sense of engagement with the cultural debates of both the past and the present in *The*

*Dunciad* enabled Pope to create a satire that was at once particular and general. On the one hand, the list of 'friends and enemies' presented in the poem was founded on local and personal likes and dislikes. Writers became dunces because of some particular slight or insult.[9] Yet, on the other hand, the poem also attempted to translate these local issues into a more universal story about the decline of culture.[10] As a number of critics have noted, Pope's use of an extended set of parallels with the *Aeneid* and the *Odyssey*, in addition to verbal echoes of Horace and allusions to *Paradise Lost*, all locate the concerns of the poem within a wider literary culture.[11]

As this summary suggests, the *Dunciad*s are poems whose precise reference points are both evolving, and, often, obscure. The most common response for modern readers coming to the poem for the first time is bewilderment at the ever-expanding cast of dunces (named but infinitely forgettable), the layers of commentary and prefatory material, and the changes of satirical focus. The editors of a 2000 reassessment of the poem comment that 'whether approached from the perspective of student or scholar, the act of reading the poem potentially reinscribes its literary hierarchy. The text often proves daunting and threatens to exclude those who lack the biblical, classical, and historical knowledge central to its meaning'.[12] Pope's accompanying notes seem to shift in tone and purpose; sometimes they are genuine self-aggrandizement, as Pope signals the literary models with which he is engaged, while at others they mock the art of annotation itself. A lot of this confusion is purposeful. In creating a world full of busy writers without memorable identities, and the sense of an author who has lost control over the spiralling apparatus of his own text, Pope mimics his major criticisms of the literary culture of his day. And yet, as so often with such satires on the art of misreading, it could not always be guaranteed that even the right readers could get the intended point.

## How Do You Deal with *The Dunciad*?

*The Dunciad*'s flipping between general and particular, the sense that it had very specific targets yet demanded familiarity with a broad range of cultural reference, makes it a challenging read. Editorial approaches to the poem's taxing combination of particular and general reference have varied over time. As we have seen, James Sutherland's edition of the poem described the paradigmatic ideal reader of Pope's poem in daunting terms. By way of editorial advice, Sutherland also suggests that the reader keen to enjoy the poem should acquaint themselves with the social and literary milieu of the time:

> much of the social background may still be acquired, in the pleasantest way imaginable, by reading the *Tatler* and *Spectator* and other works of the period, and the well-informed reader can at least walk down a Grub Street of his own imagining. The effort must be made; the reward is to watch with discernment one of the great masters of satire at his chosen task.[13]

It is, he implies, the role of the reader to upskill themselves to the point at which they can imaginatively inhabit the world of Grub Street. But is this in fact what we need to do? Other critics have cautioned that in seeking to pin down identities and places we neglect the fact that the dunces are really just metaphors. Aubrey Williams, offering his 1955 study of the meaning of the poem, cautions against the dangers of too much literal historical decoding:

> Every editor since Pope's time has heaped successive layers of apparatus and commentary upon the original, fanciful apparatus. Thus it has become extremely difficult for a reader to disentangle Pope's fiction from later editorial facts, to see his imaginative gloss undisturbed by corrections and additions which only succeed in turning his feigned history into true – but lifeless – history. [. . .] The simple fact is that historical truth is distorted by Pope so as to be more metaphorical.[14]

Williams observes here that in adding columns of footnotes to the pages of the poem, editors literalize persons whose real value is rhetorical and symbolic. But rather than chasing the footnote reference, it is crucial, he argues, to recognize that Pope's dunces are a product of his fancy:

> he alters the personages of his poem to make them appear more perfect vehicles for his subject [. . .] But where the reality leaves off and

the fancy begins is difficult for the reader to discover; we are faced with dunces who are neither wholly here – in the poem – nor there – in history.[15]

In *The Dunciad* we have a poem which pushes us to seek closure by identifying sources and insinuated allegations in which such pinned down references might also be a chimera. Aubrey Williams's advice to look for the metaphorical rather than the biographical is not shared by all scholars. Valerie Rumbold, the most recent editor of the poem, offers this advice on how to cope with the plethora of persons:

> How, though, is the first-time reader of *The Dunciad in Four Books* to cope with this crowd of unfamiliar names? A practicable approach would be to start by getting familiar with a few of the most central figures [...] and then to read the verse for the first time without pausing over the detail of the original or editorial annotation. In subsequent readings more attention can be paid to the original and editorial commentaries. Thus more detail about issues and individuals can be absorbed and can adjust the reader's general sense of the shape of the work.[16]

While Williams suggests that the dunces have symbolic rather than historical significance, and that the reader does not need to load up on biographical and historical detail, Rumbold's implication, like Sutherland's, is that the reader needs to learn more to understand the poem correctly (but that they can probably wait until the second read-through to do this).

All these critics offer responses which aim to solve a text that is hard to understand. But I would argue that we are not intended to solve Pope's *Dunciad* – a sense of bewilderment at the names and the references, the confusions of the apparatus, was and is part of the design of the poem. These strategies are not unique to this work; as we have seen, much early eighteenth-century literature both generated and depended on readerly confusion. *The Dunciad* is a work that pushes this to its limits. The first note to the first line of the poem reads: 'Wonderful is the stupidity of all the former Cricks and Commentators on this Poem!'[17] From here on in, Pope plays with his readers' befuddlement, wrongfooting them and suggesting that there is a world of retrievable reference, when the reality is that it is a work with moving targets, which throughout its textual evolution mocked the process of understanding and the application of knowledge. Names were constantly being dropped from the text and others substituted. The use of pseudonyms, classical nicknames, and cryptic initials tends towards individual anonymity at the same time that Pope seeks to identity particular persons, times, and places. We are supposed to be foxed.

## Creating Confusion: Early Versions of the Poem

The nature of this extended tease can be seen in the evolution of early versions of the poem. The first three-book 1728 version of the poem encountered by London readers took no prisoners.[18] Most of the names of the dunces were blanked out with initial letters and dashes, or asterisks, while other names of historical figures were left complete.

Pope offered some pointers to meaning in the text. At various moments in the poem, footnotes were supplied to clarify cultural or literary context. Figure 11 shows an example from Book II. It has to be said that the notes do not really help.[19] If we look at what is explained and what is not, we can see that the poem uses annotation in ways that exacerbate interpretative difficulty. The single footnote ('This, I presume, alludes to the extravagancies of the Farces of this author . . .') helps us comprehend the line about Gods and Daemons, but we are left rudderless as to the identities of the host of blanked-out names above in lines 92–94.

Such a combination of explanation and refusal of explanation creates a particularly unsettling reading experience. The presence of some notes suggests that other elements of the poem, left unannotated, should be obvious to the reader – which they are not. Through the presentation of this first version of his poem, Pope creates an illusion of an informed inner circle of readers who ought to be able to make sense of the host of allusions and coded identities. The heavy use of blanks, dashes, and asterisks within the poem was partly a way of mocking the typography of contemporary print culture, but the lacunae also demanded a lot of

6        The DUNCIAD.

She faw with joy the line immortal run,
Each fire impreft and glaring in his fon ;
So watchful *Bruin* forms with plaftic care
90 Each growing lump, and brings it to a Bear.
She faw old *Pryn* in reftlefs *Daniel* fhine,
And *E—n* eke out *Bl—*'s endlefs line ;
She faw flow *P—s* creep like *T—te*'s poor page,
And furious *D—s* foam in *W——*'s rage.

95   In each, fhe marks her image full expreft,
But chief, in *Tibbald*'s monfter-breeding breaft,
Sees Gods with Dæmons in ftrange league ingage,
And * earth, and heav'n, and hell her battles wage !

She ey'd the Bard where fupperlefs he fate,
100 And pin'd, unconfcious of his rifing fate ;
Studious he fate, with all his books around,
Sinking from thought to thought, a vaft profound !
Plung'd for his fenfe, but found no bottom there,
Then writ, and flounder'd on, in mere defpair.

* This, I prefume, alludes to the extravagancies of the Farces
of this author. *See* book III. verf. 185, &c.

He

FIGURE 11. Alexander Pope, *The Dunciad. An Heroic Poem. In Three Books,* second edition (Dublin printed; London reprinted for A. Dodd, 1728), Bodleian Library, University of Oxford, Vet.A4 f.632, p. 6.

readers who frequently found themselves unable to meet the challenge (figure 12). As we have seen, such strategies were not uncommon, but in the context of a poem which is all about judging and condemning others for their cultural competence, they add to the impression of a work which seeks to exclude its readers.

34          The DUNCIAD.

Then down are roll'd the books; ſtretch'd o'er 'em
lies
Each gentle clerk, and mutt'ring ſeals his eyes.
As what a *Dutchman* plumps into the lakes,
360 One circle firſt, and then a ſecond makes,
What dulneſs dropt among her ſons impreſt
Like motion, from one circle to the reſt;
So from the mid-moſt the nutation ſpreads
Round, and more round, o'er all the ſea of heads.
365 At laſt *C—re* felt her voice to fail,
And \*\*\* himſelf unfiniſh'd left his Tale.
*T—s* and *T—* the church and ſtate gave o'er,
Nor \*\*\* talk'd, nor *S----* whiſper'd more.
Ev'n *N———n*, gifted with his mother's tongue,
370 Tho' born at *Wapping*, and from *Daniel* ſprung,
Ceas'd his loud bawling breath, and dropt the head;
And all was huſh'd, as *Folly*'s ſelf lay dead.

Thus the ſoft gifts of *Sleep* conclude the day,
And ſtretch'd on bulks, as uſual, Poets lay.
375 Why ſhould I ſing what bards the Nightly Muſe
Did ſlumbring viſit, and convey to ſtews?

Or

FIGURE 12. Alexander Pope, *The Dunciad. An Heroic Poem. In Three Books*, second edition (Dublin printed; London reprinted for A.Dodd, 1728), Bodleian Library, University of Oxford, Vet.A4 f.632, p. 34.

The matter of how to understand the poem is foregrounded within *The Dunciad* itself. In the preface to the 1728 three-book version of the poem, Pope addressed the matter of readerly confusion in a letter from 'The Publisher to the Reader'. The 'publisher' began by explaining that he needed to get the book out because had he delayed in doing so, '*those*

Names *which are its chief Ornaments, die off daily so fast, as must render it too soon unintelligible*.[20] Thus from the very beginning, the poem raised the question of its own obscurity. The prefatory letter continued to expound on this theme:

> *But there may arise some obscurity in Chronology from the* Names *in the Poem, by the inevitable removal of some Authors, and Insertion of others, in their Niches. For whoever will consider the Unity of the whole Design, will be sensible, that the* Poem *was not made for these Authors, but these Authors for the Poem. And I should judge they were clapp'd in as they rose, fresh and fresh, and chang'd from day to day, in like manner as when the old boughs wither, we thrust new ones into a chimney.*
>
> *I would not have the reader too much troubled or anxious, if he cannot decypher them; since when he shall have found them out, he will probably know no more of the Persons than before.*
>
> *Yet we judg'd it better to preserve them as they are, than to change them for fictitious names, by which the Satyr would only be multiplied; and applied to many instead of one. Had the Hero, for instance, been called* Codrus, *how many would have affirm'd him to be Mr.* W—Mr. D—Sir R— B—, *&c.*[21]

Pope plays hard with the concept of referentiality. As we have seen, the literature of his era had used missing information, names, and identities to suggest important and clandestine content, or to create a fiction of intimacy with a particular social group. But here Pope suggests that the reader should not bother with all this decoding – the targets themselves were unstable and shifted over time, and even if one were to find out who was intended, their real-world insignificance would render their name more or less meaningless. But, at the same time, there is nonetheless a nagging sense that we ought to be able to work out who even insignificant figures are. In refusing to allow his readers to fulfil their side of the interactive bargain of contemporary print culture and frustrating their role in making meaning, Pope cements his assault on a culture and a group of writers which, he suggests, have no real meaning.

## Helping the Reader

*The Dunciad* exploits the interpretative dynamics of the print culture of its time to foreground acts of misunderstanding and puzzlement and to suggest that names are irretrievable because they are insignificant. But for all Pope's reassurance that the identities of the dunces were immaterial, early readers were unable to let go of the challenge staged by the poem. One of the most famous early responses is Jonathan Swift's letter of July 1728:

> I have often run over the *Dunciad* in an Irish edition (I suppose full of faults) which a gentleman sent me. The notes I could wish to be very large, in what relates to the persons concern'd; for I have long observ'd that twenty miles from London no body understands hints, initial letters, or town-facts and passages; and in a few years not even those who live in London. I would have the names of those scriblers printed indexically at the beginning or end of the Poem, with an account of their works, for the reader to refer to. I would have all the Parodies (as they are call'd) referred to the author they imitate – When I began this long paper, I thought I should have fill'd it with setting down the several passages I had mark'd in the edition I had, but I find it unnecessary, so many of them falling under the same rule. After twenty times reading the whole, I never in my opinion saw so much good satire, or more good sense, in so many lines. How it passes in Dublin I know not yet; but I am sure it will be a great disadvantage to the poem, that the persons and facts will not be understood, till an explanation comes out, and a very full one. I imagine it is not to be published till towards winter, when folks begin to gather in town.
>
> Again I insist, you must have your Asterisks fill'd up with some real names of real Dunces.[22]

Swift's response is intriguing. His testament that there would be many unable to comprehend the satire was correct, and, as it turned out, his suggestions for clarification were incorporated by Pope in subsequent versions. One of the points he makes here is that outside London, or in Dublin, there will be problems of comprehension. As so often in discussions of readerly competence, difficulty is axiomatically attributed to geography. Authors and editors suggested that it was non-metropolitan readers who would struggle to get the meaning of their works, and this became a way of seeing reading as an urban in-joke. Yet the reality was that, as we have seen, all kinds of readers were kept out of the books they read. Delariviere Manley worried that the Lord Treasurer himself would not understand her satire in the political scandal narratives, and the Trumbull family, close as they were to the centre of government, believed that they could not understand contemporary pamphlets without keys and codes. Narcissus Luttrell made himself an expert on the pamphlet satires of his time, yet always struggled to pin down their references. Swift's comments suggest that he considers himself an insider: 'I never in my opinion saw so much good satire, or more good sense, in so many lines'. But even if he was exaggerating, the fact that the poem demanded 'twenty times reading the whole' seems to indicate that its meaning and value were not immediately obvious even to him, a figure close to the author. Swift's answer to the problem of clarity within The Dunciad is the addition of supplementary material – an index, or the filling in of names. He was to reiterate the point in a later letter: 'I had reason to put Mr. Pope on writing the Poem, called the Dunciad, and to hale those Scoundrels out of their Obscurity by telling their Names at length, their Works, their Adventures, sometimes their Lodgings, and their Lineage; not with A—'s and B—'s according to the old Way, which would be unknown in a few Years'.[23] The Dunciad shows us the way in which, again, incomprehension is generative of more text – a pattern played out ad absurdum in Pope's poem.

Swift was not alone in identifying difficulties with reading The Dunciad. Pope's correspondence reveals that other friends had asked him to identify figures within the poem:

Its true, I gave a Correct Copy of it with the blanks filld up, at the request of 2 or 3 Friends, who were willing to attend it with some Illustrations and pieces of their own. But I have desired 'em now to put it off, and let the Gentlemen write and confederate as they please, they should for me at present rest (if they are wise enough to rest) with their Iniquities Cover'd.[24]

One of those friends, Edward Harley, second Earl of Oxford, wrote to Pope shortly after the first edition appeared: 'I see curl has advertised a Key to the *Dunciad*, I have been asked for one by several I wish the True one was come out'.[25]

These early responses to the poem all sought additional information to help readers orient themselves in the poem. Opportunistic publishers were not slow to seize the commercial opportunities presented by Pope's confection of confusion. Edmund Curll's *A Compleat Key to the Dunciad* (1728), which appeared in three editions over the course of the year, offers an index of the historical persons alluded to – or not – in the poem. Some of the names supplied by Curll were accompanied by descriptive phrases indicating their profession or accomplishments. The key, like those accompanying the secret histories of the time, does not address the larger critique offered by the work. In this case, it reads the poem as a catalogue of personal insults. So '*Juno*, of Majestic Size' is identified in the key as 'Mrs. *Mary Hearne*, Authoress of Two Novels. I. The *Lover's Week*, 2. The *Female Deserters*'.[26] 'Ch—d and C—l' are '*William Rufus Chetwood*, predecessor to Mr. *Francklin* in *Russell*-Street, *Covent*-Garden, and Mr. *Curll*, with whom Mr. *Francklin* served his Apprenticeship'.[27] The reader is locked into a series of fixed meanings as a way of navigating their way through the poem. Yet, as elsewhere, the biographical information is pretty useless. It does not really add to our understanding of what is going on in the poem. It does not help to know the names of Hearne's novels any more than it does to know the location of Chetwood's shop. Ultimately Curll's *Key*, like much of the later commentary on the poem, added to the proliferation of confusing information surrounding the work. Moreover, the quality of the intelligence provided by the key was variable. The three London 1728 editions of Curll's *Compleat Key* reveal the process of elimination and consolidation in readings of the poem. As the key progressed through its various versions within the space of the year, Curll changed some of his initial guesses at persons indicated by Pope's initials and blanks, partly in response to Pope's changing text, which altered its targets between editions.[28] 'Westley, Watts and Brome' was replaced by 'Withers Quarles and Brome' in the second and third editions. The meaning of

'Something betwixt a H—and an Owl' was a complete mystery to the author of the first and second key, and answered as 'Heidegger and an Owl' in the third. The reference to 'Lady Marys' in Book II of *The Dunciad* was only linked to Lady Mary Wortley Montagu in the third edition of the key, and 'Old Bavius' of Book III was identified as John Dennis in the first edition and Thomas Shadwell in the latter two.[29] Did readers notice these changes? It is hard to know how much confidence they had in an explanatory tool which was itself constantly mutating and updating its interpretations. The perils of these topical hermeneutics were further exacerbated by Pope's decision to change some of the names of his victims in subsequent editions. In 1728, in the third version published that year, line 91 was changed to a new set of characters ('She saw old Pryn in restless Daniel shine') and Dunton was changed to Dennis.[30] Multiplication of keys alongside the constant revision of the poem ensured that no reader could have much confidence in the stability of any meaning-making.

Curll was not the only entrepreneur to see Pope's obscurity as a gap in the market. Dublin publishers were prompt in issuing their own pirated duodecimo edition of the three-book *Dunciad*.[31] This edition supplied names in the places of the names left blank by Pope, rather than using footnotes to indicate likely meaning. This had the effect that readers were not given any room for speculation or warned of any degree of tentativeness, but were given the names in the reading text. The identities supplied were pretty hit and miss – if we compare with later authorized versions or other editions, there is some discrepancy between the guesses of the Dublin reader who supplied the names, printed in the edition, and those intended by Pope. We can also see the instances in which that reader was not able to complete all the asterisked names. In Book I of the first three-book London edition, Pope had supplied only blanks in his listing of earlier bad writers:

She saw in *N—n* all his father shine,
And *E—n* eke out *Bl—*'s endless line;
She saw slow *P—s* creep like *T—te*'s poor page,
And furious *D—n* foam in *Wh—*'s rage.[32]

The unauthorized Dublin version obliged its reader by filling in the gaps. So the edition confirmed that 'N' was Nelson, 'E—n' was Eusden, 'Bl—' was Blackmore, 'P—s' was Philips, 'T—te' was Tate, 'D—n' was Dryden and 'Wh—' was Wharton.[33] Some of these were right – Eusden, Blackmore, Philips, and Tate – but others were way off the mark. As it turned out, 'N' should have been Norton (Daniel Defoe's son, Norton Defoe), while 'Wh—' was the journalist Stephen Whatley. 'D—n' was the Whig journalist John Dunton. These print interventions in meaning-making did not please the poem's author. Pope was evidently embarrassed by the Dublin printers' identification of John Dryden as one of his litany of dunces, and in his note to *The Dunciad Variorum* was later to comment on the misattribution.[34]

The early print history of *The Dunciad* and its responses manifests a clear tension between readers' and publishers' desire to fix, however erroneously, the meaning of the satire, and Pope's frustration of those impulses through obscured reference and ever-shifting satirical targets. So what did readers make of this puzzling array of information? Swift said that 'twenty miles from London' no one would be able to work out what was going on in *The Dunciad*. We have at least one example of a reader consulting the first edition of the poem more than twenty miles from London and probably several years after its initial publication. John Cale, born in 1722, was a provincial lawyer, who studied at Hart Hall, Oxford, before going on to the Inner Temple and then a career as a barrister in the parish of Barming in Kent. His surviving book collection reflects the interests of a provincial gentleman: theology and law but also practical books on gardening and horticulture. And his library also contained a marked-up copy of the second edition of the 1728 *Dunciad*, along with a copy of Curll's 1728 *Key* to the *Dunciad*, bound separately.[35] Cale was a man who did not seem to write much on his books. In the case of *The Dunciad*, he, or perhaps his father, also named John Cale, has partially completed the blanked-out names in Pope's text, and the way in which they have done so gives some insight into how readers might have used keys and typographical prompts to navigate the works that they read. Cale Jr must have been reading *The Dunciad* some years after its initial publication; he was only six when it came out, and perhaps he inherited the early edition in his library. If he was annotating in his twenties or older, he would have been doing so after later versions of the poems had appeared with all the names completed. It could be that the book and the annotation are his father's. Either way, the Cale annotator is keen to rectify the absences in the pages in front of him, and it looks as though he used the key that he had access to in order to do this. All the names he has filled in correspond with the answers given in the Curll *Key*. But his approach to 'solving' the mystery of Pope's poem is to interact with its verse only where he can see an overt prompt, that is, when there is a line or hyphenated line to indicate a missing identity. So he fills in 'Cooke' or 'Concanen' because the page seems to ask him to with their prompts of 'C—'. But where the lines contain an allusion, such as 'Tom the First' or 'Tom the second' or a fictional identity such as 'Corinna' or 'old Bavius', he does not gloss these figures with the correct names, even though this information is actually contained within the key he owned. It is as though his interaction and his reading is driven by the typographical form of the text he is reading. He knows he needs to fill in information when there is literally a gap in the text, but not when the words are all there, even if those words have an unclear meaning.

The other intriguing feature of Cale's reading or annotation practice is that he was evidently trying to unlock the door with the wrong key, or rather, to navigate his edition of *The Dunciad* using explanations made for a different text. It was nearly right, but not right enough. The Curll *Key* in his collection correlates with the first edition of *The Dunciad*, whereas Cale owned the second edition. And, as we know, Pope changed some of the targets of his satire between the two imprints. This presented a challenge for John Cale. The 'answers' given by the key did not fit the work he had in front of him. But he seems to have been determined to use those answers anyway, even if they fitted a version of the poem that was now superseded. So, for example, in Book I he came across the lines 'Well-purg'd, and worthy *W—s, Q—s*, and *Bl—*'.[36] Pope seems to have intended those figures as 'Withers, Quarles and Bloom'. But looking at his key, the key to a different version of the poem, Cale discovered that the names in this line were '*Westley, Watts,* and *Brome*' – or at least, those were the answers to the gaps in the first edition of the lumes, whofe fize the fpace exactly fill'd;

which fond authors were fo good to gild;

where, by Sculpture made for ever known,

e page admires new beauties, not its own.

re fwells the fhelf with *Ogleby* the *great*,

ere, ftamp'd with arms, *Newcaftle* fhines compleat,

re all his fuff'ring brotherhood retire,

d 'fcape the martyrdom of jakes and fire;

*Gothic* Vatican! of *Greece* and *Rome* *Us, walls*    *Brome*

ell-purg'd, and worthy *W—s*, *Q—s*, and *Bl—*

But high above, more folid Learning fhone,

e *Clafficks* of an Age that heard of none;

ere * *Caxton* flept, with *Wynkin* at his fide,

e clafp'd in wood, and one in ftrong cow-hide:

ere fav'd by fpice, like mummies, many a year,

d Bodies of philofophy apppear:

e *Lyra* there a dreadful front extends,

nd there, the groaning Shelves § *Philemon* bends.

| Printers.        § *Philemon Holland*.                        Of

FIGURE 13. Alexander Pope, *The Dunciad. An Heroic Poem. In Three Books. The Second Edition.* (Dublin printed; London reprinted for A. Dodd, 1728), Hertford College Library, University of Oxford, XXX.2.20(2), p. 7. Annotated by John Cale. Reproduced with the permission of the Principal, Fellows and Scholars of Hertford College, University of Oxford.

poem (figure 13).[37] So, despite the fact that those 'answers' were both out of date and manifestly did not fit the clues given in the text he was reading, he wrote them in. There is a genuine muddling of right and wrong reading, authority, and authorial intention in this practice, revealing the degree to which *The Dunciad* prompted readerly desire to solve its puzzles, often in ways that were clearly problematic.

## Annotation and Further Muddle

As *The Dunciad* evolved, so did the nature of its challenge. The four-book *Dunciad Variorum* of 1729 filled in some of the absences of the 1728 text, and Pope completed its aposiopesis and partial blanks with the names of historical figures. Yet, while one kind of interpretative puzzle was removed, perhaps partly in response to the clamour from bamboozled readers, another kind of difficulty was introduced. *The Dunciad Variorum* significantly increased the length of the work by adding a whole set of introductory and explanatory apparatus to the poem, which offered new opportunities for Pope to foreground the folly of acts of explanation and clarification.

From the title page onwards of this new version of *The Dunciad*, we are made aware of the poem's positioning within a debate about scholarly presentation and interpretation. The 1729 *Dunciad, Variorum. With the Prolegomena of Scriblerus* listed in the contents 'The Prolegomena of Martinus Scriblerus', 'Notes Variorum', 'A Dissertation of the Poem', 'Dunciados Periocha', and 'Testimonies of Authors'. It is pages and pages before we get to the actual poem. The title page is followed by 'The Publisher's Advertisement', 'A Letter to the Publisher', 'The Prolegomena of Martinus Scriblerus', 'Testimonies of Authors', 'A Dissertation of the Poem', and 'Dunciados Periocha: Or, Arguments to the Books'. Pope parades the technical paraphernalia of contemporary print culture as a form of critique. This display also involved the satiric redeployment of his critics' earlier attacks on his work, reworking their texts to bolster his own.[38] The 'Testimonies of Authors' which preface the poem present a parody of the apparatus of a learned edition, a self-important announcement of the text within, which had appeared from the 1729 edition onwards. Within those testimonies we find a recurring interest in interpretation and misinterpretation. Some of the extracts show Pope's glee at the ways in which his enemies have overread his work and found in it seditious tendencies. So, for example, we hear that 'Mr. *Dennis* himself hath written to a *Minister*, that he [Pope] is one of the most *dangerous Persons in this kingdom* [...] A third gives Information of Treason discover'd in his Poem'.[39]

Here is the same joy in excessive hermeneutical suspicion that Pope had exercised in *A Key to the Lock*. The phrases Pope cited in his poem were taken from earlier published responses to his writings, and in this context their charges against the poet seem palpably ridiculous. As the poem progressed and amassed more and more detailed commentary, Pope used similar principles of highly selective quotation to turn criticism into praise. So, for example, there is a testimony from the Whig historian John Oldmixon, who declares 'the purity and perfection of the *English* language to be found in his [Pope's] *Homer*; and, saying there are more good verses in *Dryden's Virgil* than in any other work, excepts this of our author only'.[40] This is sort of true. The quotation is indeed from Oldmixon. But what Pope has left out in his citation is all the context. These lines accompany Oldmixon's slighting suggestion made in the original piece that Pope's Homer has only a surface elegance which doesn't really make up for a profound lack of substance. Oldmixon's commentary on Pope's translation of Homer was, in fact, rather more critical of his work:

> I have hinted more than once, that such Poets, and their Admirers, almost always mistake Affectation for Beauty, and I wonder the Translator of *Homer* should give them the least Countenance by his Example; for I am very much deceiv'd if there is a more affected Period in the *English* Tongue than what follows.[41]

No one reading the 'Testimonies of Authors' could really have thought that the kinds of excerpts cited by Pope really were the opinions of Gildon, Dennis, or Oldmixon – authors whose critical acumen was roundly rubbished within the mock-heroic poem that followed. The role of the testimonies was not to affirm the poem through the judgements of Pope's critics but to showcase the ingenuity of his wilful manipulation, his ability to make his enemies say the very opposite of what they intended. Deliberate misreading is here used to showcase intellectual and literary prowess. Pope's misquotations brought their own comebacks. Although he disavowed his authorship of the notes, readers were nonetheless keen to assign blame for the perceived slights that the comments offered, and when they did so, they pointed their fingers at Pope himself.

The dramatist Aaron Hill took issue with 'a paragraph in the notes of a late edition of the *Dunciad*' which seemed to slight him using the initials 'A.H.', linking him to an unnamed contestant in the mud-diving contest.[42] Pope replied that he had not intended Hill as a target, and was not in any case the author of the notes. Hill responded angrily and threatened to publish an attack on Pope, entitled '*An Essay on Propriety and Impropriety in Thought, Design and Expression* [. . .] *from the Writings of Mr. Pope*'.[43] Pope responded, promising to leave out the note and specify that Hill was not meant in the initials 'A.H.'.[44] Part of Pope's defence for himself was that he did not write the notes and so was not responsible for Hill being identified as a character in them. Hill challenged him: 'If the initial Letters *A.H.* were not meant to stand for my Name, yet, they were, everywhere, read so, as you might have seen in *Mist's Journal*, and other publick Papers; and I had shewn Mr. *Pope* an example, how reasonable I thought it to clear a Mistake, publickly, which had been publickly propagated'.[45] We circle back on the questions of accountability raised in contemporary libel litigation. Even if Pope had not intended Hill to be a target, the fact that the rest of the world assumed that Hill was being attacked made the matter of his intention more or less irrelevant. In this case, misreading was reading, and like Defoe and others before him, Pope also faced the consequences of the misunderstanding of his works.

## How Not to Read? *The Dunciad* and Its Notes

The annotations to *The Dunciad* developed the satirical layers of Pope's polyvalent text, and they also offered a reading and a misreading of the poetry they abutted. A collaborative effort among various friends, the crowd-sourced nature of their content probably adds to their confusing nature. Even the loyal editor James Sutherland, generally so keen to explain away the obscurities of the poem, comments on William

Warburton's notes that 'Pope may sometimes have failed to realize that what, after due explanation was crystal clear to his friend, might not be readily intelligible to the general public who had not Warburton's advantage'.[46] The status of the notes is double-edged. Like the other texts produced by the Scriblerian group, the proliferation of commentary around *The Dunciad* parodied what Pope, Swift, Gay, and Arbuthnot saw as the pedantry and narcissism of professional scholars like Richard Bentley and William Wotton, whose editions of classical texts were littered with 'conjectural emendations' and 'variant readings'. In this sense, the *mise en page* of *The Dunciad* set itself against the new scholarly traditions of text that generated a documentary and interpretative tradition. But, at the same time, in mocking approaches to Greek and Latin texts, Pope also paraded a prowess in classical learning, a familiarity and confidence with authors like Homer, Virgil, and Horace and their works, so long lauded as the cornerstones of Western civilization. For Pope, this appearance of assurance with the classics was particularly important. A self-taught scholar, his translation of Homer's *Iliad* had been attacked by many for the quality of the translation. *The Dunciad's* presentation of learning and reading is very much a combination of parody and display.

The new puzzles of the poem extended beyond biographical allusions to Pope's recruitment of classical sources and parallels; individual passages amply illustrate the ways in which Pope staged different forms of interpretative play as he pretended to clarify the poem for its readers. We can see from the example of an individual episode the way in which the reader's challenge changed as the poem evolved. In the funeral games episode of Book II, the Queen of Dulness has appointed Bays, representing the poet laureate Colley Cibber, as her chosen son. To celebrate his accession, she orders the other dunces to perform games in his honour. Pope imagines the contemporary rivalry among book publishers, endemic to the book trade, as a ridiculous race to capture a nonexistent poet. Bernard Lintot and Edmund Curll chase the phantom poet, and Curll slips in a puddle of excrement made by his mistress, Elizabeth Thomas, or Corinna as she is named in the poem. In the first version of the poem, the names of Curll and Bernard were omitted from the text. Contemporary keys explained that they referred to Curll and Lintot, and that Corinna was Elizabeth Thomas. The passage reads:

Full in the middle way there stood a lake,
Which Curl's Corinna chanc'd that morn to make,
(Such was her wont, at early dawn to drop
Her evening cates before his neighbour's shop,)
Here fortun'd Curl to slide: loud shout the band,
And Bernard! Bernard! rings thro' all the Strand.
Obscene with filth the Miscreant lies bewray'd,
Fal'n in the plash his wickedness had lay'd.[47]

The episode is pure slapstick; a buffoon slipping and sliding in excrement becomes a trope for the degraded state of the literary marketplace. In this edition of *The Dunciad Variorum* the names of Curll and Lintot were spelled out, but the passage acquired a heavy dose of annotation. The new notes to the passage exposed multiple relationships between Pope's mock-heroic verse and its classical antecedents, but in doing so they further confused the sense of what or who was being satirized in the poem. The annotation to line 69 of Book II offers a comparison from Virgil's description of funeral races in Book V of the *Aeneid*, given only in Latin: '*Labitur infelix, caesis ut forte juvencis / Fusus humum viridisque; super madefecerat herbas– / Concidit, immundoque fimo, sacroque cruore*'.[48] As elsewhere in the text, the absence of translation reminds us of the assumption at the heart of the poem's engagement with its readers, that only those with a gentlemanly knowledge of classical literature might know the reference and get the joke, and be included in its interpretative games. The quotation translates as: 'the unlucky man slipped, as by chance the blood poured out where cattle had been slaughtered and had soaked the ground and green grass – He fell right in the filthy dung and the blood of sacrifice'. Pope gives us a fragment of classical literature as a counterpoint to Curll's fall, and in doing so he emphasizes the differences between his own culture and that of ancient Greece and Rome. The comparison with the *Aeneid* stresses the essentially unheroic state of contemporary culture. Pope takes Virgil's description and compares it to a ridiculous contest between two book publishers. The referents are all wrong – Virgil is concerned with warriors and martial honour, while Pope is talking about grasping Grub Street booksellers and illusory poets.

But, at the same time, the epic comparison doesn't entirely confirm the superiority of classical culture. The fall in the *Aeneid* (or for that matter the fall of Ajax in the *Iliad*), where the leading runner slips on blood and entrails left from sacrifices, represents a deeply unappealing and alien aspect of ancient civilization, a pagan world in which animals are slaughtered to appease the gods and their butchered entrails litter the ground. While Curll and Lintot's mucky race is purely a fantasy, the slipping and sliding of the *Aeneid* testifies to a genuine immersion in filth and superstition. From this perspective, classical culture looks barbaric and primitive compared to modern society, and the relationship between the mock-epic and the genre it mimics becomes deeply problematic. It's unclear whether the poem offers a celebration or a critique of classical culture.

This question of the relation between *The Dunciad* and classical epic is pursued in the note to line 71. Pope mounts a pseudo-scholarly defence of his lines on Curll sliding in Corinna's filth:

> Tho' this incident may seem too low and base for the dignity of an Epic poem, the learned very well know it to be but a copy of *Homer* and *Virgil*; the very words ονθος and *Fimus* are used by them, tho' our poet (in compliance to modern nicety) has remarkably enriched and colour'd his language, as well as rais'd the versification, in these two Episodes.[49]

Here the annotations question the relationship between epic and mock-epic from another perspective. The note plays with the reader's desire to have their own classical education gratified, asserting that 'the learned very well know' that the muck is justified by two references to dung as *onthos* and *fimus* in Homer and Virgil. But this points to the spuriousness of the annotation here. Book II of the Dunciad is literally awash with human excrement, and it's hard to see this as explained solely by a couple of references to dung in the *Iliad* and *Aeneid*. The notes both gratify readerly erudition and mock its irrelevance. Just at the moment where we think we have arrived at clarity, we are forced to doubt the validity of our reading. Have these notes in fact taken us into a misreading of the poem, a false projection of learning? *The Dunciad* is a work which simultaneously exalts and mocks classical culture, which parodies works of learning while parading its own scholarship, and which both laments and thrives on the proliferation of contemporary literary forms. Rather than being the explanatory tools that they seem to be, the annotations compound this multi-layering, and it's clear that while considering the text as a whole opens up a number of areas for discussion, it doesn't provide us with a unified reading of the poem. In some ways, all readers of the poem become dunces, perplexed but intrigued by Pope's textual virtuosity.

It is illuminating to compare this process of obfuscation with the overt discussion of readership within the poem's materials. Pope claimed that his annotations of the classical 'Imitations' in *The Dunciad Variorum* were included 'to gratify those who either never read, or may have forgotten them'.[50] Yet the feint is not really sincere. *The Dunciad* is constantly discriminating between those who are and aren't able to read correctly. In 'Ricardus Aristarchus of the Hero of the poem' the fictional misinterpreter, Scriblerus, claims to have identified classical allusions which even the poet and original annotator were blind to:

> particular allusions infinite, many whereof have escaped both the commentator and poet himself; yea divers by his exceeding diligence are so alter'd and interwoven with the rest, that several already have been, and more will be, by the ignorant abused, as altogether and originally his own.[51]

The effect of *The Dunciad* is to create a profoundly paranoid reading experience: are we overreading or underreading? Scriblerus's words offer an invitation to competent readers to enjoy allusion-spotting, but at the same time they mock incompetent readers whose mistaken sense of classical parallels merely reveals their own stupidity and lack of taste. James Sutherland said of the poem that the 'uninformed reader' who needed footnotes would never really get the poem: 'The Dunciad can make its full effect only upon one who is already sufficiently familiar with the classical poets to feel that small shock of delighted surprise which Pope intended by his irreverent shifting of the context'.[52] I would beg to differ. *The Dunciad* only really makes sense (or not) if we situate it within the wider culture of confusion and expectation that surrounded print publication at this time, and that this book explores. It has often been argued that Pope loved or needed the subjects he mocked; so, for example, the *Dunciad* is dependent on the folly and energy of the dunces to inspire its crazy flights of fantasy.[53] And this dependence is also true of Pope and his early readers. It is not that his work is based on a readership that knows everything. Rather, it is dependent on a more flawed and intellectually vulnerable audience, one that has been trained to feel wrongfooted and potentially outside the charmed circle evoked within the text. It is a poem that hinges on its readers' expectation that they might know some but not all of the answers, that they were being teased at the same time that they were invited to contribute to meaning-making. Like so many other works of the time, *The Dunciad* offers tantalizing fictions of inclusion which might also be a fantasy. It seems to rest on the assumption that difficult books sorted out competent readers from incompetent ones – except that, as we have seen, at this time there was little consensus on who the 'competent' readers were. *The Dunciad* forces its readers to engage with a poem that arrives with its own set of interpretative guidelines, a poem that is already subversive and is undercut by the text that surrounds it. It offers a complex example of literary misunderstanding; complex not only because of its constant revision, but also because Pope seems to celebrate both the art of reading and misreading in his poem, and sometimes it is hard to tell which is which.

## Notes and their Readers

The combination of obscurity and proliferating annotation within the poem was a source of comment for contemporary readers, who perceived in the work, and in Pope's continued revision, a desire on his part to control the way the poem was read. The novelist Samuel Richardson, himself an arch-manipulator of the reading experience, commented that:

> Mr Pope in the Height of his Fame, tho' he had made himself, by Arts only He (as a Man of Genius) could stoop to, the *Fashion*, could not trust his Works with the Vulgar, without Notes longer than the Work, and Self-praises, to tell them what he meant, and that he *had* a Meaning in this or that Place. And thus every-one was taught to read with his Eyes.[54]

Richardson's observation that Pope wanted to tell readers 'what he meant' and 'to read with his Eyes' is astute (and ironic given Richardson's interventions in his own fictional works). He was right that Pope's annotations created a particularly loaded reading experience for the poem. This sense of a text dwarfed by its notes was amplified by the further layers of commentary that the poem accrued at the hands of subsequent editors. Later editions of Pope's works through the next half-century added to the poem's already abundant explication, and readers like the Suffolk diarist Thomas Green, who 'Read the Dunciad, with Warton's and Wakefield's Annotations', clearly mediated their encounters with the poem through this material.[55] *The Dunciad* was a poem born with its own bewildering instruction manual, a manual that got ever longer and more contradictory with each new edition both during and after Pope's lifetime. Not everyone thought this accretive process made for the best reading experience. A 1753 letter from the bluestocking Frances Boscawen to Elizabeth Montagu declares that:

> At present I live upon M$^r$. Botham's Charity who has lent me a new Edition of M$^r$ Pope's Works. Not that I can pretend to be much edify'd by M$^r$ W[arburton's]: Commentary on the contrary it makes me dig deep for Meanings w$^{ch}$ I us'd to find (right or wrong I can't say) among the flowers upon the enamel'd surface: and except one note which informs me why the Isle's of an old Cathedral are like / the \ Walks in Old Groves (& that they are so I had long since observ'd) I don't meet with any thing very instructing or entertaining in the said M$^r$ W.[56]

What's particularly interesting about this response is that Boscawen is a reader who does not like to 'dig deep for meaning'. The plethora of commentary provided by Warburton is not, for her, instructive or entertaining. We come back to what to do with Pope's text.[57] We might ask if it is, in fact, the role of the editor to further explain the intellectual and satirical contexts that inform the poem, or whether there is a danger that in seeking to do so, we create the impression that this is a text that can be solved – when in fact it cannot. The goal of the editor and the teacher is to make the works of the past accessible, but if the aim of the work is to bamboozle and wrongfoot the reader, perhaps we need a different approach, one which acknowledges the limits of explication and the role of partial comprehension.

# Afterword

Students who come to my literature classes, I find, read in all the ways they aren't supposed to.

—MICHAEL WARNER, 'UNCRITICAL READING'

THIS IS A BOOK that began with my experience of trying to teach eighteenth-century literature to twenty-first-century students. For years I have watched them wade through references to Whigs and Tories and conspiracy theories and bizarre society disputes in order to understand what was on the pages before them. I would say that if they read the books in scholarly editions and looked at all the footnotes, then they would be able to read them right. They would get all the jokes, could pat themselves on the back for their decoding. They would, in short, learn to read just like eighteenth-century readers had done.

This book shows that I was wrong. Or at least, it shows that partial comprehension was central to the experience of being an early reader. It was also a dynamic built into many of the major texts of the period, which played with their own accessibility and depended on readers' incomprehension. Such works frequently mocked those trying to understand, at the same time that they offered guidance in how to unpick meaning. This can be read as an exercise in cultural gatekeeping. But it was also often entertainment: a playful engagement among reading communities, real or virtual, who wanted to be taxed. People seem to have liked scribbling all over their books and pamphlets, excitedly exchanging guesses and answers with their friends. Maybe the cryptic crossword or Wordle work on the same basis.[1] And they wouldn't be fun if they were too easy.

As I try to understand the original appeal of the works and the reading practices described here, it helps to think about parallels with the present day. There are clear links between the contemporary appeal of the counterfactual and the secret histories of the Augustan age. Both depend on the idea that there might be an alternative political reality ripe for exposure, ready to be unpicked by a canny reader or viewer, given the right material. A populist hermeneutics of suspicion has come to shape geopolitical realities in ways that would have seemed unthinkable even three decades past. But it was very much thinkable three hundred years ago. And there is the whole question of new forms and new, often unknowable readers. Part of the backstory to the culture of muddle I describe in *Reading It Wrong* is mass circulation and the impact of commercial print and its reach. There are powerful resonances with our own moment of media shift and the advent of the digital. Both eras are defined by newly available forms of access to information: the democratization of knowledge through the search engine offers compelling connections with the generalist writings in all fields in the Augustan era. But there is also the wider question of the challenges of anonymous cultural transmission afforded by the digital: in both the early eighteenth century and the early twenty-first, writers and readers find themselves trying to navigate a vast, unknowable world of ideas, people, and responses made accessible through commercial print and through online engagement. In both cases, we also find the flourishing of what appear to be much more focused subsets of readers: coteries and implied coteries of knowing readers in the 1700s, and online 'affinity spaces' or communities of shared values and interests in our own time. Perhaps these have a common dynamic. Recent work on the 'imagined reader' of online postings shows that writers commonly deal with the enormity of the potentially limitless and utterly unknowable audience of the internet by imagining they are writing for smaller audiences with whom they have personal or communal ties, even though in reality they are posting content to a much more diverse and unknown group.[2] This might be another way of understanding the appeals to exclusivity and specificity that we see across so many eighteenth-century works. The idea of the knowable small group, even the fiction of a small group, offers a way of negotiating the newly expanded, unpredictable, and anonymous spaces of print culture. All these analogies are useful in understanding why the texts I describe here worked as they did, why people enjoyed them – and how they sometimes went wrong. And identifying prehistories for what often feel like uniquely contemporary cultural concerns also has its value, reminding us of the ways in which changing forms of communication and access can alter the basics of the ways we understand what we read.

But coming back to the confused students I started with, what about them? If we are still to study, edit, and teach the complex satirical and fictional texts that characterize so much of early eighteenth-century literary culture, what does learning about reading wrong have to offer? My own recent experience of redescribing the kinds of works discussed in this book as literature which is meant to be a puzzle, perhaps intended to make its readers feel a bit left out or left behind, is that this news can come as something of a relief. The writings of the early eighteenth century are challenging in the seminar room for many reasons, but one of them is surely the sense they give, in the words of one recent master's student, that they are 'books written by clever Dicks for clever Dicks'. Maybe we would teach and edit more effectively if we better acknowledged difficulty and uncertainty. If in this period and elsewhere students were enabled to be bewildered by what they found, rather than having to feign a steady grip on the most evasive of texts, those materials might seem a bit less alienating and a bit more likeable, more of a game than a test to be failed. And the contemporary parallels can help here: for a Gen Z audience the idea of memes that spin out into their own anonymous metajokes, often divorced from the intentions of an original creator and purposefully incomprehensible to many, is both deeply familiar and closely related to the kinds of interpretative play described in this book.[3] So too might be the similarities between the group problem-solving of true crime cases among online communities and the collective decoding of scandal narratives and secret histories in the early eighteenth century.[4] Do we get involved out of a desire for truth, justice, or voyeurism, or the desire to be part of a quest? Engagement is driven by the fact that we are puzzled, and we want and need to work out the answer for ourselves.

In terms of critical practice, one of the things that this book shows is how the kinds of qualitative evidence gathered as part of the history of reading – letters, diaries, marginalia – can be used to drive bigger conceptual questions about interpretation. These sorts of materials have been mined extensively and with huge effect by early modern scholars, but not so much by those working in the period just after them. Although the literature of the early eighteenth century is peculiarly, uniquely interactive, empirical reader-based evidence in marginalia, letters, diaries, and commonplace books has not been so well-mined, other than in constructing reception histories for individual writers or texts. But when we move away from generalized readers to actual ones we start to glimpse the works we thought we knew rather differently. We don't always need to hypothesize about what a reader might have gleaned from a contemporary satire: in some cases there is evidence on the page to tell us, or at least to unsettle some of the assumptions we bring to the text. The practice of scholarly editing, as we have seen, has long been invested in ideas of expertise and precise interpretation: footnotes are rarely question marks. But maybe they could be, and maybe the hazarding of guesses would be a more appropriate response to works which are designed to slip away from us. Recognizing that we are supposed to be foxed by much eighteenth-century literature, and that being puzzled is part of its pleasure, might not be a desirable endpoint for many readers, but it is probably an authentic one.

# NOTES

## Reading It Wrong: An Introduction

1. Versions of this argument can be found in Mark Bauerlein, *The Dumbest Generation: How the Digital Age Stupifies Young Americans and Jeopardizes Our Future* (New York: Penguin, 2008); *To Read or Not to Read: A Question of National Consequence*, Research Report 47, National Endowment for the Arts (Washington: NEA, 2007); Lennard Davis, Trisha Pender, Robert Eaglestone, Elleke Boehmer, Alexander Dick, Patricia Badir, and Michael O'Sullivan, 'The State of the Discipline: English Studies', *Times Higher Education*, 2 May 2019, https://www.timeshighereducation.com/features/state-discipline-english-studies.

2. For a summary of these changes, see Dustin Griffin, 'The Rise of the Professional Author?' *The Cambridge History of the Book in Britain, 1695–1830*, vol. 5, ed. Michael F. Suarez, S.J., and Michael L. Turner (Cambridge: Cambridge University Press, 2010), 132–45; Jurgen Habermas, *Structural Transformation of the Public Sphere* (Cambridge, MA: MIT Press, 1989); Brean Hammond, *Professional Imaginative Writing in England, 1670–1740* (Oxford: Clarendon Press, 1997); Isobel Grundy, 'Women and Print: Readers, Writers and the Market', *Cambridge History of the Book in Britain*, vol. 5, 146–60; Erin Mackie, *Market à la Mode: Fashion, Commodity, and Gender in the Tatler and Spectator Papers* (Baltimore, MD: Johns Hopkins University Press, 1997); Alvin Kernan, *Samuel Johnson and the Impact of Print* (Princeton, NJ: Princeton University Press, 1987).

3. Roger Cocks, *An Answer to a Book Set forth by Sir Edward Peyton, Carrying this Title, A Discourse concerning the fitnese of the Posture, necessary to be used, in taking the Bread and Wine at the Sacrament* (London, 1642), 1.

4. Mark Rose, 'Copyright, Authors and Censorship', *Cambridge History of the Book in Britain*, vol. 5, 118–31.

5. David Cressy, *Literacy and the Social Order: Reading and Writing in Tudor and Stuart England* (Cambridge: Cambridge University Press, 1980), 47.

6. Peter Hinds, 'The Book Trade at the Turn of the Eighteenth Century', *The Oxford Handbook of the Eighteenth-Century Novel*, ed. James Alan Downie (Oxford: Oxford University Press, 2016), 5–22, 10.

7. Cressy, *Literature and the Social Order*, 176.

8. Cressy, *Literature and the Social Order*, 175–77; David Cressy, 'Levels of Illiteracy in England, 1530–1730', *The Historical Journal* 20, no. 1 (March 1977): 1–23.

9. Michael F. Suarez, 'Introduction', *Cambridge History of the Book*, vol. 5, 1–36, 3.

10. For much fuller discussion see Suarez, 'Introduction', 8–11.

11. Suarez, 'Introduction', 11.

12. 'Lucinda's Day', *The Female Tatler*, no. 60 (23 November 1709).

13. Jonathan Swift, 'The Importance of the Guardian Considered', *The Prose Works of Jonathan Swift*, vol. 8, ed. Herbert Davis (Oxford: Basil Blackwell, 1939–1968), 14–15.

14. *The M——'d C——b; or, the L——th. Consultation* (London, 1704).

15. *The M——'d C——b*, title page. William Shakespeare, *Julius Caesar*, ed. David Daniell (London: Arden Shakespeare, 1998), 237. Virgil, *Aeneid VII–XII*, transl. H. Rushton Fairclough, revised by G. P. Goold (Cambridge, MA: Harvard University Press, 2000), 24–25.

16. *The M——'d C——b*, 6.

17. Isaac Hawkins Browne, *A Pipe of Tobacco: In Imitation of Six Several Authors* (London, 1736).

18. Browne, *A Pipe of Tobacco* (London, 1736), William Andrews Clark Memorial Library, UCLA, PR3326.B95 P6*, 7, 11, 13, 16, 19, 21.

19. Jane Brereton, *Poems on Several Occasions: by Mrs Jane Brereton. With letters to her friends, and an account of her life* (London, 1744), front matter advertisement, a2.

20. Jonathan Swift, *Gulliver's Travels*, ed. David Womersley (Cambridge: Cambridge University Press, 2012), 282–84.

21. On the hard and soft debate, see James L. Clifford, 'Gulliver's Fourth Voyage: "Hard" and "Soft" Schools of Interpretation', *Quick Springs of Sense: Studies in the Eighteenth Century*, ed. Larry S. Champion (Athens: University of Georgia Press, 197), 33–49.

22. Robert Darnton, '"What is the history of books?" revisited', *Modern Intellectual History* 4, no. 3 (2007): 495–508, 506.

23. Alan Roper, 'Who's Who in *Absalom and Achitophel*?' *Huntington Library Quarterly* 63, no. 1 (2000): 93–138.

24. John Dryden, *Absalom and Achitophel: A Poem* (1682), National Trust, Townend Library, Troutbeck, 3075367.3. The marginal notes identify 'D Monmouth', 'Parliamt', 'D Buckingham', 'Bethell', and 'Oates'.

25. See also Alan Roper, 'Drawing Parallels and Making Applications in Restoration Literature', *Politics as Reflected in Literature: Papers Presented at a Clark Library Seminar, 24 January 1987*, ed. Richard Ashcraft (Los Angeles: University of California Press, 1989), 31–52.

26. Observations on Jonathan Swift, *Travels into Several Remote Nations of the World* (London, 1726), National Library of Wales Ottley Papers, uncatalogued volume MS, N.20.n.p. My thanks to Juan Christian Pellicer for this reference.

27. Gertrude Savile, diary entry for 29 January 1728, *Secret Comment: The Diaries of Gertrude Savile, 1721–1757*, ed. Alan Saville (Devon: Kingsbridge History Society, 1997), 100; Dudley Ryder, diary entry for 8 December 1715, *Diary of Dudley Ryder*, ed. William Matthews (London: Methuen, 1939), 146–47.

28. 'ce qui est un jeu singulier, qui regne dans tout le Livre, où l'on ne sait souvent si l'Auteur se moque, ou non, ni à qui il en veut, ni quel est son dessein'. Jean Le Clerc, *Bibliotheque Ancienne et Moderne*, vol. 15 (Amsterdam, 1721), 443.

29. Jonathan Swift to Alexander Pope, 16 July 1728, *The Correspondence of Alexander Pope*, vol. 2, ed. George Sherburn (Oxford: Clarendon Press, 1956), 504.

30. Jonathan Swift to John Gay, 28 March 1728, *The Correspondence of Jonathan Swift, D.D.*, vol. 3, ed. David Woolley (Frankfurt am Main: Peter Lang, 2003), 170.

31. Doctor John Arbuthnot to Jonathan Swift, 5 November 1726, *Correspondence of Jonathan Swift*, vol. 3, ed. Woolley, 44.

32. Mather Byles to Alexander Pope, 25 November 1728, *The Correspondence of Alexander Pope*, vol. 2, ed. Sherburn, 528.

33. Alexander Pope, *The Dunciad, Variorvm. With the Prolegomena of Scriblerus* (London, 1729), National Art Library, Victoria and Albert Museum, Dyce M 8vo 7742, 20, 41.

34. Alexander Pope, *The Dunciad, in Four Books* (London, 1743), Bodleian Library, University of Oxford, Vet. A4 c.429, 137.

35. Daniel Defoe, *The Shortest-Way with the Dissenters: or Proposals for the Establishment of the Church* (London, 1702), National Library of Scotland, NG.1559. c.29 (6).

36. *A Pair of Spectacles for Oliver's Looking-Glass Maker* (London, 1711), Beinecke Library, Yale University College Pamphlets 906 9, 38.

37. Alexander Pope, *Of the Use of Riches: An Epistle to the Right Honourable Lord Bathurst* (London, 1732), British Library C.59.h.9.(3.), 4.

38. Alexander Pope, *An Essay on Man: in Epistles to a Friend* (London: J. Wilford, 1733), Bodleian Library, University of Oxford, Vet. A4 c.389. For a similar example of a reader correcting their edition of the *Essay* against the later version, see Pope, *Essay* (Dublin, 1733 [1734]), Bodleian Library, University of Oxford, 2799 f.192.

39. *Rocks and Shallows Discovered: Or, the Ass Kicking at the Lyons in the Tower* (London, 1716), British Library, 8132.bb.14(1), 14.

40. *Poetical Miscellanies: The Fifth Part: Containing a Collection of Original Poems, with Several New Translations. By the Most Eminent Hands* (London, 1704), Beinecke Library, Yale University, Osborn Collections, pb119c.

41. Roger L'Estrange, *Aesop's Fables, With Morals and Reflections, as Improv'd by Sir Roger L'Estrange Done into Variety of English Verse*, 2nd ed. (London, 1718), Beinecke Library, Yale University, 20041522, 237.

42. Alexander Pope, *The Works of Alexander Pope Esq, with explanatory notes and additions never before printed*, vol. 1 (London, 1736), Beinecke Library, Yale University, Osborn pc305 1,10.

43. *The Grove; or, A Collection of Original Poems, Translations, &c.* (London, 1721), Worcester College Library, University of Oxford, Godwyn Collection, KK.8.34 (7), 12.

44. John Dryden, *Mr Limberham: or the Kind Keeper. A Comedy as it was Acted at the Duke's Theatre* (London, 1690), Cardiff University Library, Rare Books Collection, PR3415.K4.C9, a2r.

45. Seth Lehrer has written insightfully of the history of scholarship in particular as intrinsically linked to the correction of error: Seth Lehrer, *Error and the Academic Self: The Scholarly Imagination, Medieval to Modern* (New York: Columbia University Press, 2002). See also Andrew Murphy, '"Came errour here by mysse of man": Editing and the Metaphysics of Presence', *Yearbook of English Studies* 29 (1999): 118–37; Ann Blair, 'Errata Lists and the Reader as Corrector', *Agent of Change: Print Culture Studies after Elizabeth L. Eisenstein*, ed. Sabrina Alcorn Baron, Eric N. Lindquist, and Eleanor F. Shevlin (Amherst: University of Massachusetts Press, 2007), 21–41.

46. On Thomas Turner's reading habits, see Naomi Tadmor, ' "In the Even my Wife Read to Me": Women, Reading and Household Life in the Eighteenth Century', *The Practice and Representation of Reading in England*, ed. James Raven, Helen Small, and Naomi Tadmor (Cambridge: Cambridge University Press, 1996), 162–74. See also Abigail Williams, *The Social Life of Books: Reading Together in the Eighteenth-Century Home* (New Haven, CT: Yale University Press, 2017), 247–51.

47. Thomas Turner, diary entry for 4 December 1756, *The Diary of Thomas Turner, 1754–1765*, ed. David Vaisey (Oxford: Oxford University Press, 1984), 73.

48. Thomas Turner, diary entry for 16 December 1756, *Diary of Thomas Turner*, ed. Vaisey, 74.

49. John Cannon, Χρονεχα *seu Annales: Or: Memoirs: Of the Birth, Education, Life and Death of: Mr. John Cannon*, 1741–42, John Cannon's Diary, Somerset Heritage Centre, Taunton, DD/SAS/C1193/4. The memoir has been edited in an abridged edition as *The Chronicles of John Cannon, Excise Officer and Writing Master*, ed. John Money, 2 vols (Oxford: Oxford University Press, 2010).

50. John Hervey, *The court-Spy; Or, Memoirs of St J–M–S'S* (London, 1744), British Library, BL 1415 f.17, 4.

51. Colley Cibber, *The Secret History of Arlus and Odolphus, Ministers of State to the Empress of Grandinsula* (London, 1710), 2.

52. For a more extensive discussion of the social function of book reading and sharing in the period, see Williams, *Social Life of Books*.

## Chapter 1: The Good Reader

1. Bruce Robbins, 'Reading Bad', *Los Angeles Review of Books*, 21 January 2018, https://lareviewofbooks.org/article/reading-bad/.

2. Harold Bloom, *A Map of Misreading* (Oxford: Oxford University Press, 1975), 3–4.

3. Bloom, *Map of Misreading*, 128.

4. Paul de Man, *Blindness and Insight: Essays on the Rhetoric of Contemporary Criticism* (New York: Oxford University Press, 1971), 102–3.

5. Jacques Rancière, 'Literary Misunderstanding', transl. Mary Stevens, *Paragraph* 28, no. 2 (July 2005): 91–103.

6. Ricoeur first coined the phrase in *Freud and Philosophy: An Essay in Interpretation*, transl. Denis Savage (New Haven, CT: Yale University Press, 1970).

7. For a thoughtful study of the role of writerly error, see Erica McAlpine, *The Poet's Mistake* (Princeton, NJ: Princeton University Press, 2020).

8. See, for example, Rancière's description of the 'stultifying' master and the 'circle of power' in *The Ignorant Schoolmaster*, transl. Kristin Ross (Stanford, CA: Stanford University Press, 1991), 1–18. For a lucid account of the gendered dynamics of the student-teacher exchange, see Amia Srinivasan, *The Right to Sex* (London: Bloomsbury, 2021), 128–36.

9. See Maren S. Aukerman, 'When Reading it Wrong is Getting it Right: Shared Evaluation Pedagogy among Fifth Grade Readers', *Research in the Teaching of English* 42, no. 1 (August 2007): 56–103. On the post-colonial dimensions of this approach, see also Sayan Dey, 'Why

a Pedagogy of the Stupid is Smart and Liberating', *University World News*, 4 April 2020, https://www.universityworldnews.com/post.php?story=20200401114425376.

10. Michael Warner has described this emphasis on particular kinds of taught critical reading as 'an invisible norm', which remains at the heart of university teaching practices even while other elements of the discipline, such as the canon or the notion of literature itself, are increasingly questioned. Michael Warner, 'Uncritical Reading', *Polemic: Critical or Uncritical*, ed. Jane Gallop (New York and London: Routledge, 2004), 13–38, 20.

11. I.A. Richards, *Practical Criticism* (London: Routledge, 1929), 346.

12. E.D. Hirsch, *Validity in Interpretation* (New Haven, CT: Yale University Press, 1967), 207.

13. Stanley Fish, *Is There a Text in this Class? The Authority of Interpretive Communities* (Cambridge, MA: Harvard University Press, 1980), 338.

14. Rita Felski, 'Context Stinks', *New Literary History* 42, no. 4 (Autumn 2011): 573–591, 574.

15. Bonamy Dobrée, *English Literature in the Early Eighteenth Century, 1700–1740* (Oxford: Clarendon Press, 1959), 198.

16. David Worcester, *The Art of Satire* (Cambridge, MA: Harvard University Press, 1940).

17. Worcester, *The Art of Satire*, 13.

18. For a survey of twentieth-century critical approaches to satire, see: Claire Bucknell, 'Satire, Morality and Criticism, 1930–1965', *The Oxford Handbook of Eighteenth-Century Satire*, ed. Paddy Bullard (Oxford: Oxford University Press, 2019), 696–711.

19. Dustin Griffin, *Satire: A Critical Reintroduction* (Lexington: University Press of Kentucky, 1994), 29. For examples, see Ian Jack, *Augustan Satire: Intention and Idiom in English Poetry, 1660–1750* (Oxford: Clarendon Press, 1952); Maynard Mack, 'The Muse of Satire', *Yale Review* 41 (1951): 80–92.

20. Alvin Kernan, *The Cankered Muse: Satire of the English Renaissance* (New Haven, CT: Yale University Press, 1959), 16.

21. For an excellent summary of these approaches, see Catherine Ingrassia and Claudia N. Thomas, Introduction to *'More Solid Learning': New Perspectives on Alexander Pope's Dunciad*, ed. Catherine Ingrassia and Claudia N. Thomas (Lewisburg, PA: Bucknell University Press, 2000), 24–32.

22. Brean Hammond, *Professional Imaginative Writing in Britain, 1670–1740: Hackney for Bread* (Oxford: Oxford University Press, 1997), 9.

23. Peter Stallybrass and Allon White, *The Politics and Poetics of Transgression* (Ithaca, NY: Cornell University Press, 1986).

24. Michael Seidel, 'Satire, lampoon, libel, slander', *The Cambridge Companion to English Literature, 1650–1740*, ed. Steven N. Zwicker (Cambridge: Cambridge University Press, 1998): 33–57, 38.

25. Ashley Marshall, *The Practice of Satire in England, 1658–1770* (Baltimore, MD: Johns Hopkins University Press, 2013), 74.

26. Marshall, *The Practice of Satire in England*, 117.

27. Marshall, *The Practice of Satire in England*, 157–58. On the notion of Augustan coterie writing as a mutually understood small world, see also Robert D. Hume, 'Satire in the Reign of Charles II', *Modern Philology* 102, no. 3 (2005): 332–371, 341.

28. Paddy Bullard, ed., *The Oxford Handbook of Eighteenth-Century Satire* (Oxford: Oxford University Press, 2019).

29. For acknowledgements of the potential diversity of audience response, see articles by Marcus Walsh and David Taylor in *The Oxford Handbook of Eighteenth-Century Satire*.

30. 'the painful shock . . .' Helen Deutsch, 'The Body of Thersites: Misanthropy and Violence': 420–36, 430; 'the task of identifying . . .' James Fowler, 'Moralizing Satire: Cross-Channel Perspectives': 595–612, 603; 'it is through the reader's laughter . . .' Alexis Tadié, 'Quarrelling': 542–56, 553; 'the reader is encouraged . . .' Jon Mee, 'Satire in the Age of the French Revolution': 661–78, 671; '"general satire" . . .' Paddy Bullard, 'Against the Experts: Swift and Political Satire': 403–19, 403. All are in *The Oxford Handbook of Eighteenth-Century Satire*.

31. Robert Phiddian, 'Satire and the Limits of Literary Theories', *Critical Quarterly* 55, no. 3 (2013): 44–58, 48.

32. Phiddian, 'Satire and the Limits of Literary Theories', 49.

33. Phiddian, 'Satire and the Limits of Literary Theories', 53.

34. On error, see, for example, Seth Lehrer, *Error and the Academic Self* (New York: Columbia University Press, 2003); Daniel Wakelin, *Scribal Correction and Literary Craft* (Cambridge: Cambridge University Press, 2014); Julian Yates, *Error, Misuse and Failure: Object Lessons from the English Renaissance* (Minneapolis: Minnesota University Press, 2002).

35. There is some correction of this in the work of Heidi Brayman Hackel, who says that marginalia studies have tended to emphasize 'goal-oriented, professional, and contestatory readings' and that the activities of women have remained relatively under studied. Heidi Brayman Hackel, *Reading Material in Early Modern England: Print, Gender, and Literacy* (Cambridge: Cambridge University Press, 2005), 196–97.

36. Anthony Grafton and Lisa Jardine, '"Studied for Action": How Gabriel Harvey Read his Livy', *Oxford: Past and Present Society* 129, no. 1 (1990): 30–78; William H. Sherman, *Used Books: Marking Readers in Renaissance England* (Philadelphia: University of Pennsylvania Press, 2007); Hackel, *Reading Material*.

37. Sherman, *Used Books*, 16–17.

38. Geoff Baker, *Reading and Politics in Early Modern England: The Mental World of a Seventeenth-Century Catholic Gentleman* (Manchester, UK: Manchester University Press, 2010), 120, 125; Kevin Sharpe, *Reading Revolutions: The Politics of Reading in Early Modern England* (New Haven, CT: Yale University Press, 2000), 105–6, 276–77; Carlo Ginzburg, *The Cheese and the Worms: The Cosmos of a Sixteenth-Century Miller*, transl. John and Anne C. Tedeschi, (Baltimore, MD: Johns Hopkins University Press, 1980, new ed. 2013), 34, 45, 49.

39. Heather Jackson, *Marginalia: Readers Writing in Books* (New Haven, CT: Yale University Press, 2001), 248.

40. Martin C. Battestin, 'A Rationale of Literary Annotation: The Example of Fielding's Novels', *Studies in Bibliography* 34 (1981): 1–22, 19–20.

41. Michael Edson, 'Annotator as Ordinary Reader: Accuracy, Relevance and Editorial Method', *Textual Cultures* 11 (2017), 42–69, 65. Edson is not the only recent critic to have aired the question of the problematic relationship among text, context, and the urge to over-annotate historical works. Discussing theoretical implications of textual scholarship, David Greetham has argued that a fully recognized and articulated context will always provide a rival set of data

from that putatively placed in a text by the author, and these rival sets will inevitably invoke various theories of authorial prerogative, 'readability', and social construction. The rivalry expressed as a conflict between text and context can therefore be seen as a struggle for control of the text between the constructed author-function and the reader (that is, the editor, in the role of 'ideal reader'). David Greetham, 'Context and the "Impossibility Trope"', *New Literary History* 42, no. 4 (2011), 719–38, 731.

42. Ian Small, 'The Editor as Annotator as Ideal Reader', *The Theory and Practice of Text-Editing*, ed. Marcus Walsh and Ian Small (Cambridge: Cambridge University Press, 1991): 186–209, 189.

43. Catherine Nicolson, *Reading and Not Reading the Faerie Queene: Spenser and the Making of Literary Criticism* (Princeton, NJ: Princeton University Press, 2020), 15.

44. Nicolson, *Reading and Not Reading*, 21.

45. Warner, 'Uncritical Reading', 13–16.

46. Merve Emre, *Paraliterary: The Making of Bad Readers in Post-War America* (Chicago: University of Chicago Press, 2017).

## Chapter 2: The Christian Reader

1. John Geree, 'The Preface: Containing the Grounds, and Use of the Additions, in this New Edition', Nicholas Byfield, *Directions for the Private Reading of the Scriptures*, 4th ed. (London, 1648).

2. Quoted by John Locke, 'Of the Imperfection of Words', *The Clarendon Edition of the Works of John Locke: An Essay Concerning Human Understanding*, ed. Peter H. Nidditch (Oxford: Clarendon Press, 1975), 475–90, 481. For an example of this quotation being apocryphally attributed to St Jerome, see 'The words "Si non vis intelligi non debes legi" were, I believe, the exclamation of St Jerome, as he threw his copy of Persius into the fire in a fit of testiness at being unable to construe some tough lines of that tough author. I set down this reply from memory, and am unable to give authority for it', W. Fraser, 'Quotation in Locke', *Notes and Queries* 7, no. 166 (1 January 1853): 23.

3. For some discussion of late seventeenth-century debates over Biblical interpretation, see Scott Mandelbrote, 'Writing the History of the English Bible in the Early Eighteenth Century', *Studies in Church History* 38 (2004): 268–78.

4. Ariel Hessayon and Nicholas Keene, 'Introduction', *Scripture and Scholarship in Early Modern England* (Aldershot, UK: Ashgate, 2006), 1–4, 4.

5. Justin Champion, '"Directions for the Profitable Reading of the Holy Scriptures": Biblical Criticism, Clerical Learning, and Lay Readers, c. 1650–1720', *Scripture and Scholarship*, 208–30, 208–9.

6. Francis Roberts and Edmund Calamy, *Clavis Bibliorum. The Key of the Bible, Unlocking the Richest Treasury of the Holy Scriptures*, 2nd ed. (London, 1649), title page.

7. *A Key to Catechisms: or An Easie and Familiar Help for the True and Right Understanding of the Principal Substance of all Catechisms Whatsoever* (London, 1682), title page.

8. See Hans W. Frei, *The Eclipse of Biblical Narrative: A Study in Eighteenth and Nineteenth Century Hermeneutics* (New Haven, CT: Yale University Press, 1980).

9. Henry St John, Viscount Bolingbroke, *The Works of Lord Bolingbroke, with a Life, Containing Additional Information Relative to his Personal and Public Character*, vol. 3 (Farnborough, UK: Gregg, 1969), 464.

10. See Champion, "'Directions for the Profitable Reading of the Holy Scriptures'". Examples of popular works engaging in these debates include William Lowth, *Directions for the Profitable Reading of the Scriptures* (London, 1708); Byfield, *Directions for the Private Reading of the Scriptures*.

11. Francis Hare, *The Difficulties and Discouragements which attend the Study of the Scriptures in the Way of Private Judgement* (London, 1714), 45.

12. Hare, *Difficulties and Discouragements*, 45–46.

13. William Lowth, *Vindication of the Divine Authority and Inspiration of the Writings of the Old and New Testament* (Oxford, 1692), 9.

14. John Williams, *Of the Perspicuity of Scripture, and Rules for Interpretation of It* (London, 1696), 12.

15. Joseph Johnston, *A Reply to the Defence of the Exposition of the Doctrine of Church of England* (London, 1687), 133.

16. Locke, 'Of the Imperfection of Words', 481.

17. John Locke, 'The Preface an Essay for the Understanding of St Paul's Epistles by Consulting St Paul Himself', *The Clarendon Edition of the Works of John Locke: A Paraphrase and Notes on the Epistles of St Paul*, ed. Arthur W. Wainwright, vol. 1 (Oxford: Clarendon Press, 1987), 102–116, 103.

18. Locke, 'The Preface an Essay for the Understanding of St Paul's Epistles', 103.

19. Locke, 'The Preface an Essay for the Understanding of St Paul's Epistles', 105.

20. Edmund Calamy, 'An Epistle to the Reader', *Clavis Bibliorum. The Key of the Bible, Unlocking the Richest Treasury of the Holy Scriptures*, Francis Roberts and Edmund Calamy, 2nd ed. (London, 1649), 1–7, 5.

21. For an overview of Blundell's reading interests and publication, see Geoff Baker, *Reading and Politics in Early Modern England: The Mental World of a Seventeenth-Century Catholic Gentleman* (Manchester, UK: Manchester University Press, 2010), 11–19. For a thorough account of Blundell's responses to his religious reading, see 136–70.

22. William Blundell, Historica, Lancashire County Record Office, DDBL acc. 6121, Box 4, Historica; William Blundell, Adversaria, Lancashire County Record Office, DDBL acc. 6121, Box 4, Adversaria.

23. Blundell, Historica, fol. 152v.

24. Blundell, Adversaria, fol. 32v.

25. Blundell, Adversaria, fol. 85r. He is writing here specifically of the story of Samson. For examples of these passages of difficulty, see fols 14–15; 32v; 36v–7r; 44r; 49v; 56r; 62; 94v–5; 112r–v; 135v.

26. Blundell, Adversaria, fol. 32r.

27. Blundell, Adversaria, fol. 96r.

28. Blundell, Adversaria, fol.188v.

29. Blundell, Adversaria, fol. 135r.

30. Blundell, Adversaria, fol. 95r

31. Blundell, Adversaria, fol. 321r.

32. Blundell, Adversaria, fol. 273r.

33. Blundell, Adversaria, fols 37v–9, 41v.

34. Byfield, 'The Preface Containing Directions How to Use the Booke Following With Most Profit', *Directions for the Private Reading of the Scriptures*, a2v–a3r.

35. Geree, 'The Preface Containing the Grounds', Byfield, *Directions for the Private Reading of the Scriptures*.

36. Byfield, *Directions for the Private Reading of the Scriptures*, 4th ed. (London, 1648), British Library, Wing B6383.

37. 'Dr Merryweather's Directions to a young Student in the University', Commonplace Book, Beinecke Library, Yale University, Osborn c581. There are two other surviving manuscript copies of this work: MS Rawl D 200 at the Bodleian Library, Oxford, and Emmanuel MS 78 at Emmanuel College, Cambridge. I am extremely grateful to Ben Card for his insights into this material. For discussion of Holdsworth's authorship, see: John A. Trentman in 'The Authorship of "Directions for a Student in the Universitie"', *Transactions of the Cambridge Bibliographical Society* 7, no. 2 (1978): 170–83.

38. On the manuscript's intellectual significance, see Scott Mandelbrote, 'Early Modern Natural Theologies', *The Oxford Handbook of Natural Theology*, ed. John Hedley Brooke, Russel Re Manning, and Fraser Watts (Oxford: Oxford University Press, 2013), 75–92, 85; Eugene E. White, 'Master Holdsworth and "A Knowledge Very Useful and Necessary"', *The Quarterly Journal of Speech* 53, no. 1 (Feb 1967): 1–16, 16.

39. 'Dr Merryweather's Directions', 125–27.

40. 'Dr Merryweather's Directions', 129.

41. 'Dr Merryweather's Directions', 154.

42. *The Book of Common Prayer, and Administration of the Sacraments, . . . together with the Psalter* (Cambridge, 1748), Bodleian Library, University of Oxford, Buchanan e.111.

43. *The New Testament of our Lord and Saviour Jesus Christ, Newly Translated out of the Original Greek* (Oxford, 1679), Bodleian Library, University of Oxford, Vet A3 e.2217, inscriptions on inside of upper cover and recto of frontispiece portrait.

44. *The Holy Bible Containing the Old Testament and the New, Newly Translated out of ye Original Tongues* (London, 1671), Bodleian Library, University of Oxford, Bib. Eng 1671. e.1.

45. *The Holy Bible Containing the Old Testament and the New*, Bib. Eng 1671. e.1, Numbers 11:25–26.

46. Richard Allestree, *The Causes of the Decay of Christian Piety. Or An Impartial Survey of the Ruines of Christian Religion* (London, 1674). National Trust Townend Library, Troutbeck, 3075555.

47. Allestree, *The Causes of the Decay of Christian Piety*, Townend Library 3075555, 19.

48. Allestree, *The Causes of the Decay of Christian Piety*, Townend Library 3075555, preface, n.p.

49. Allestree, *The Causes of the Decay of Christian Piety*, Townend Library, 3075555, preface, 7, preface, 4, 53.

50. Allestree, *The Causes of the Decay of Christian Piety*, Townend Library 3075555, 12.

51. B.J. McMullin, 'The Bible Trade', *The Cambridge History of the Book in Britain*, vol. 4, ed. John Barnard, D.F. McKenzie, and Maureen Bell (Cambridge: Cambridge University Press, 2002), 455–73.

52. W.E. Slights, '"Marginall Notes that Spoile the Text": Scriptural Annotation in the English Renaissance', *Huntington Library Quarterly* 55 (1992): 255–278, 270.

53. Samuel Blackwell, *Several Methods of Reading the Holy Scriptures in Private; Seriously Recommended to Consideration and Use*, 2nd ed. (London, 1720), 4.

54. Alexander Beresford to John Locke, 24 March 1695, *The Correspondence of John Locke*, vol. 5, ed. Esmond de Beer (Oxford: Clarendon Press), 314.

55. Calamy, 'An Epistle to the Reader', *Clavis Bibliorum*, 6–7.

56. Benjamin Keach, 'The Epistle to the Reader', *Tropologia: A Key to Open Scripture-Metaphors. Wherein the most Significant Tropes, (as Metaphors, &c.) And Express Similitudes, Respecting the Father, Son, & Holy Spirit, As Also such as respect the Sacred Word of God Are opened, and Parallel-wise applied, together with the Disparities: From which Practical Inferences are deduced, for Edification of the Reader* (London, 1681).

57. Keach, 'The Word of God Compared to Light', *Tropologia*, book 3: 1–40, 1.

58. Keach, 'Of an Allegory', *Tropologia*, book 1: 200.

59. Keach, 'The Epistle to the Reader', *Tropologia*.

60. Keach, 'The Epistle to the Reader', *Tropologia*.

61. Keach, 'Metaphors taken from Things Growing out of the Earth', *Tropologia*, book 1: 135–39, 136.

62. Anthony Horneck, *Delight and Judgment, or the Great Assize. Represented in a Discourse Concerning the Great Day of Judgment. And its Power to Damp and Imbitter Sensual Delights, Sports and Recreations* (London, 1705), 4.

63. Thomas Blackwell, *Schema Sacrum, or, a Sacred Scheme of Natural and Revealed Religion* (Edinburgh, 1710), 50.

64. Charles Brent, *An Essay Concerning the Nature and Guilt of Lying* (London, 1702), 19.

65. *The Bible*, 3pt. Tomson's Geneva Bible (London, 1615), e.1 (2).

66. Byfield, 'The Preface Containing Directions', *Directions for the Private Reading of the Scriptures*, a3r.

67. 'Dr Merryweather's Directions', 162.

68. John Owen, *Vindiciae Evangelicae, or the Mystery of the Gospell Vindicated.* (Oxford: Leon. Lichfield, 1655), William Andrews Clark Memorial Library, UCLA, BZ O97vi 1655.

69. *Vindiciae Evangelicae*, BZ O97vi 1655, 40, 128, 545.

70. *Vindiciae Evangelicae*, BZ O97vi 1655, 60, 61, 68.

71. *Vindiciae Evangelicae*, BZ O97vi 1655, 65.

72. William Molyneux to John Locke, 20 July 1697, *The Correspondence of John Locke*, vol. 6, ed. E.S. De Beer (Oxford: Clarendon Press, 1981), 165.

73. For an engaging account of the role of marginalia as a site of sociable exchange, see Matthew Sangster, 'Copyright Literature and Reading Communities in Eighteenth-Century St Andrews', *Review of English Studies* 68 (2017), 945–67, 964–67.

74. Browne's is a particularly rich example of a reader marking up his copy of *Tale of a Tub* with the points of reference and clarification that the text seemed to him to demand. Jonathan Swift, *Tale of a Tub: Written for the Universal Improvement of Mankind* (London, 1711), National Trust Library, Townend, NT3074454, note to p. 177.

75. On the circulation of manuscript and printed keys, see Robert M. Adams, 'Jonathan Swift, Thomas Swift, and the Authorship of "*A Tale of a Tub*"', *Modern Philology* 64 (1967): 198–232.

76. *A Tale of a Tub. Written for the Universal Improvement of Mankind. The Fourth Edition Corrected* (London, 1705), Yale University, Beinecke Library, Osborn pc265.

77. Jonathan Swift, *A Tale of a Tub: Written for the Universal Improvement of Mankind*, 4th ed. (London: John Nutt, 1705), Beinecke Library, Yale University, Osborn pc265. There are annotations which seem to suggest some uncertainty as to whether the *Tale* was the work of Thomas or of Jonathan Swift.

78. *A Tale of a Tub*, Osborn pc265, inside front leaf.

79. *A Tale of a Tub*, Beinecke Osborn pc265, 37; 41.

80. *A Tale of a Tub*, Osborn pc265, 125.

81. *A Tale of a Tub*, Osborn pc265, 106.

82. The annotations and explanations transcribed in the copy bear a complex relation to other existing keys to the *Tale*, with some overlap of content. For a discussion of the various extant manuscript sources for the key, see Dipak Nandy, 'Jonathan Swift, Thomas Swift, and the Authorship of "A Tale of a Tub,"' *Modern Philology* 66, no. 4 (1969): 333–37.

83. *A Tale of a Tub*, Osborn pc265, 59.

84. *A Tale of a Tub*, Beinecke Osborn pc265, note to unpaginated page immediately preceding The Battel of the Books.

## Chapter 3: The Classical Reader

1. See, for example, Paul Hammond, *Dryden and the Traces of Classical Rome* (Oxford: Oxford University Press, 1999); Stuart Gillespie, *English Translation and Classical Reception: Towards a New Literary History* (Oxford: Blackwell, 2011); Stuart Gillespie, *Newly Recovered English Classical Translations, 1600–1800* (Oxford: Oxford University Press, 2019); *The Oxford History of Classical Reception in English Literature, 1660–1790*, vol. 3, ed. Charles Martindale and David Hopkins (Oxford: Oxford University Press, 2012).

2. See Anthony Walker-Cook, review of Martindale and Hopkins, *The Oxford History of Classical Reception*: 'it is hoped that later volumes may give a greater voice to authors on the margins, especially those women whose instrumental role in the development of the literature of the period has long been recognised'. *Notes and Queries* 65, no. 3 (2018): 451–53, 451.

3. Bonamy Dobrée, *English Literature in the Early Eighteenth Century, 1700–1740* (Oxford: Clarendon Press, 1959), 160.

4. Roger D. Lund, 'The Eel of Science: Index Learning, Scriblerian Satire, and the Rise of Information Culture', *Eighteenth-Century Life* 22, no. 2 (1988): 19–39, 21.

5. *Clavis Virgilianæ: Pars Prima: A Numerical Key to the Bucolics of P Virgilius Maro* (London, 1715), title page.

6. *Clavis Virgilianæ*, Preface, A2r.

7. For an overview of the range of advice material, see Lance Bertelsen, 'Popular Entertainment and Instruction', *The Cambridge History of English Literature, 1660–1780*, ed. John Richetti (Cambridge: Cambridge University Press, 2005): 61–86, 69–70. See also Natasha Glaisyer and

Sara Pennell, 'Introduction', *Didactic Literature in England, 1500–1800*, ed. Glaisyer and Pennell (London: Routledge, 2016): 1–18. Important studies of secular education include Helen M. Jewell, *Education in Early Modern England* (Basingstoke, UK: Macmillan, 1998); Rosemary O'Day, *Education and Society, 1500–1800: The Social Foundations of Education in Early Modern Britain* (London: Longman, 1982); Kenneth Charlton, *Education in Renaissance England* (London: Routledge and Kegan Paul, 1965); Margaret Spufford, *Contrasting Communities: English Villagers in the Sixteenth and Seventeenth Centuries* (London: Cambridge University Press, 1974), 173–205.

8. It was also possible to buy *Clavis Horatiana* (1715), *Clavis Ovidiana* (1715), and *Clavis Terentiana* (1697).

9. John Gallagher, *Learning Languages in Early Modern England* (Oxford: Oxford University Press, 2019), 16.

10. Bathsua Makin, *An Essay to Revive the Ancient Education of Gentlewomen in Religion, Manners, Arts & Tongues* (London, 1673).

11. Makin, *An Essay to Revive the Ancient Education*, E3v.

12. Makin, *An Essay to Revive the Ancient Education*, E3v.

13. Makin, *An Essay to Revive the Ancient Education*, E3r.

14. On Westmorland schools at this time, see P.J. Wallis, 'Westmorland Schools about 1676: Christopher Wase's survey', *Transactions of the Cumberland & Westmorland Antiquarian & Archaeological Society* 67 (1967): 168–85. I am extremely grateful to Dr Edward Taylor for helping me understand the evidence of these notebooks and their background.

15. Both notebooks are in the Cumbrian archives at Kendal Archive Centre: Latin and Greek notebook of Benjamin Browne, Kendal Archive Centre, WDTE/Box 16/3; Latin notebook of George Birkett, WD/TE/Box 16/25.

16. On humanist Latin education, see Emily Hansen, 'From "Humanist" to "Godly"?: The Changing Social Function of Education in Early Modern English Grammar Schools', unpublished PhD thesis, University of York, 2015, 7–56, 153–67.

17. Latin and Greek notebook of Benjamin Browne, Kendal Archive Centre, WDTE/Box 16/3, np.

18. Richard Bernard, *Terence in English. Fabulæ Comici Facetissimi et Elegantissimi Poetæ Terentii Omnes Anglicæ Factæ* (Cambridge, 1598, last edition, 1641).

19. *Post Boy*, no. 853 (24–26 September 1700).

20. Gallagher, *Learning Languages*, 102–3.

21. See Geoff Baker, *Reading and Politics in Early Modern England: The Mental World of a Seventeenth-Century Catholic Gentleman* (Manchester, UK: Manchester University Press, 2010), 122.

22. William Blundell, Historica, Lancashire County Record Office, DDBL acc. 6121, Box 4, fol.87b.

23. *Gulliver Decypher'd* (London, 1727), British Library, C.116.b.1.(1.), 17.

24. Matthew Concanen, *A Supplement to the Profund* (London, 1728), British Library, C.116.b.2.(4.), v.

25. *The Censor*, no. 1 (11 April 1715), *The Censor*, vol. 1 (London: Jonas Brown, 1717): 4–5.

26. *The Female Tatler*, no. 81 (9–11 January 1710).

27. Matt. Morgan, dedication 'To The Highly Honour'd, the Lady M.S.', *A Poem to the Queen, Upon the King's Victory in Ireland, and his Voyage to Holland* (Oxford, 1691), A1r.

28. Mary Granville Pendarves Delany to Anne Granville Dewes, 5 January 1759, *The Autobiography and Correspondence of Mrs. Delany*, vol. 2 (Boston, 1879), 65–66.

29. Mary Granville Pendarves Delany to Anne Granville Dewes, 9 June 1757 , *The Autobiography and Correspondence of Mrs. Delany*, vol. 2, 37.

30. Voltaire [François Marie Arouet] to Nicolas Claude Thieriot, 26 May 1732, *Digital Correspondence of Voltaire*, ed. N. Cronk and T.D.N. Besterman, 2008, https://doi.org/10.13051 /ee:doc/voltfrVF0860191a1c.

31. Samuel Bury, *An Account of the Life and Death of Mrs Elizabeth Bury, Who Died, May the 11th 1720. Collected Chiefly out of her own Diary*, 2nd ed. (London, 1721), 7.

32. See Penelope Wilson, 'Women Writers and the Classics', *The Oxford History of Classical Reception*, vol. 3.

33. Kathryn Shevelow, *Women and Print Culture: The Construction of Femininity in the Early Periodical* (London: Routledge, 1989), 34–35.

34. Sarah Lindenbaum, 'Hiding in Plain Sight: How Electronic Records Can Lead Us to Early Modern Women Readers', *Women's Bookscapes in Early Modern Britain: Reading, Ownership, Circulation*, ed. Leah Knight, Micheline White, and Elizabeth Sauer (Ann Arbor: University of Michigan Press, 2018), 193–213; Sarah Lindenbaum, 'Memorializing the Everyday: The Evidence of the Final Decade of Frances Wolfreston's Life', *The Seventeenth Century* 37, no. 3 (2022): 449–76.

35. John Dryden, *The Satires of Decimus Junius Juvenalis. Translated into English Verse* (London: Jacob Tonson, 1693), Milner Library, Illinois State University, Special Collections PA6447. E5 D7 1693. Sarah Lindenbaum and Tara Lyons, 'John Dryden, Satires of Juvenal and Persius (1693)', *Early Modern Female Book Ownership*, 24 August 2020, https://earlymodernfemaleboo kownership.wordpress.com/2020/08/24/anne-wolferstan-dryden/.

36. Dryden, *The Satires of Decimus Junius Juvenalis*, lii.

37. Dryden, *The Satires of Decimus Junius Juvenalis*, 87.

38. Amanda Vickery, *The Gentleman's Daughter: Women's Lives in Georgian England* (New Haven, CT: Yale University Press, 1998), 226; Rosemary Sweet, *Cities and the Grand Tour: The British in Italy c.1690–1820* (Cambridge: Cambridge University Press, 2012), 30–31.

39. Matthew Prideaux, 'To the Reader', *An Easy and Compendious Introduction for Reading All Sorts of Histories Contrived in a More Facile Way Then Heretofore Hath Been Published*, 5th ed. (Oxford: Leon Lichfield, 1672).

40. We now know more about the culture of amateur translation in this period, the golden age of English neoclassicism, but even so, this work of retrieval of 'ordinary' classicism has privileged accuracy and aesthetic quality, obscuring the bumbling, the inaccurate, or the uninspired classical author, and offering little sense of the amateur reader in this period. In *Newly Recovered English Classical Translations, 1600–1800*, Stuart Gillespie rejects the 'feebly prosaic' and states that 'this edition is by no means intended to rescue translations which went unprinted because they were not good enough', 7.

41. See Gallagher, *Learning Languages*, 11. Peter Burke, '"Heu Domine, Adsunt Turcae": A Sketch for a Social History of Post-Medieval Latin', *The Art of Conversation* (Cambridge: Polity, 1993), 34–65; Burke, 'Latin: A Language in Search of a Community', *Languages and*

*Communities in Early Modern Europe* (Cambridge: Cambridge University Press, 2004): 43–60; J.W. Binns, *Intellectual Culture in Elizabethan and Jacobean England: The Latin Writings of the Age* (Leeds, UK: Francis Cairns, 1990).

42. Francoise Waquet, *Latin, or, the Empire of a Sign: From the Sixteenth to the Twentieth Centuries,* transl. John Howe (London: Verso, 2001), 132–34. On Greek in early modern England, see Micha Lazarus, 'Greek Literacy in Sixteenth-Century England', *Renaissance Studies* 29, no. 3 (2015): 433–58.

43. James Binns, 'The Decline of Latin in Eighteenth-Century England', *Britannia Latina: Latin in the Culture of Great Britain from the Middle Ages to the Twentieth Century,* ed. Charles Burnett and Nicholas Mann (London: Warburg Institute, 2005), 170–77.

44. Binns, 'The Decline of Latin', 175–77.

45. For a thoughtful discussion of the background to eighteenth-century neoclassicism, see Joseph M. Levine, 'Why Neoclassicism? Politics and Culture in Eighteenth-Century England', *British Journal for Eighteenth-Century Studies* 25 (2002), 75–101.

46. See, for example, Lazarus, 'Greek Literacy in Sixteenth Century England'.

47. On the material form of the Chronicles, see Anna Marar and Abigail Williams, '"The Tennis Ball of Fortune": Print, Manuscript, and Provincial Literacies in the Chronicles of John Cannon', forthcoming 2023/4 in special issue of *Eighteenth-Century Life* on 'The Manuscript Book', ed. Betty Schellenberg and Alexis Chema.

48. John Cannon, *The Chronicles of John Cannon, Excise Officer and Writing Master,* 2 vols, vol. 1, ed. John Money (London: British Academy/Oxford University Press, 2010), cxxxi.

49. *Chronicles of John Cannon*, vol. 1, 174.

50. *Chronicles of John Cannon*, vol. 1, 28–29.

51. *Chronicles of John Cannon*, vol. 1, 174, note 376.

52. The stricture before 'Sing not . . .', for instance, reads: 'Put not thy hand in the presence of others to any part of thy body, not ordinarily discovered'. John Garretson, *The School of Manners. Or Rules for Childrens Behaviour: At Church, at Home, at Table, in Company, in Discourse, at School, abroad, and among Boys,* 4th ed. (London, 1701), 38–39.

53. *Chronicles of John Cannon*, vol. 2, 308, 312.

54. *Chronicles of John Cannon*, vol. 1, 156.

55. *Chronicles of John Cannon*, vol. 2, 312.

56. *Chronicles of John Cannon*, vol.2, 567–8.

57. *Chronicles of John Cannon*, vol. 2, 332.

58. *Chronicles of John Cannon*, vol. 2, 332.

59. Paul Davis, *Translation and the Poet's Life: The Ethics of Translating in English Culture, 1646–1726* (Oxford: Oxford University Press, 2008); David Hopkins, *Conversing with Antiquity: English Poets and the Classics from Shakespeare to Pope* (Oxford: Oxford University Press, 2009); *Oxford History of Literary Translation in English, 1660–1790,* vol. 3, ed. Stuart Gillespie and David Hopkins (Oxford: Oxford University Press, 2005); Robin Sowerby, *The Augustan Art of Poetry: Augustan Translation of the Classics* (Oxford: Oxford University Press, 2006).

60. Alexander Pope, *The First Satire of the Second Book of Horace, Imitated in Dialogue* (London, 1734), William Andrews Clark Memorial Library, UCLA, Clark Library UCLA, f PR3630. H8 F5 1734 *.

61. On the classical models influencing the poem, see Thomas E. Maresca, 'Pope's Defense of Satire: The First Satire of the Second Book of Horace, Imitated', *ELH* 31, no. 4 (Dec. 1964): 366–94, 379–80.

62. Pope, *The First Satire of the Second Book of Horace*, William Andrews Clark Memorial Library, UCLA, Clark Library UCLA, f PR3630.H8 F5 1734 *, A2, 5, 9.

63. Pope, *The First Satire of the Second Book of Horace*, William Andrews Clark Memorial Library, UCLA, Clark Library UCLA, f PR3630.H8 F5 1734 *, 11.

64. Pope, *The First Satire of the Second Book of Horace*, William Andrews Clark Memorial Library, UCLA, Clark Library UCLA, f PR3630.H8 F5 1734 *, 13, 35.

65. See Joseph M Levine, *The Battle of the Books: History and Literature in the Augustan Age* (Ithaca, NY: Cornell University Press, 1991); Steven Shapin, '"A Scholar and a Gentleman": The Problematic Identity of the Scientific Practitioner in Early Modern England', *History of Science* 29, no. 3 (Sep. 1991): 279–327.

66. For a fuller discussion, see Levine, *Battle of the Books*, 2.

67. Sir William Temple, 'Essay Upon Ancient and Modern Learning', *Miscellanea. The Second Part in Four Essays*, 2nd ed. (London, 1690), A4–75, 57.

68. Temple, 'Essay Upon Ancient and Modern Learning', 61.

69. Temple, 'Essay Upon Ancient and Modern Learning', 61.

70. Charles Boyle, *Phalaridos Akragantinōn tyrannou Epistolai* (Oxford, 1695).

71. Richard Bentley, *A Dissertation upon the Epistles of Phalaris, Themistocles, Socrates, Euripides, and Others, and the Fables of Æsop* (London, 1697), 16.

72. Bentley, *Dissertation*, 51.

73. Bentley, *Dissertation*, 58, 62.

74. See Shapin, '"A Scholar and a Gentleman"'.

75. George Smalridge to Walter Gough, 22 February 1697–98, in John Nichols, *Illustrations of the Literary History of the Eighteenth Century: Consisting of Authentic Memoirs and Original Letters of Eminent Persons*, 8 vols, vol. 3 (London, 1818): 268–69.

76. Charles Boyle, *Dr. Bentley's Dissertations on the Epistles of Phalaris, and the Fables of Æsop* (London, 1698), 223.

77. Boyle, *Dr. Bentley's Dissertations*, 225–26.

78. Alexander Pope, preface to *The Iliad of Homer: Translated by Mr Pope*, 6 vols, vol. 1 (London, 1715).

79. For a fuller discussion of the edition, see Kristine Haugen, *Richard Bentley: Poetry and Enlightenment* (Cambridge, MA: Harvard University Press, 2011), 125–54.

80. Haugen, *Richard Bentley: Poetry and Enlightenment*, 130–31. On the enduring appeal of Horace for elite English readers, see E.J. Kenney, '"A Little of it Sticks": the Englishman's Horace', *Britannia Latina: Latin in the Culture of Great Britain from the Middle Ages to the Twentieth Century*, ed. Charles Burnett and Nicholas Mann (London: Warburg Institute, 2005), 178–93.

81. Haugen, *Richard Bentley: Poetry and Enlightenment*, 132.

82. From Richard Bentley's preface to Horace, *Q. Horatius Flaccus*, ed. Richard Bentley (Cantabrigiae, 1711), C2r: '*Horum* [Bentley's readers] *ego ut praejudicio &ανθολκη occurrerem; fuse pleraque & prolixe praeter morem meum in adnotationibus deduxi: ut vel indignantes ac*

*reluctantes cum rationum pondere tum exemplorum numero obruerem, inque meam tandem sententiam vel obtorto eos collo traherem'.* Cited in Haugen, *Richard Bentley: Poetry and Enlightenment*, 133.

83. Jonathan Swift, *A Tale of a Tub. Written for the Universal Improvement of Mankind*, 5th ed. (1710), *A Tale of a Tub and Other Works*, ed. Marcus Walsh (Cambridge: Cambridge University Press, 2010), 82.

84. On the textual evolution of the *Tale*, see Walsh, Introduction to *A Tale of a Tub and Other Works*, xxxii–xxxv.

85. Charles Boyle, *Dr. Bentley's Dissertations on the Epistles of Phalaris, and the Fables of Æsop*, 2nd ed. (London, 1698).

86. Boyle, *Dr. Bentley's Dissertations*, 2nd ed., 145.

87. William King, 'A Short Account of Dr. Bentley by Way of Index', in Charles Boyle, *Dr. Bentley's Dissertations on the Epistles of Phalaris, and the Fables of Aesop*, 4th ed. (London, 1745).

88. On the history of the index in this period, see Dennis Duncan, *Index, a History of the: A Bookish Adventure* (London: Allen Lane, 2021).

## Chapter 4: The Literary Reader

1. For a summary of the evolution of criticism and of the nature of the critic, see Douglas Lane Patey, 'The Institution of Criticism in the Eighteenth Century', *The Cambridge History of Literary Criticism*, vol. 4, ed. H.B. Nisbet and Claude Rawson (Cambridge: Cambridge University Press, 1997), 3–31. On the idea of taste and the reading public, see David Marshall, 'Shaftesbury and Addison: Criticism and the Public Taste', *Cambridge History of Literary Criticism*, vol. 4, 633–57. For Habermas's account, see: Jürgen Habermas, *The Structural Transformation of the Public Sphere: An Inquiry into a Category of Bourgeois Society* (Darmstadt: Hermann Luchterhand, 1962), trans. Thomas Burger with Frederick Lawrence (Cambridge, MA: MIT Press, 1989), 56. For accounts endorsing a Habermasian view of the public sphere, see Scott Black, 'Social and Literary Form in the Spectator', *Eighteenth-Century Studies* 33, no. 1 (1999): 21–42; Michael Ketcham, *Transparent Designs: Reading, Performance and Form in the Spectator Papers* (Athens: University of Georgia Press, 1985).

2. On critical interest in the rise of public discourse, see the special issue of *Eighteenth-Century Studies* on 'The Public and the Nation', *Eighteenth-Century Studies* 29, no. 1 (1995).

3. John Periam, annotations to Mark Akenside, *The Pleasures of Imagination: A Poem in Three Books*, 3rd ed. (London: 1744), William Andrews Clark Memorial Library, UCLA, PR3312 .P71 1744 *, 45, 40, 105, 133.

4. Thomas Turner, diary entry for 14 June 1758, *The Diary of Thomas Turner, 1754–1765*, ed. David Vaisey (Oxford: Oxford University Press, 1984), 153.

5. Thomas Turner, diary entry for Saturday, Mar 1 1755, Transcript of Thomas Turner's Diaries, East Sussex Record Office, AMS 6532/1, 33.

6. Turner, diary entry for 28 February 1756, *Diary of Thomas Turner*, ed. Vaisey, 32.

7. Hugh Dalrymple Murray Kynynmound, Minto Papers, National Library of Scotland, MS 12811 15–30, fol. 19v.

8. John Dryden, 'Life of Lucian', *The Works of John Dryden: Prose 1691–1698*, ed. A Wallace Maurer and George R. Guffey (Berkeley: University of California Press, 1989), 223. The Life was probably written in 1696 but not published until after Dryden's death in 1711. See *Works of John Dryden: Prose 1691–1698*, 370.

9. John Dryden, 'The Authors Apology for Heroique Poetry; and Poetique Licence', preface to *The State of Innocence* (1677), *The Works of John Dryden: Plays; Amboyna; The State of Innocence; Aureng-Zebe*, ed. Vinton A. Dearing (Berkeley: University of California Press, 1994), 86.

10. Dryden, 'The Authors Apology for Heroique Poetry; and Poetique Licence', 87.

11. Henry Felton, *A Discussion of Reading the Classics and Forming a Just Style* (London, 1713), 76.

12. On the evolution of the concept of criticism in this period, see Patey, 'The Institution of Criticism in the Eighteenth Century', 3–4.

13. Patey, 'The Institution of Criticism in the Eighteenth Century', 6. For a good discussion of the tension between generalist and expert criticism in the period, see Jonathan Brody Kramnick, 'Literary Criticism Among the Disciplines', *Eighteenth-Century Studies* 35, no. 3 (2002): 343–60.

14. See Helen Berry, *Gender, Society and Print Culture in Late-Stuart England: The Cultural World of the Athenian Mercury* (Aldershot, UK: Ashgate 2003); Rachael Scarborough King, '"Interloping with my Question-Project": Debating Genre in John Dunton's and Daniel Defoe's Epistolary Periodicals', *Studies in Eighteenth-Century Culture* 44, no. 1 (2015): 121–42, 128.

15. 'Advertisement', *The Athenian Gazette* 1, no. 1 (17 March 1690 [1691]).

16. *The Athenian Gazette: Or Casuistical Mercury. Resolving all the most Nice and Curious Questions Proposed by the Ingenious*, vol. 1 (London, 1691), title page.

17. 'Quest. 4', *Athenian Mercury* 20, no. 1 (14 May 1697).

18. 'Quest. 3', 'Quest. 4', 'Quest. 6', *Athenian Mercury* 20, no. 3 (21 May 1697).

19. 'Quest. 4', *Athenian Mercury* 20, no. 4 (24 May 1697).

20. Charles Gildon, *The History of the Athenian Society, For the Resolving all Nice and Curious Questions* (London, 1692), 4.

21. 'Quest. 7', *Athenian Mercury* 20, no. 1 (14 May 1697).

22. 'Quest. 5', *Athenian Mercury* 20, no. 3 (21 May 1697).

23. On the evolution of the various volumes of the *Art of Poetry* from 1702 onwards, see A. Dwight Culler, 'Edward Bysshe and the Poet's Handbook', *PMLA* 63, no. 3 (1948): 858–85, 861–62.

24. Edward Bysshe, *The Art of English Poetry*, vol. 1 (London, 1702), title page.

25. Bysshe, *Art of English Poetry*, vol. 1, 201–3.

26. P. Dixon, 'Edward Bysshe and Pope's "Shakespear"', *Notes and Queries* 11, no. 8 (1964): 292–93; Michael E. Connaughton, 'Richardson's Familiar Quotations: "Clarissa" and Bysshe's "Art of English Poetry"', *Philological Quarterly* 60, no. 2 (1981): 183–95.

27. See Connaughton, 'Richardson's Familiar Quotations'.

28. Bysshe, *Art of English Poetry*, vol. 1, dedication.

29. Bysshe, *Art of English Poetry*, vol. 1, preface.

30. On the history of commonplacing in the early modern period and its continuation into the eighteenth century, see Ann Moss, *Printed Commonplace-books and the Structuring of*

*Renaissance Thought* (Oxford: Clarendon Press, 1996); David Allan, *Commonplace Books and Reading in Georgian England* (Cambridge: Cambridge University Press, 2010).

31. John Dryden, *Aureng Zebe, or the Great Mogul. A Tragedy* (London, 1690), Cardiff University Library, Rare Books Collection PR3415.A8.C90, 18–19.

32. Dryden, *Aureng Zebe*, Cardiff University Library, PR3415.A8.C90, 15.

33. Dryden, *Aureng Zebe*, Cardiff University Library, PR3415.A8.C90, title page, verso.

34. Henry Felton, *A Discussion of Reading the Classics and Forming a Just Style* (London, 1713), 41–42.

35. *The Works of Mr. William Shakespear; in eight volumes. Adorn'd with cutts. Revis'd and corrected, with an account of the life and writings of the author, by N. Rowe, Esq; to this edition is added, a table of the most sublime passages in this author* (London, 1714), National Trust Townend Library, Troutbeck, 3074274.1–9.

36. *The Works of Mr. William Shakespear*, vol. 6, Townend Library, Troutbeck, 3074274.6, 125.

37. *The Works of Mr. William Shakespear*, vol. 6, Townend Library, Troutbeck, 3074274.6, 18.

38. *The Works of Mr. William Shakespear*, vol. 6, Townend Library, Troutbeck, 3074274.6, 70.

39. *The Works of Mr. William Shakespear*, vol. 6, Townend Library, Troutbeck, 3074274.6, 72.

40. *The Works of Mr. William Shakespear*, vol. 6, Townend Library, Troutbeck, 3074274.6, 74.

41. *The Works of Mr. William Shakespear*, vol. 6, Townend Library, Troutbeck, 3074274.6, 361.

42. As Lawrence E. Klein has observed, there is a 'fuzzy boundary' around authorship of these periodicals and their various essays. The *Tatler* and *Spectator* were produced collaboratively but often attributed to Addison alone by contemporaries and later eighteenth-century readers. In the discussion that follows, I use 'Addison' as a shorthand while recognizing the broader group of writers involved in the *periodicals*. Lawrence E. Klein, 'Addisonian Afterlives: Joseph Addison in Eighteenth-Century Culture, *Journal for Eighteenth-Century Studies* 35 (2012), 101–18.

43. See Lawrence E. Klein, 'The political significance of "politeness" in early eighteenth-century Britain', in Gorden J. Schochet, ed., *Politics, Politeness and Patriotism*, The Folger Institute Center for the History of British Political Thought Proceedings, vol. 5 (Washington DC, 1993), 73–108; Klein, *Shaftesbury and the Culture of Politeness: Moral Discourse and Cultural Politics in Early Eighteenth-Century England* (Cambridge: Cambridge University Press, 1994). For a qualification of the idea of politeness as an exclusively Whiggish concept, see Markku Peltonen, 'Politeness and Whiggism, 1688–1732', *Historical Journal* 48 (2005), 391–414.

44. *The Spectator*, no. 1 (1 March 1711), *The Spectator*, vol. 1, ed. Donald F. Bond (Oxford: Oxford University Press, 1987), 2.

45. *The Spectator*, no. 1 (1 March 1711), *The Spectator*, vol. 1, ed. Bond, 2.

46. *The Spectator*, no. 1 (1 March 1711), *The Spectator*, vol. 1, ed. Bond, 5.

47. *The Spectator*, no. 58 (7 May 1711), *The Spectator*, vol. 1, ed. Bond, 244–45.

48. On the tension between the denigration of pedantry and the role of virtuosic culture in the periodical, see Brian Cowan, 'The Curious Mr Spectator: Virtuoso Culture and the Man of Taste in the Works of Addison and Steele', *Media History* 14, no. 3 (2008): 275–92.

49. *The Spectator*, no. 58 (7 May 1711), *The Spectator*, vol. 1, ed. Bond, 246.

50. *The Spectator*, no. 4 (5 March 1711), *The Spectator*, vol. 1, ed. Bond, 21.

51. Kathryn Shevelow, *Women and Print Culture: The Construction of Femininity in the Early Periodical* (London: Routledge, 1989).

52. As Kathryn Shevelow has argued, the explicit claim to orient the publication towards women's reading levels also established a common denominator of both male and female reading levels: the female reader could be a shorthand for a class-based lack of higher education. Shevelow, *Women and Print Culture*, 34–35.

53. *The Spectator*, no. 10 (12 March 1711), *The Spectator*, vol. 1, ed. Bond, 44. Following the Stamp tax of August 1712, the price was raised to 2 pence. At this price it was no longer viable, and it closed within four months.

54. *The Spectator*, no. 10 (12 March 1711), *The Spectator*, vol. 1, ed. Bond, 44.

55. See Anthony Pollock: 'these normative principles functioned as a kind of pervasive fantasy or cultural fiction that served to perpetuate particular forms of hierarchy and exclusion'. Anthony Pollock, *Gender and the Fictions of the Public Sphere, 1660–1755* (London: Routledge, 2009), 6.

56. *The Spectator*, no. 568 (16 July 1714), *The Spectator*, vol. 4, ed. Bond, 540.

57. 'T.G.' *The Female Tatler*, no. 81 (9–11 January 1710).

58. See Pollock, *Gender and the Fictions of the Public Sphere*, 1–5.

59. *The Female Tatler*, no. 81 (9–11 January 1710).

60. Bonamy Dobrée, *English Literature in the Early Eighteenth Century, 1700–1740* (Oxford: Clarendon Press, 1959), 8. Brean S. Hammond, *Professional Imaginative Writing in England, 1670–1740: 'Hackney for Bread'* (Oxford: Oxford University Press, 1997), 185. T.S. Eliot, *The Use of Poetry and the Use of Criticism* (London: Faber and Faber, 1933, 7th ed., 1955), 62. Brian Cowan has argued persuasively that Addison and Steele's periodicals in fact sought to limit and tame Habermas's 'political public-ness'. Brian Cowan, 'Mr Spectator and the Coffeehouse Public Sphere', *Eighteenth-Century Studies* 37, no. 3 (Spring 2004): 345–66.

61. See Michael G. Ketcham: '*The Spectator*'s whole program embraces an expanding readership while it creates the balance of an intimate community'. Michael G. Ketcham, *Transparent Designs: Reading, Performance and Form in the Spectator Papers* (Athens: University of Georgia Press, 1985), 676. Iona Italia argues that over the course of *The Spectator*'s evolution the sociable fiction of the club of editors gives way to a more prominent use of the club of reader-correspondents. Iona Italia, *The Rise of Literary Journalism in the Eighteenth Century: Anxious Employment* (Abingdon, UK: Routledge, 2005), 66–92.

62. On the role of polite conversation as an embodiment of urbane sociability in this period, see: Lawrence E. Klein, *Shaftesbury and the Culture of Politeness: Moral Discourse and Cultural Politics in Early Eighteenth-Century England* (Cambridge: Cambridge University Press, 1994).

63. Margaret J.M. Ezell, 'The *Gentleman's Journal* and the Commercialization of Restoration Coterie Literary Practices', *Modern Philology* 89, no. 3 (Feb. 1991): 323–40.

64. Ezell, 'The *Gentleman's Journal* and the Commercialization of Restoration Coterie Literary Practices'.

65. James Boswell, journal entry for 1 December 1762, James Boswell, *Boswell's London Journal, 1762–1763*, ed. Frederick A. Pottle (London: Heinemann, 1950), 62.

66. Boswell, journal entry for 11 December 1762, Boswell, *London Journal*, 76.

67. For a longer discussion of the rhetoric of friendship and sociable exchange within the print culture of this period, see Dustin Griffin, 'The Social World of Authorship 1660–1714', *The Cambridge History of English Literature, 1660–1780*, ed. John Richetti (Cambridge: Cambridge University Press, 2005): 37–60.

68. Rachel Aroesti, 'Tragic but True: How Podcasters Replaced Our Real Friends', *The Guardian*, 7 June 2021, https://www.theguardian.com/tv-and-radio/2021/jun/07/tragic-but -true-have-podcasters-replaced-our-real-friends.

69. Dudley Ryder, diary entry for 13 October 1716, Dudley Ryder, *Diary of Dudley Ryder: 1715–1716*, ed. William Matthews (London: Methuen, 1939), 346.

70. Dudley Ryder, diary entry for 11 October 1715, *Diary of Dudley Ryder*, 117.

71. Dudley Ryder, diary entry for 18 June 1715, *Diary of Dudley Ryder*, 38.

72. Dudley Ryder, diary entry for 18 April 1716, *Diary of Dudley Ryder*, 223.

73. Dudley Ryder, diary entry for 2 July 1715, *Diary of Dudley Ryder*, 46.

74. Thomas Turner, diary entry for 26 June 1754, *Diary of Thomas Turner*, ed. Vaisey, 3.

75. William Shakespeare, *Othello, the Moor of Venice: A tragedy. As it hath been divers times acted at the Globe, and at the Black-Friars* (London, 1695), Cardiff University Library, Rare Books Collection, PR2829.A1.C95, title page, title page verso.

76. Joseph Addison and Richard Steele, *The Guardian*, no. 37 (Thursday 23 April 1713), *The Guardian*, vol. 1 (London, 1714), 149.

77. Joseph Addison and Richard Steele, *The Spectator* 9th ed. (London, 1729), National Trust Townend Library, Troutbeck, 3075055.1–8.

78. *The Spectator*, National Trust Townend Library, Troutbeck, 3075055.7, 165; 3075055.6, 141.

79. *The Spectator*, National Trust Townend Library, Troutbeck, 3075055.6, 18; 3075055.5, 249; 3075055.6, 99; 3075055.5, 126.

## Chapter 5: Mind the Gap: Reading Topically

1. George deF. Lord, 'Preface', *Poems on Affairs of State: Augustan Satirical Verse, 1660–1714*, vol. 1 (New Haven, CT: Yale University Press, 1963), vii–xiv, vii.

2. *The Country Parson's Advice to Those Little Scriblers Who Pretend to Write Better Sense Than Great Secretaries: Or, Mr Stephen's Triumph over the Pillory* (London, 1706); *Poor Robins Dream, or the Visions of Hell: with a Dialogue Between the Two Ghosts of Dr. T. and Capt. B.* (London, 1681).

3. *An Answer to the Great Noise about Nothing: or, a Noise about something* (London, 1705); *The Litany of The D. of B.* (c. 1679); *The Dog in the Wheel. A Satyr* (London, 1705); *Mordecai's Memorial: or, There's Nothing done for him. Being A Satyr upon Some-body, but I name No-body: (or, in plainer English, A Just and Generous Representation of Unrewarded Services, by which the Protestant Succession has been sav'd out of Danger)* (London, 1716).

4. *The Plotters; A Satire* (London, 1722), title page.

5. *The Plotters*, 1.

6. *The Plotters*, 10.

7. *The Plotters*, 4.

8. Paul Whitehead, *The State Dunces: Inscribed to Mr. Pope* (London, 1733), William Andrews Clark Memorial Library, UCLA, f PR3765.W3 S7 1733 *.

9. Abel Evans, *The Apparition. A Poem. A Dialogue Betwixt the Devil and a Doctor Concerning a Book Falsly call'd, The Rights of the Christian Church*, 2nd ed. (London, 1710), title page.

10. There were two editions in 1710, and two more in 1726.

11. According to the ESTC there are twenty-six copies of the first edition (ESTC T22250) in UK libraries, thirty-eight in North American research libraries, and two in Australia. There are sixteen copies of the second edition (ESTC T22251) in UK research libraries, thirteen in North American libraries, and two in Australia and New Zealand.

12. On the controversy around Tindal and his writings, see Dmitri Levitin, 'Matthew Tindal's *Rights of the Christian Church* (1706) and the Church-State Relationship', *The Historical Journal* 54, no. 3 (2011): 717–40.

13. Abel Evans, *The Apparition. A Poem* (London, 1710), Bodleian Library, Oxford, G. Pamph 1600 (2).

14. Abel Evans, *The Apparition. A Poem* (London, 1710), 4.

15. The following copies share this identification of each of the three missing names and words in the passage: *The Apparition*, 2nd ed. (London, 1710), Bodleian Library, University of Oxford, G. Pamph 61 (4); *The Apparition* (Oxford, 1710), British Library, 11623 d.2. The owner or reader of the following pirated edition was only able to complete the name 'Burgess': *The Apparition* (Dublin, 1710), Bodleian Library, University of Oxford, Vet.A4f.2039.

16. *The Apparition* (London, 1710), 22, 16, 24.

17. Copies consulted include *The Apparition*, 2nd ed. (London, 1710), Bodleian Library, University of Oxford, G. Pamph 61 (4); *The Apparition* (Oxford, 1710), British Library, 11623 d.2; *The Apparition* (Dublin, 1710), Bodleian Library, University of Oxford, Vet.A4f.2039; *The Apparition* (London, Oxford, 1710), British Library, 11642.bb.58; *The Apparition* (London, 1710), St John's College, Oxford, HB4/Folios.3.4.Box(21); *The Apparition*, Bodleian Library, Oxford, G. Pamph 1600 (2).

18. *The Appartion* [*sic*] (London, Oxford, 1710), British Library, 11642.bb.58.

19. *The Apparition* (Oxford, 1710), British Library, 11623.d.2, 6.

20. Evans, *The Apparition*, Bodleian Library, Oxford, G. Pamph 1600 (2).

21. Evans, *The Apparition*, Bodleian Library, Oxford, G. Pamph 1600 (2), 13, 15, 18, 20, 22, 26.

22. *The Apparition* (London, 1710), St John's College, Oxford, HB4/Folios.3.4.Box(21).

23. *Poems on Affairs of State: Augustan Satirical Verse, 1660–1714*, ed. George deF. Lord, 7 vols (New Haven, CT: Yale University Press, 1963–75).

24. Robert D. Hume, '"Satire" in the Reign of Charles II', *Modern Philology* 102, no. 3 (Feb. 2005): 332–71, 343–44.

25. DeF. Lord, 'Introduction', *Poems on Affairs of State*, vol. 1, xxxii.

26. Bonamy Dobrée, *English Literature in the Early Eighteenth Century, 1700–1740* (Oxford: Clarendon Press, 1959), 129.

27. Frank H. Ellis, headnote to *The Dispensary*, *Poems on Affairs of State*, vol. 6, 61.

28. John F. Sena, 'Samuel Garth's *The Dispensary*', *Texas Studies in Literature and Language* 15, no. 4 (Winter 1974): 639–48, 640.

29. *A Compleat Key to The Dispensary* (London, 1726); *A Compleat Key to the Seventh Edition of The Dispensary* (London, 1714); *A Compleat Key to the Eighth Edition of the Dispensary* (London, 1718). There are many surviving keys that survive; see *Poems on Affairs of State*, vol. 6, 62.

30. 'The Preface', Samuel Garth, *The Dispensary: A Poem in Six Cantos*, 2nd ed. (London, 1699).

31. Editorial footnote to *The Dispensary*, *Poems on Affairs of State*, vol. 6, 75–76.

32. Editorial footnote to *The Dispensary, Poems on Affairs of State*, vol. 6, 64–65.

33. Samuel Garth, *The Dispensary. A Poem. In Six Canto's*, 6th ed. (London, 1706), Wadham College Library, University of Oxford, A33.9, 46.

34. Michael McKeon, 'What Were Poems on Affairs of State?' *1650–1850: Ideas, Aesthetics, and Inquiries in the Early Modern Era* 4 (1997): 363–82, 367.

35. Narcissus Luttrell, *A Brief Historical Relation of State Affairs from September 1678 to April 1714, six vols* (Oxford: University Press, 1857).

36. Edmond Malone, *The Critical and Miscellaneous Prose Works of John Dryden, now first collected: with notes and illustrations; an account of the life and writings of the author, grounded on original and authentick documents; and a collection of his letters, the greater part of which has never before been published*, vol. 1, part 1 (London, 1800), 156.

37. On Luttrell's reading habits and engagement with political culture, see Tim Somers, 'The "Impartiality" of Narcissus Luttrell's Reading Practices and Historical Writing, 1679–1710', *The Historical Journal* 62, no. 4 (December 2019): 921–41.

38. James M. Osborn, 'Reflections on Narcissus Luttrell 1657–1732', *The Book Collector* 6 (1957), 15–27, 22.

39. Edmund Stacy, *The Black-Bird's Second Tale. A Poem* (London, 1710), British Library, 164.k. 35, title page; Francis Quarles, *The Whig's Exaltation; A Pleasant New Song of 82. To an Old Tune of 41* (1682), Huntington Library, call no. 135827, 49.

40. *An Address to the Honorable City of London . . . Concerning their Choice of a New Parliament* (1681), copy owned by Narcissus Luttrell, annotation cited by Osborn, 'Reflections on Narcissus Luttrell', 23.

41. *Commendatory Verses on the Author of the Two Arthurs, and the Satyr against Wit; By some of his particular friends* (London, 1700), William Andrews Clark Memorial Library, UCLA, f PR3318.B5 Z8c \*, title page.

42. Paul Nash, 'The "Wits" who beset Sir Richard Blackmore', *St Edmund Hall Magazine* 18, no. 6 (October 2015): 143–49, 144.

43. Luttrell owned and annotated a copy of: Daniel Kenrick, *A New Session of the Poets, Occasion'd by the Death of Mr. Dryden* (London, 1700), William Andrews Clark Memorial Library, UCLA, f PR3539.K22 N5 \*.

44. *Commendatory Verses on the Author of the Two Arthurs*, William Andrews Clark Memorial Library, UCLA, f PR3318.B5 Z8c \*, 1, 8, 16, 25.

45. For examples of this kind of annotation, see *A Trip to Nottingham. With a Character of Mareschal Tallard and the French-Generals* (London, 1705), William Andrews Clark Memorial Library, UCLA, f PR3291.T823 \*; *Almonds for Parrots: Or, A Soft Answer To a Scurrilous Satyr, call'd, St James's Park. With a Word or two in Praise of Condons* (London, 1708), William Andrews Clark Memorial Library, UCLA, f PR3291.A452 \*; Ned Ward, *The Devil's Journey to London: Or, The Visit Repaid* (London, 1700), William Andrews Clark Memorial Library, UCLA, f PR3757. W8 Z8d \*.

46. *The Tune to the Devonshire Cant: or, An answer to the Parliament dissolved at Oxford* (1681), Huntington Library, call no. 135792, 14.

47. *The Irish Rendezvouz, or a Description of T——ll's Army of Tories and Bog-Trotters* (London, 1689), British Library, BL C.107.k.19.

48. *Corona Civica, A Poem, To The Right Honourable the Lord-Keeper of the Great Seal of England* (London, 1706), William Andrews Clark Memorial Library, UCLA, f PR3745.V75 C8 *.

49. *A New Collection of Poems Relating to State Affairs, from Oliver Cromwel To this present Time: by the Greatest Wits of the Age* (London, 1705), British Library, C 28.e.15.

50. *A New Collection of Poems Relating to State Affairs*, British Library, C 28.e.15, 100, 133.

51. For good examples of individual readers reading across political or religious divides, see Geoff Baker, *Reading and Politics in Early Modern England: The Mental World of a Seventeenth-Century Catholic Gentleman* (Manchester, UK: Manchester University Press, 2010), 112; on the evidence of eclectic tastes in the reading of religious works in early modern England and Europe, see Kevin Sharpe, *Reading Revolutions: The Politics of Reading in Early Modern England* (New Haven, CT: Yale University Press, 2000), 283–84.

52. On the emergence of the online filter bubble and its consequences, see Eli Pariser, *The Filter Bubble: What the Internet is Hiding from You* (New York: Penguin, 2011).

53. The Yale POAS editors remark of Alexander Pope's annotations in his copy of Garth's *Dispensary* at the Huntington Library, 'disappointing [. . .] he offers nothing worth recording'. *Poems on Affairs of State*, vol. 6, 726.

54. *A Collection of Poems Relating to State Affairs* (London, 1705), Osborn Collection, Beinecke Library, Yale University, pc268.

55. Samuel Garth, *The Dispensary. A Poem in Six Cantos*, 6th ed. (London, 1706), British Library, 1162.h.17(1).

56. *The Dispensary. A Poem in Six Canto's*, 5th ed. (London, 1703), British Library, 991.k.27.

57. *The Dispensary*, British Library, 991.k.27, 44.

58. *The Story of the St Alb-ns Ghost, or The Apparition of Mother Haggy*, 4th ed. (London, 1712), William Andrews Clark Memorial Library, UCLA, PR3747 .W5 S8 1712b *.

59. *The Story of the St Alb-ns Ghost*, William Andrews Clark Memorial Library, PR3747 .W5 S8 1712b *, title page, verso.

60. *The Seditious Insects: or, The Levellers Assembled in Convocation. A Poem* (London, 1708), William Andrews Clark Memorial Library, UCLA, f PR3291 .S448.

61. Richard Blackmore, *A Satyr Against Wit* (London, 1700), William Andrews Clark Memorial Library, UCLA, f PR3318.B5 S2 1700a *.

62. *Manlius or the Brave Adventurer: A Poetical Novel* (Edinburgh, 1749), British Library, General Reference Collection 1600/66.

63. *Manlius*, British Library, GRC 1600/66, 3.

64. *Manlius*, British Library, GRC 1600/66, 24.

## Chapter 6: The Intimacy of Omission

1. On approaches to teaching the poem, see Arlene Wilner, 'Text and Theory: Teaching *The Rape of the Lock*', CEA Critic 62, no. 1 (Fall 1999): 45–60, 47.

2. For a discussion of the challenges of interpreting the poem for students, see Wilner, 'Text and Theory: Teaching *The Rape of the Lock*'.

3. John Gay, *Trivia, John Gay: Poetry and Prose*, vol. 1, ed. Vinton A Dearing with Charles E Beckwith (Oxford: Clarendon Press, 1974), 134–81, 159.

4. Charles Gildon, *A New Rehearsal, or Bays the Younger* (London, 1714), 42.

5. William Hazlitt, 'On Dryden and Pope', *Lectures on the English Poets* (London, 1818): 135–67, 143.

6. Maynard Mack, *Alexander Pope: A Life* (New Haven, CT: Yale University Press, 1985), 248.

7. Aubrey Williams, 'The "Fall" of China and *The Rape of the Lock*', *Philological Quarterly* 41, no. 2 (April 1962): 412–25, 425.

8. John Dixon Hunt, 'Introduction', *Pope: The Rape of the Lock, A Selection of Critical Essays* (Basingstoke, UK: Macmillan, 1968): 11–20, 20.

9. Laura Brown, 'Imperialism and Poetic Form: *The Rape of the Lock* (1712, 1714, 1717), *Windsor-Forest* (1713)', in *Alexander Pope* (Oxford: Blackwell, 1985), 6–45; Stewart Crehan, '"The Rape of the Lock" and the Economy of "Trivial Things,"' *Eighteenth-Century Studies* 31, no. 1 (Fall 1997): 45–68.

10. Ellen Pollak, *The Poetics of Sexual Myth: Gender and Ideology in the Verse of Swift and Pope* (Chicago: Chicago University Press, 1985); Rebecca Ferguson, '"Quick as Her Eyes, and as unfix'd as those": Objectification and Seeing in Pope's *Rape of the Lock*', *Critical Survey* 4, no. 2 (1992): 140–46. More recently these considerations of gender have responded to the developing field of animal studies and the material turn. See, for example Laura Brown's arguments about the role of the lap dog in 'The Lady, The Lap Dog and Literary Alterity', *The Eighteenth Century* 52, no. 1 (2011): 31–45, 35–36; Elizabeth Kowaleski Wallace, 'The Things Don't Say: *The Rape of the Lock*, Vitalism, and New Materialism', *The Eighteenth Century* 59, no. 1 (2018): 105–22. See also Don Nichol, *Anniversary Essays on Alexander Pope's The Rape of the Lock* (Toronto: University of Toronto Press, 2016).

11. For a fuller description of the background to the poem and its conception, see: Geoffrey Tillotson (ed.), introduction to *The Rape of the Lock*, Alexander Pope, *The Rape of the Lock, and Other Poems* (London: Methuen, 1966): 81–105; Paul Baines and Julian Ferraro (eds), editors' headnote to *The Rape of the Locke*, Alexander Pope, *The Poems of Alexander Pope*, vol. 1 (London: Routledge, 2019), 477–84.

12. Joseph Spence, *Observations, Anecdotes, and Characters, of Books and Men* (London, 1820), 20–21.

13. On the composition and publication history of the poem, see Baines and Ferraro, *The Poems of Alexander Pope*, 478.

14. Spence, *Observations*, I, 44. Cited by Joseph Hone, *Alexander Pope in the Making* (Oxford: Oxford University Press, 2021), 49. Authors could use the real or invented threat of piracy to their own advantage. In Pope's case, he had little to gain financially from the manuscript circulation, but with the authorized second print five-canto version he made a considerable profit.

15. Alexander Pope to John Caryll, 8 November 1712, *The Correspondence of Alexander Pope*, vol. 1, ed. George Sherburn (Oxford: Clarendon Press, 1956), 151.

16. *The Plotters; a Satire* (London, 1722), 3–4.

17. Pope to Caryll, 8 November 1712, *Correspondence of Alexander Pope*, vol. 1, ed. Sherburn, 151; Pope, *The Rape of the Locke*, *The Poems of Alexander Pope*, vol. 1, ed. Baines and Ferraro: 477–520, 506. Further references to *The Rape of the Locke* in parenthesis in main text are to this edition.

18. Pope to Caryll, 12 June 1713, *Correspondence of Alexander Pope*, vol. 1, ed. Sherburn, 177.

19. Pope to Caryll, 12 March 1714, *Correspondence of Alexander Pope*, vol. 1, ed. Sherburn, 214.

20. Pope to Caryll, 15 December 1713, *Correspondence of Alexander Pope*, vol. 1, ed. Sherburn, 203.

21. Pope, 'To Mrs. Arabella Fermor', *The Rape of the Lock*, ed. Tillotson, 142.

22. Pope to Caryll, 9 January 1714, *Correspondence of Alexander Pope*, vol. 1, ed. Sherburn, 207.

23. Pope to Caryll, 25 February 1714, *Correspondence of Alexander Pope*, vol. 1, ed. Sherburn, 210.

24. J. Paul Hunter, 'Poetry of Occasions', *A Concise Companion to the Restoration and Eighteenth Century*, ed. Cynthia Wall (Oxford: Wiley, 2005): 202–25, 216.

25. Alexander Pope, *The Rape of the Lock: An Heroi-Comical Poem in Five Canto's*, 2nd ed. (London, 1714), The Queen's College Library, University of Oxford, PP.e.187[1], 1.

26. *The Rape of the Lock, an Heroi-Comical Poem, in Five Canto's*, 3rd ed. (London, 1714), Bodleian Library, University of Oxford, 12 Theta 1145, 7, 20. It is possible the 'R Stewart/Steurt' might stand for 'Regina Stuart'—i.e., Queen Anne. In *Alexander Pope in the Making* Joe Hone discusses the political readings on offer in *Key to the Lock*, and the way in which the *Key* identified Belinda as the late Queen Anne. Joseph Hone, *Alexander Pope in the Making* (Oxford: Oxford University Press, 2021), 145–50.

27. The tradition seems to stem from Joseph Warton's late eighteenth-century edition of Pope's works: in a note to book 1 of the poem, he makes the connection and identifies his manuscript source: '"Thalestris was Mrs. Morly; Sir Plume was her brother, Sir George Brown, of Berkshire". Copied from a MS. in a book presented by R. Lord Burlington, to Mr. William Sherwin'. *The Works of Alexander Pope, Esq. In nine volumes, complete. With notes and illustrations by Joseph Warton, D.D. and others* (London, 1797), vol. 1, 284. The Reverend William Sherwin dedicated a manuscript entitled 'Some remarks upon Bishop (Gilbert) Burnet's History of His Own Times' to Dorothy, Countess of Burlington in 1725 and corresponded with the Burlingtons about health matters in the early 1730s (Cambridge University Library, GBR/0012/MS Add.4022; Chatsworth, GB 2495 CS1/199). He was probably the William Sherwin, chaplain to Charles, second Duke of Richmond and Lennox, who was buried at St James's church, Bath, on 5 May 1735 (William Sherwin | Bath Record Office, batharchives.co.uk). I am very grateful to Valerie Rumbold for sharing this emerging research with me.

28. Robert Carruthers, ed., *The Poetical Works of Alexander Pope*, 4 vols (London, 1853–54), vol. II, 218–19. Neither of the two documents sometimes called in evidence about Mrs Morley (a will in which Sir George Browne's uncle names a niece called Elisabeth Morley, and the register of Sir George's marriage to a Gertrude Morley) identifies the Morley family (or families) involved. In the absence of further evidence, this suggests that the claimed links to John Morley result from his celebrity, his attested friendship with Pope, and his having the same surname (Frederick Brown, *Abstracts of Somersetshire Wills, third series*, ed. Arthur Crisp (privately printed, 1889), 66–67; F. Collins, *The Registers and Monumental Inscriptions of Charterhouse Chapel* (1892), 10).

29. Pope, 'To Mrs Arabella Fermor', *The Rape of the Lock*, ed. Tillotson, 143.

30. For a fuller discussion of the publication of this second edition, see James McLaverty, *Pope, Print, and Meaning* (Oxford: Oxford University Press, 2001), 14–24.

31. Wilner, 'Text and Theory: Teaching *The Rape of the Lock*', 48.

32. Pope, 'To Mrs Arabella Fermor', *The Rape of the Lock*, ed. Tillotson, 142.

33. Joseph Warton, *An Essay on the Writings and Genius of Pope* (London, 1756), 220.

34. Gildon, *A New Rehearsal*, 43; John Oldmixon, *The Catholick Poet; Or, Protestant Barnaby's Sorrowful Lamentation: An Excellent New Ballad* (London, 1716), 1.

35. Esdras Barnivelt [Alexander Pope], *A Key to the Lock. Or, a Treatise proving, beyond all Contradiction, the dangerous Tendency of a late Poem, entituled, The Rape of the Lock, To Government and Religion* (London, 1715).

36. For a summary of modern critical discussion of the political subtexts of the poem, see Hone, *Alexander Pope in the Making*, 146–48.

37. For a comprehensive guide to the many printed attacks on Pope at this time, see J.V. Guerinot, *Pamphlet Attacks on Alexander Pope, 1711–1744: A Descriptive Bibliography* (London: Methuen, 1969).

38. Pope, *A Key to the Lock*, 7.

39. Melinda Alliker Rabb, *Satire and Secrecy in English Literature from 1650–1750* (New York: Palgrave Macmillan, 2007), 141.

40. David Brewer, 'Secret History and Allegory', *The Secret History in Literature, 1660–1820*, ed. Rebecca Bullard and Rachel Carnell (Cambridge: Cambridge University Press, 2017): 60–73, 66.

41. Pope, *A Key to the Lock*, 9–10.

42. Jonathan Swift to Alexander Pope, 28 June 1715, *The Correspondence of Jonathan Swift, D.D.*, vol. 2, ed. David Woolley (Frankfurt am Main: Peter Lang, 2001), 133. On the topicality of the revised *Key*, see Hone, *Alexander Pope in the Making*, 148–49.

43. Mather Byles to Alexander Pope, 25 November 1728, *Correspondence of Alexander Pope*, vol. 2, ed. Sherburn, 528.

44. On the reinforcing of authorial attribution through annotation on title pages, see David A. Brewer, 'The Tactility of Authorial Names', *The Eighteenth Century* 54, no. 2 (Summer 2013): 195–213.

45. Hunter, 'Poetry of Occasions', 207–8.

46. *The Celebrated Beauties: Being an Heroick Poem, Made on the Colledge Green and Queen's Square Ladies* (Bristol, 1720).

47. *The Celebrated Beauties*, 5.

48. *The Celebrated Beauties: Being an Heroick Poem, Made on the Colledge Green and Queen's Square Ladies* (Bristol: Joseph Penn, 1720), Beinecke Library, Yale University, 2006 144.

49. Richard Poekrich, *The Temple-Oge Ballad* (Rathfarnham [Dublin], 1730).

50. See James E. May, 'False and Incomplete Imprints in Swift's Dublin, 1710–35', in *Reading Swift: Papers from the Seventh Muenster Symposium on Jonathan Swift*, ed. Janika Bischof, Kirsten Juhas, and Hermann J. Real (Munich: Wilhelm Fink, 2019): 59–99.

51. *The Temple-Oge Ballad*, 4.

52. *The Temple-Oge Ballad*, 7.

53. Richard Poekrich, *The Temple-Oge Ballad* (Rathfarnham [Dublin], 1730), British Library, 11631.a.36.

54. Elijah Fenton, *Oxford and Cambridge Miscellany Poems* (London, 1708).

55. According to the ESTC, there are fifteen copies of the volume in the UK, thirty-three in the US, and six elsewhere.

56. *Musapædia, Or Miscellany Poems, Never Before Printed. By Several members of the Oxford Poetical Club, late of Eton and Westminster* (London, 1719).

57. There are thirteen surviving copies of the first edition and eight of the second, a reissue.

58. On the inaccessibility of university references from one college to another, see Thomas Gray to Horace Walpole, 31 October 1734: 'For Gods sake send me your Quære's, & I'll do my best to get information upon those Points, you don't understand: I warrant, you imagine that People in one College, know the Customs of others; but you mistake, they are quite little Societies by themselves: ye Dresses, Language, Customs &c are different in different Colledges: what passes for Wit in one, would not be understood if it were carried to another: thus the Men of Peter-house, Pembroke & Clare-hall of course must be Tories; those of Trinity, Rakes; of Kings, Scholars; of Sidney, Wigs; of St Johns, Worthy men & so on'. *Correspondence of Thomas Gray*, ed. Paget Toynbee and Leonard Whibley, with corrections by H.W. Starr, 3 vols, vol. 1 (Oxford: Clarendon Press, 1971), 3.

59. *Musapædia, Or Miscellany Poems*, 6.

60. *News from both Universities. Containing, I. Mr. Cobb's Tripos Speech at Cambridge, with a Complete Key inserted. II. The Brawny Priest: Or, the Captivity of the Nose. A Poem* (London, 1714).

61. For a fuller exploration of this area, see Kathleen Keown, 'Sociable Productions: Women's Poetry, 1730–1760', unpublished DPhil, University of Oxford, 2018.

62. Keown, 'Sociable Productions'; Betty Schellenberg, *Literary Coteries and the Making of Modern Print Culture* (Cambridge: Cambridge University Press, 2016).

63. Jane Brereton, *Poems on Several Occasions: by Mrs Jane Brereton. With Letters to her Friends, and an Account of her Life* (London, 1744), Sig.A2.

64. Paula R. Backscheider, *Eighteenth-Century Women Poets and Their Poetry: Inventing Agency, Inventing Genre* (Baltimore, MD: Johns Hopkins University Press, 2008), 219.

65. *Musapædia, Or Miscellany Poems, Never Before Printed. By Several members of the Oxford Poetical Club, late of Eton and Westminster* (London, 1719), Beinecke Library, Yale University, 1998.1566, 57–58, 86.

66. Margaret Portland to Catherine Collingwood, 16 September 1734, WRO Throckmorton Papers, Tribune CR 1998/CD/Folder 49. Cited in Abigail Williams, 'Nothing Better than Mirth and Hilarity: Happiness, Unhappiness, Jest and Sociability in the Eighteenth Century', *English Literature* 2, no. 1 (June 2015): 123–43, 134–35.

67. Swift to Knightley Chetwode, 17 December 1715, *Correspondence of Jonathan Swift*, vol. 2, ed. Woolley, 149.

68. Edward Ward, *The Diverting Muse, or the Universal Medly. Written by a Society of Merry Gentlemen, for the Entertainment of the Town* (1707), final leaf.

69. Paul Baines and Pat Rogers, *Edmund Curll, Bookseller* (Oxford: Oxford University Press, 2007), 48.

70. Baines and Rogers, *Edmund Curll*, 48.

71. Mary Chandler, *A Description of Bath. A Poem* (Bath, 1734), 15, 18.

72. Chandler, *A Description of Bath*, 15, 14, 11.

73. Chandler, *A Description of Bath*, 18.

74. On the link between gender, geography, and provincial society in women's writing in this period, see Elizabeth Child, ' "To Sing the Town": Women, Place and Print Culture in Eighteenth-Century Bath', *Studies in Eighteenth-Century Culture* 28, no. 1 (1999): 155–72.

## Chapter 7: Unlocking the Past

1. For a fuller study of the secret history across the long eighteenth century, see Rebecca Bullard and Rachel Carnell (eds), *The Secret History in Literature, 1660–1820* (Cambridge: Cambridge University Press, 2017); Rebecca Bullard, *The Politics of Disclosure, 1674–1725: Secret History Narratives* (London: Pickering & Chatto, 2009).

2. The first work published in English with the title 'secret history' is *The Secret History of the Court of the Emperor Justinian* (1674). On the context of conspiratorial plotting, see Melinda S. Zook, *Radical Whigs and Conspiratorial Politics in Late Stuart England* (University Park, PA: Penn State University Press, 1999); R. Greaves, *Secrets of the Kingdom: British Radicals from the Popish Plot to the Revolution of 1688–89* (Stanford, CA: Stanford University Press, 1992); Gordon S. Wood, 'Conspiracy and the Paranoid Style: Causality and Deceit in the Eighteenth Century', *William and Mary Quarterly* 39, no. 3 (July 1982): 401–44; Rachel Weil, *A Plague of Informers: Conspiracy and Political Trust in William III's England* (New Haven, CT: Yale University Press, 2013). For theories about the implications of this plotting for fiction, see Richard Braverman, *Plots and Counterplots: Sexual Politics and the Body Politic in English Literature, 1660–1730* (Cambridge: Cambridge University Press, 1993).

3. Eve Tavor Bannet, ' "Secret History": Or, Talebearing Inside and Outside the Secretorie', *Huntington Library Quarterly* 68, no. 1–2 (2005): 375–96, 368.

4. Bullard, 'Introduction: Reconsidering Secret History', *Secret History in Literature*, ed. Bullard and Carnell, 1–14.

5. John McTague, *Things that Didn't Happen: Writing, Politics and the Counterhistorical, 1678–1743* (Woodbridge, UK: Boydell Press, 2019).

6. On the relationship between historical writing and secret history, see Martine W. Brownley, 'Secret History and Seventeenth-Century Historiography', *Secret History in Literature*, ed. Bullard and Carnell, 33–45.

7. Eliza Haywood, *The Female Spectator*, vol. 2 (London, 1745), 119.

8. On the satire of Mr Politico and the 'bad' political reader in this episode, see Kathryn R. King, *A Political Biography of Eliza Haywood* (London: Pickering and Chatto, 2012), 118–21.

9. Haywood, *The Female Spectator*, vol. 2, 124–25.

10. King, *A Political Biography of Eliza Haywood*, 198.

11. Eliza Haywood, *The Perplex'd Dutchess: or, Treachery Rewarded. Being some Memoirs of the Court of Malfy* (Dublin, 1727), 16–17.

12. *The True Secret History of the Lives and Reigns of all the Kings and Queens of England, from King William the First, Called, the Conquerour* ([London], 1702), a2 r–v; Joseph Browne, *The Secret History of Queen Zarah and the Zarazians; Being a Looking-glass for——In the Kingdom of Albigion* (Albigion [London], 1705), title page.

13. René Rapin, *Instructions for History: With A Character of the most Considerable Historians, Ancient and Modern* (London, 1680), 59.

14. Eliza Haywood, *The British Recluse: or, the Secret History of Cleomira, Suppos'd Dead. A Novel* (London, 1722), 2.

15. See, for example, *The Popish Damnable Plot against our Religion and Liberties Fairly laid open and discover'd in the Breviats of Threescore and Four Letters and Papers of Intelligence past . . .* (London, 1680); *A Secret Collection of the Affairs of Spain During the Negotiations between the Courts of England and Madrid* [. . .] *With several curious and valuable pieces under their own hands, to be found no where extant, but in this Book* (London, 1720); John Oldmixon, *The Secret History of Europe* [. . .] *taken from the Memoirs of a Person of Quality, never before printed* (London, 1713).

16. See Nicola Parsons' excellent study of the currency of gossip in print and political culture of the era in Nicola Parsons, *Reading Gossip in Early Eighteenth-Century England* (Basingstoke, UK: Palgrave Macmillan, 2009).

17. On the use of 'Atalantis' as a shorthand for secret history, see Stephen Karian, 'Who was Swift's "Corinna"?' *Reading Swift: Papers from the Sixth Münster Symposium*, ed. Kirsten Juhas, Josef Hermann Real, and Sandra Simon (Munich: Wilhelm Fink, 2013): 417–31, 429.

18. Parsons, *Reading Gossip in Early Eighteenth-Century England*, 8; Bradford K. Mudge, *The Whore's Story: Women, Pornography and the British Novel, 1684–1830* (Oxford: Oxford University Press, 2003), 137.

19. Delariviere Manley, *Secret Memoirs and Manners of Several Persons of Quality of Both Sexes. From the New Atalantis, An Island in the Mediterranean*, 2nd ed. (London, 1709), 224–25.

20. On the link between sex and politics in Manley's work, see Rachel Weil, *Political Passions: Gender, the Family and Political Argument in England, 1680–1714* (Manchester, UK: Manchester University Press, 1999), 176.

21. *Anekdota heteroūiaka. Or, The Secret History of the House of Medicis, Written Originally by that Fam'd Historian, the Sieur de Varillas. Made English by Ferrand Spence* (London, 1686), sig. a6r.

22. On the dual appeal of the erotic narrative, see Catherine Gallagher, *Nobody's Story: The Vanishing Act of Women Writers in the Marketplace, 1670–1820* (Berkeley: University of California Press, 1995), 102–3.

23. *Palace Amours: Or, The Genuine History of Alexis. Containing An Exact Account of his Amorous Adventures among Ladies of Quality, and Fair Ones of inferior Rank. Diversified with Original Letters, Poems, and very curious Discoveries in the Beau Monde. To which is Annexed, Something about Somebody's second Reckoning, with some shrewd Guesses when it will be out* (London, 1733), title page.

24. *Palace Amours*, 16.

25. *Palace Amours*, 18.

26. On the role of the anecdote within the genre, see Nicola Parsons, 'The Miscellaneous New Atalantis', *New Perspectives on Delarivier Manley and Eighteenth-Century Literature: Power, Sex and Text*, ed. Aleksondra Hultquist and Elizabeth J. Mathews (New York: Routledge, 2017): 201–13; Joel Fineman, 'The History of the Anecdote: Fiction and Fiction', *The New Historicism*, ed. H. Aram Veeser (New York: Routledge, 1989): 49–76.

27. Delariviere Manley to Robert Harley, 12 May 1710, British Library, Add Ms 70026, fol. 24v.

28. John Hervey, *The court-Spy; Or, Memoirs of St J–M–S'S*. (London, 1744), 4.

29. Colley Cibber, 'A Word to the Reader', *The Secret History of Arlus and Odolphus, Ministers of State to the Empress of Grandinsula* (1710), A2r. The owner of a surviving annotated copy in the British Library has keyed all the references in the piece: British Library, 1415. b.12.

30. Quoted in Patrick Spedding, *A Bibliography of Eliza Haywood* (London: Pickering & Chatto, 2004), 716.

31. Bullard, 'Introduction: Reconsidering Secret History', *Secret History in Literature*, 3.

32. See Steven Plunkett, 'Turning the Key: Keys, Supplemental Glossing, and the Range of Literary Interpretation in the First Half of the Eighteenth Century', unpublished PhD thesis, Brandeis University, 2015, 21.

33. See, for example, *The Distiller of London: With the Clavis to unlock the deepest Secrets of that Mysterious Art. With many additions of the most excellent Cordial Waters Which have been Pen'd by our most able Doctors and Physitians, Ancient and Modern, Foreign and Domestick* (London, 1652); *Enchiridium Being a Key to Italian Book-Keeping, Shewing briefly how to give the true Title of Debitor and Creditor, upon Sixty three Articles, &c.* (Dublin, 1724); Thomas Harby, *The Key of Sacred Scripture, And, Leading to It. First, an Answer to Some Objections Given to the Author, by a Person of great Learning and Piety* (London, 1679); *A Key to the Art of Letters: Or, English a Learned Language. Full of Art, Elegancy and Variety* (London, 1705).

34. Plunkett estimates that between 1700 and 1740 about three dozen or so printed interpretive keys were published. Plunkett, 'Turning the Key', 27.

35. *The Key to Atalantis. Part I* (London, 1709); *The Key to Atalantis. Part II* (London, 1709).

36. Delariviere Manley, *A Key to the Third Volume of Atalantis, call'd, Memoirs of Europe* (London, 1712).

37. On the digressive and interpretative challenges of the narrative, see Gallagher, *Nobody's Story*, 127.

38. *The Secret History of Mama Oello, Princess Royal of Peru. A New Court Novel* (London, 1733), British Library, 14.18.d.40.

39. Lady Mary Wortley Montagu to Frances Hewet, 12 November 1709, *The Complete Letters of Lady Mary Wortley Montagu*, vol. 1, ed. Robert Halsband (Oxford: Oxford University Press, 1967), 18.

40. Ralph Bridges to Sir William Trumbull, 31 October 1709, British Library, Add. Ms 72494, fol. 139r.

41. Ralph Bridges to Sir William Trumbull, 11 November 1709, British Library, Add. Ms 72494, fol. 142v.

42. Ralph Bridges to Sir William Trumbull, 18 November 1709, British Library, Add. Ms 72494, fol. 144r–v.

43. Ralph Bridges to Sir William Trumbull, 7 December 1709, British Library, Add. Ms 72494, fol. 145r.

44. Anne Bynn to Sir William Trumbull, 8 March 1710, British Library, Add. Ms 725515, fol. 98r.

45. Anne Bynn to Sir William Trumbull, 27 March 1710, British Library, Add. Ms 725515, fol. 100r.

46. *A Complete Key to the Four Parts of Law is a Bottomless-Pit, and the story of the St Alban's Ghost*, 3rd ed. ([London], 1712). For other examples of the use of blanked-out names in the 'answers', see also *A Key to the Third Volume of the Atalantis; Court Tales: or, a History of the Amours of the Present Nobility. To which is added, a Compleat Key* (London, 1717).

47. *A Complete Key to the Four Parts of Law is a Bottomless-Pit, and the Story of the St Alban's Ghost*, 3rd ed. ([London], 1712), Bodleian Library, University of Oxford, G.Pamph.1145(17).

48. On the difficulty of assigning authorial responsibility for a key, see Plunkett, 'Turning the Key', 59.

49. Anne Bynn to Sir William Trumbull, 27 March 1710, British Library, Add. Ms 725515 fol. 100r.

50. Texts published with the key included are Richard Brome, *A Jovial Crew: or, the Merry Beggars. A Comedy. Acted both at the Queen's Theatre, and the Theatre-Royal, at the same Time, with the Actors Names who Play'd it at both Houses: And after, upon the Uniting both Companys into One, in Drury-Lane. Likewise all the Songs, and a Key to the Beggars Cant* (London, 1708); *A Dream: or, The Force of Fancy. A Poem, containing Characters of the Company now at the Bath. With a Key Incsrted [sic]* (London, 1710); *An Answer to Duke upon Duke, &c. with a key. Set to Musick by the same Hand* (1720); *Verres and his Scribblers; A Satire in Three Cantos. To which is added an Examen of the Piece, and a Key to the Characters and obscure Passages* (London, 1732).

51. George Villiers, *The Rehearsal; A Comedy. Written by his Grace, George late Duke of Buckingham. To expose some Plays then in Vogue, & their Authors. With a Key & Remarks, necessary to Illustrate the most material passages, of this piece, & to point out the Authors & Writings here exposed. Never printed with it before* (London [i.e., The Hague], 1710), a4r. The following text was also intended to expose the references embedded within Buckingham's burlesque play, *The Rehearsal*, first published a half-century previously: *A General Key to the Writings of the Poets of the Last Age. Wherein their Beauties and Excellencies, Are fairly and impartially pointed out, and display'd, and their Follies and Blunders, Expos'd and Ridicul'd in the Rehearsal* (London, 1723).

52. *The Tatler* 2, no. 187, 17–20 June 1710.

53. Jeffrey Todd Knight, *Bound to Read: Compilations, Collections, and the Making of Renaissance Literature* (Philadelphia: University of Pennsylvania Press, 2013).

54. On the difficulty of establishing a reception history for secret history, see Bullard, *Politics of Disclosure*, 10–11.

55. Rachel Carnell, *A Political Biography of Delarivier Manley* (London: Pickering and Chatto, 2008), 173.

56. Delariviere Manley, *Secret Memoirs and Manners of Several Persons of Quality, of Both Sexes, from the New Atalantis, an Island in the Mediteranean* (London, 1709), Bodleian Library, University of Oxford, Vet.A4e.1020.

57. Delariviere Manley, *Secret Memoirs and Manners of Several Persons of Quality, of Both Sexes, from the New Atalantis, an Island in the Mediteranean*, 2nd ed. (London, 1709), Bodleian Library, University of Oxford, Rawl.8° 4.

58. Manley, *Secret Memoirs and Manners of Several Persons of Quality*, Bodleian Library, Rawl.8° 4, 158.

59. Anthony Hamilton, *A Key to Count Grammont's Memoirs* (London, 1715), British Library, 614.h.2.

60. Hamilton, *A Key to Count Grammont's Memoirs*, British Library, 614.h.2., 4, 7, 5, 2.

61. Cited in Plunkett, *Turning the Key*, 62.

62. Joseph Browne, *The Secret History of Queen Zarah, from Her Birth to the Conclusion of her Reign* (London, 1745), British Library, 1419.c.48.

63. Delariviere Manley, *The Adventures of Rivella; or, the History of the Author of the Atalantis. With Secret Memoirs and Characters of several considerable Persons her Cotemporaries* [sic] (London, 1714), British Library, 1419.f.23.

64. Eliza Haywood, *The Perplex'd Dutchess: or, Treachery Rewarded. Being some Memoirs of the Court of Malfy* (Dublin, 1727), British Library, 1077.b.79.

65. *Palace Amours: or, The Genuine History of Alexis* (London, 1733), British Library, C.142.aa.26.

66. *Palace Amours*, British Library, C.142.aa.26., 16.

67. *Palace Amours*, British Library, C.142.aa.26., 49.

68. Paula McDowell, *The Women of Grub Street: Press, Politics and Gender in the London Literary Marketplace 1678–1730* (Oxford: Clarendon Press, 1998), 268–70. Sarah Churchill, quoted in McDowell, 271.

69. Lady Mary Wortley Montagu to Frances Hewet, 12 November 1709, *Letters of Lady Mary Wortley Montagu*, vol. 1, 18.

70. Manley, *The Adventures of Rivella*, 113.

71. Manley, *The Adventures of Rivella*, 114.

72. For a fuller discussion of evolving libel law, see Thomas Keymer, *Poetics of the Pillory: English Literature and Seditious Libel, 1660–1820* (Oxford: Oxford University Press, 2019), 124–30.

73. Kathryn Temple, 'Manley's "Feigned Scene": The Fictions of Law at Westminster Hall', *Eighteenth-Century Fiction* 22, no. 4 (2010): 573–98, 580–81.

74. On the longer-term development of libel law, see Philip Hamburger, 'The Development of the Law of Seditious Libel and the Control of the Press', *Stanford Law Review* 37, no. 3 (February 1985): 661–765.

75. Cited in Temple, 'Manley's "Feigned Scene"', 582.

76. William Hawkins, *A Treatise of the Pleas of the Crown: or, A System of the Principal Matters relating to that Subject, digested under their Proper Heads*, vol. 1 (London, 1716), 194.

77. Hawkins, *A Treatise of the Pleas of the Crown*, vol. 1, 194.

78. Lady Mary Wortley Montagu to Frances Hewet, 12 November 1709, *Letters of Lady Mary Wortley Montagu*, vol. 1., 18–19.

## Chapter 8: Out of Control

1. Lady Mary Wortley Montagu to Lady Bute, 22 September 1755, *The Complete Letters of Lady Mary Wortley Montagu*, ed. Robert Halsband, 3 vols, vol. 3 (Oxford: Oxford University Press, 1967), 89.

2. Mary Granville Pendarves Delany to Anne Granville Dewes, 20 January 1755, *The Autobiography and Correspondence of Mrs. Delany*, ed. Sarah Chauncey Woolsey, 2 vols, vol. 1 (Boston, MA: Little, Brown and Company, 1879), 462.

3. Jonathan Swift, *The Examiner*, no. 18 (23–30 November 1710).

4. *An Answer Paragraph by Paragraph, to the Memorial of the Church of England* (London, 1705), 52.

5. Henry Fielding, *Jacobites Journal*, no. 17 (March 26, 1748).

6. *The London Gazette*, no. 3879 (11–14 January 1702 [1703]).

7. On Defoe's nonconformist education and activity, see Paula R. Backscheider, *Daniel Defoe: His Life* (Baltimore, MD: Johns Hopkins University Press, 1989), 85–86.

8. Although there were relatively few Dissenters employed by the crown or military, there were a significant number in borough corporations, and the bill would bar Dissenters from legislative and judiciary branches of government and administration of laws and regulations. Backscheider, *Daniel Defoe*, 92.

9. See Paul K. Alkon, 'Defoe's Argument in "The Shortest-Way with the Dissenters"', *Modern Philology* 73, no. 4 (May 1976): S12–S23; Miriam Lerenbaum, '"An Irony Not Unusual": Defoe's "Shortest-Way with the Dissenters"', *Huntington Library Quarterly* 37, no. 3 (May 1974): 227–50.

10. High Anglican sources for the *Shortest-Way* include Henry Sacheverell, *The Political Union. A Discourse Shewing the Dependance of Government on Religion In General: And of The English Monarchy on The Church of England In Particular* (Oxford, 1702). See also Edmund Bohun, *An address to the free-Men and free-holders of the nation* (London, 1682); Edmund Bohun, *The justice of the peace, his calling and qualifications* (London, 1693), 22.

11. Daniel Defoe, *The Shortest-Way with the Dissenters: Or Proposals for the Establishment of the Church* (London, 1702), 13, 18, 21.

12. Defoe, *The Shortest-Way with the Dissenters*, 21.

13. Defoe, *The Shortest-Way with the Dissenters*, 21.

14. L.S. Horsley, 'Contemporary Reactions to Defoe's *Shortest-Way with the Dissenters*', *Studies in English Literature* 16, no. 3 (July 1976): 407–20.

15. Defoe later cited an 'eminent Church-man in the Country' who wrote to thank his London friend for sending him the pamphlet, of which he heartily approved: 'SIR, *I Receiv'd yours, and enclosed the Book, call'd* The Shortest-Way with the Dissenters, *for which I thank you; and, next to the Holy Bible, and Sacred Comments, I place it as the most Valuable Thing I can have. I look upon it as the only Method, and I pray God to put it into the Heart of our most Gracious Queen to put what is there propos'd in Execution'.* Daniel Defoe, *The Dissenters Answer to the High-Church Challenge* (London, 1704), 37–38.

16. John Tutchin, *The Observator*, no. 71 (23–26 December 1702).

17. *The Safest-Way with the Dissenters; Being in Answer to a late Book, Entituled, the Shortest-Way with the Dissenters* (London, 1703), 3.

18. Daniel Defoe to William Paterson, April 1703, *The Letters of Daniel Defoe*, ed. George Harris Healey (Oxford: Oxford University Press, 1955), 4.

19. Daniel Defoe to William Paterson, April 1703, *Letters of Daniel Defoe*, 4–5.

20. Defoe's fears for his likely punishment were not ungrounded: he would have seen what happened to those found guilty of seditious libel. Another pamphleteer, William Fuller, had only a couple of months before been sentenced to pillory three times, to hard labour and correction in Bridewell prison, and to remain in prison until he had paid a fine

of 1000 marks. Defoe knew that a man named Anderton had been executed for seditious libel. And, in 1682, Thomas DeLaune, author of *Plea for the Non-Conformists*, had his work confiscated then burned by the common hangman. DeLaune was convicted of seditious libel, and, with his wife and two children, died in Newgate unable to pay the fine. See Backscheider, *Daniel Defoe*, 101.

21. 'A Certain Criminal document, a Seditious, pernicious and Diabolical Libel Entitled The Shortest-Way', CLRO, SF 472, cited by Backscheider, *Daniel Defoe*, 104.

22. Backscheider, *Daniel Defoe*, 110.

23. For a summary of the changing legal context for the publication of satirical writing, see Joseph Hone, 'Legal Constraints, Libellous Evasions', *The Oxford Handbook of Eighteenth-Century Satire*, ed. P. Bullard (Oxford: Oxford University Press, 2019), 525–41.

24. The trial of the radical Whig writer John Tutchin had cemented this shift in the law. Tutchin's counsel had argued that 'nothing is a libel but what reflects upon some particular person', but the prosecution had successfully argued that his papers reflected on the government as a whole. 87 Eng. Rep. 1014–28, cited by Hone, 'Legal Constraints', 528.

25. Hone, 'Legal Constraints'. For further discussion, see Tom Keymer, *Poetics of the Pillory: English Literature and Seditious Libel, 1660–1820* (Oxford: Oxford University Press, 2019), 120–30.

26. Daniel Defoe, *A Brief Explanation of a Late Pamphlet, Entituled The Shortest-Way with the Dissenters* (London, 1703), 1–2.

27. Defoe, *A Brief Explanation*, 2.

28. Defoe, *A Brief Explanation*, 2.

29. Defoe, *A Brief Explanation*, 2.

30. *Remarks on the Author of the Hymn to the Pillory* (London, 1703), 2.

31. See, for example, *The Shortest-Way with the Dissenters: Or, Proposals for the Establishment of the Church., With its Author's Brief Explication Consider'd . . .* , 2nd ed. (London, 1703); Charles Leslie, *The New Association, Part II. With farther Improvements* (London, 1703). Both responses are discussed in Kate Loveman, *Reading Fictions, 1660–1740: Deception in English Literary and Political Culture* (Aldershot, UK: Ashgate, 2008), 134.

32. Loveman, *Reading Fictions*, 134.

33. *The Shortest-Way with the Dissenters: Or Proposals for the Establishment of the Church* (London, 1702), British Library, 110.f.27.

34. *The Shortest-Way with the Dissenters*, British Library, 110.f.27, verso of title page.

35. *The Shortest-Way with the Dissenters*, British Library, 110.f.27, 29.

36. See for example notes at 3, 4, 6, 10–11.

37. *The Shortest-Way with the Dissenters*, British Library, 110.f.27, 18.

38. *The Shortest-Way with the Dissenters*, British Library, 110.f.27, 18.

39. *The Fox with his Fire-brand Unkennell'd and Insnar'd: Or, a Short Answer to Mr Daniel Foe's Shortest-Way with the Dissenters* (London, 1703), 3.

40. *The Fox with his Fire-brand Unkennell'd*, 4.

41. See, for example, Leranbaum, '"An Irony not Unusual"'; Alkon, 'Defoe's Argument in "The Shortest-Way with the Dissenters"'. For a summary of critical debate over the text's purpose, see Loveman, *Reading Fictions*, 132–33.

42. J.A. Downie, 'Defoe's *Shortest-Way with the Dissenters*: Irony, Intention, and Reader-Response', *Prose Studies* 9, no. 2 (September 1986): 120–39; Ashley Marshall, 'The Generic Context of Defoe's *The Shortest-Way With The Dissenters* and the Problem of Irony', *The Review of English Studies* 61, no. 249 (April 2010): 234–58.

43. Keymer, *Poetics of the Pillory*, 130–31.

44. Daniel Defoe, *The Consolidator: or, Memoirs of sundry transactions from the world in the moon* (London, 1705), 208.

45. Defoe reiterates this view in *The Present State of the Parties in Great Britain: Particularly An Enquiry into the State of the Dissenters in England* (London, 1712), 24: 'The Case the Book pointed at, was to speak in the first Person of the *Party*, and then, thereby, not only speak their Language, but make them acknowledge it to be theirs, which they did so openly, that confounded all their Attempts afterwards to deny it, and to call it a *Scandal* thrown upon them by another'.

46. For fuller discussion of the uses of anonymity in the period, see, Gillian Paku, 'Anonymity in the Eighteenth Century', Oxford Handbooks Online (2015), http://doi.org/10.1093/oxfordhb/9780199935338.013.37.

47. Mark Vareschi, *Everywhere and Nowhere: Anonymity and Mediation in Eighteenth-Century Britain* (Minneapolis: University of Minnesota Press, 2018), 5. Leah Orr, 'Genre Labels on the Title Pages of English Fiction, 1660–1800', *Philological Quarterly* 90, no. 1 (2011): 67–95, 80–81. James Raven, 'The Anonymous Novel in Britain and Ireland, 1750–1830', *The Faces of Anonymity: Anonymous and Pseudonymous Publication from the Sixteenth to the Twentieth Century*, ed. Robert J. Griffin (New York: Palgrave Macmillan, 2003), 145.

48. Griffin (ed.), *Faces of Anonymity*, 1–2.

49. One recent critic argues that the reader should accept the text as it is and resist the readerly desire to fill the gaps left by anonymity 'to allow for a transcendent co-existence of unknown and unknowable authorship with our own acts of "countersignature"'. Mark Robson, 'The Ethics of Anonymity', *Anonymity in Early Modern England: "What's in a Name?"* ed. Janet Wright Starner and Barbara Howard Traister (Farnham, UK: Ashgate, 2011): 159–77, 170.

50. On marginalia and attribution, see David A. Brewer, 'The Tactility of Authorial Names', *The Eighteenth Century* 54, no. 2 (July 2013): 195–213; William H. Sherman, *Used Books: Marking Readers in Renaissance England* (Philadelphia: University of Pennsylvania Press, 2008); Carl James Grindley, 'Reading *Piers Plowman* C-Text Annotations: Notes toward the Classification of Printed and Written Marginalia in Texts from the British Isles, 1300–1641', *The Medieval Professional Reader at Work: Evidence from Manuscripts of Chaucer, Langland, Kempe, and Gower*, ed. Kathryn Kerby-Fulton and Maidie Hilmo (Victoria, BC: ELS University of Victoria, 2001): 73–141, 77.

51. Brewer, 'The Tactility of Authorial Names', 196.

52. Daniel Defoe, *London Post*, 9 April 1705. Quoted in Paku, 'Anonymity in the Eighteenth Century', 5.

53. Daniel Defoe, Review, *Defoe's Review Reproduced from the Original Editions*, ed. John McVeagh and Arthur Wellesley Secord, 9 vols, vol. 8 (New York: Columbia University Press, 1938), 210. Quoted in Paku, 'Anonymity in the Eighteenth Century', 5.

54. P.N. Furbank and W.R. Owens, *Defoe De-Attributions: A Critique of J.R. Moore's Checklist* (London: Hambledon, 1994). For a critique of the de-attribution project, see Maximilian E. Novak, review of *The Defoe Canon: Attribution and De-Attribution, Huntington Library Quarterly* 59, no. 1 (1996): 83–104.

55. Vareschi, *Everywhere and Nowhere*, 113.

56. H.W. Fowler, *A Dictionary of Modern English Usage*, 2nd ed. (Oxford: Clarendon Press, 1965), 305–6.

57. Herbert H. Clark and Richard J. Gerrig, 'On the Pretense Theory of Irony', *Journal of Experimental Psychology* 113, no. 1 (March 1984): 121–26.

58. Whitney Phillips and Ryan Milner, *The Ambivalent Internet: Mischief, Oddity and Antagonism Online* (Cambridge: Polity Press, 2017), 52.

59. Ryan and Milner, *The Ambivalent Internet*, 122–23.

60. Daniel Defoe, *And What If the Pretender Should Come? Or, some Considerations of the Advantages and Real Consequences of the Pretender's Possessing the Crown of Great-Britain* (London, 1713), 18.

61. Daniel Defoe, *Reasons Against the Succession of the House of Hanover, with an Enquiry How far the Abdication of King James, supposing it to be Legal, ought to affect the Person of the Pretender* (London, 1713), 21.

62. Daniel Defoe, *An Answer to a Question that No Body Things of, viz., But What if the Queen Should Die?* (London, 1713), 43.

63. On Jacobite rhetoric, see Paul Kleber Monod, *Jacobitism and the English People, 1688–1788* (Cambridge: Cambridge University Press, 1989), 36; Howard Erskine-Hill, 'Literature and the Jacobite Cause: Was There a Rhetoric of Jacobitism?' *Ideology and Conspiracy: Aspects of Jacobitism, 1689–1759*, ed. Eveline Cruickshanks (Edinburgh: J. Donald, 1982), 49–50.

64. Daniel Defoe, *Review*, no. 85, Saturday 18 April 1713, *Defoe's Review Reproduced from the Original Editions*, ed. John McVeagh and Arthur Wellesley Secord, 9 vols, vol. 9, (New York: Columbia University Press, 1938), 170.

65. Daniel Defoe, *Review*, no. 84, Thursday 16 April 1713, *Defoe's Review*, vol. 9, 167.

66. *Judas Discuver'd, and Catch'd at last: Or, Daniel de Foe in Lobs Pound. Being a Full and True Account of the Apprehending and Taking of Mr. Daniel de Foe, On Saturday last, for High-Treason against the Queen and Government. With his Examination before the Lord Chief Justice* (London, 1713), 6.

67. Lord Justice Parker to Bolingbroke, 15 April 1713, (P.R.O., S.P. 34/21/241) reproduced in *Letters of Daniel Defoe*, 411–12.

68. Daniel Defoe, 'To the Queens Most Excellent Majesty The Humble Petition of Daniel De Foe', The National Archives, SP 34/37, fo. 11, cited in Keymer, *Poetics of the Pillory*, 146.

69. Daniel Defoe to Robert Harley, Earl of Oxford, 12 April 1713, *Letters of Daniel Defoe*, 407.

## Chapter 9: Messing with Readers

1. Alexander Pope to John Caryll, 2nd Baron Caryll of Durford [the younger], 8 March 1733, *The Correspondence of Alexander Pope*, ed. George Sherburn, 5 vols, vol. 3 (Oxford: Clarendon Press, 1956), 354.

2. James Sutherland, preface to *The Dunciad*, *The Twickenham Edition of the Poems of Alexander Pope*, ed. John Butt, 11 vols, vol. 5 (London: Methuen, 1943, revised 1963), v. Hereafter referred to as 'TE'.

3. The first version, *The Dunciad*, a poem in three books, appeared in 1728 with a hero called Tibbald. The second, *The Dunciad Variorum*, came out in 1729 and was a slightly revised version, accompanied by a new commentary and apparatus. There was then a gap, until *The New Dunciad* was published in 1742. It was a new single book of verse, planned as a sequel to the previous three. And finally, in 1743, Pope issued *The Dunciad in Four Books*, a revised version of the initial three books, along with a slightly revised fourth book and revised commentary and apparatus. In this version, the hero Tibbald was replaced by a new character called Bays. For a recent summary of the other changes to the poem over this period, see Pat Rogers, 'Disappearances from *The Dunciad*: Pope's Late Use of the *Grub-Street Journal*', *The Review of English Studies* 72, no. 306 (2021): 707–31, 707–8.

4. Alexander Pope, *The Dunciad, Variorum. With the Prolegomena of Scriblerus* (London, 1729), 70. ESTC T5551. I have included ESTC reference numbers in citation of the poem to distinguish between similarly titled editions.

5. The dating of the action of the poem changes through successive versions. In the first version we are told the action of the poem takes place in 1719 or 1720.

6. Valerie Rumbold, Introduction to Alexander Pope, *The Dunciad in Four Books* (Harlow, UK: Pearson, 1999), 3.

7. Pope, *The Dunciad, Variorum*, ESTC T5551, 78.

8. Aubrey Williams, *Pope's Dunciad: A Study of its Meaning* (London: Methuen, 1955), 64.

9. For example, Pope's resentment of Giles Jacob, as revealed by James McLaverty in 'Pope and Giles Jacob's "Lives of the Poets": The *Dunciad* as Alternative Literary History', *Modern Philology* 83, no. 1 (1985): 22–32.

10. On the way in which Pope alternates between historical, mythological, and fictional representation in the poem, see John McTague, *Things that Didn't Happen: Writing, Politics and the Counterhistorical, 1678–1743* (Woodbridge, UK: Boydell Press, 2019), 184–85.

11. For a fuller account of the parallels with the *Aeneid*, see Aubrey Williams, *Pope's Dunciad: A Study of Its Meaning* (London: Methuen, 1955), 17–29. For a summary of other classical allusions, see Howard Erskine-Hill, *Pope: The Dunciad* (London: Edward Arnold, 1972).

12. Catherine Ingrassia and Claudia N. Thomas, introduction to *'More Solid Learning': New Perspectives on Alexander Pope's Dunciad*, ed. Catherine Ingrassia and Claudia N. Thomas (Lewisburg, PA: Bucknell University Press, 2000), 23. For an excellent summary of late twentieth-century approaches to the poem, see *'More Solid Learning'*, 24–32. On more recent treatments, see Emrys D. Jones, 'An Appetite for Ambivalence: Pope Studies in the Twenty-First Century', *Literature Compass* 15, no. 12 (2018), https://doi.org/10.1111/lic3.12502.

13. Sutherland, preface to *The Dunciad*, TE, vol. 5, v.

14. Williams, *Pope's Dunciad*, 64.

15. Williams, *Pope's Dunciad*, 64. For later critical discussions of the personal versus the abstract nature of the dunces' identification, see Blakey Vermeule, *The Party of Humanity: Writing Moral Psychology in Eighteenth-Century Britain* (Baltimore, MD: Johns Hopkins University Press, 2000), 95; Veronica Kelly, '"Embody'd Dark": the Simulation of Allegory

in *The Dunciad*', *Enlightening Allegory: Theory, Practice and Contexts of Allegory in the Late Seventeenth and Eighteenth Centuries*, ed. Kevin L. Cope (New York: AMS Press, 1993), 351–72, 352–53.

16. Rumbold, introduction to *The Dunciad in Four Books*, 6–7.

17. Alexander Pope, *The Dunciad, Variorum. With the Prolegomena of Scriblerus.* (London, 1729), ESTC T5551, 70.

18. Alexander Pope, *The Dunciad. An Heroic Poem. In Three Books* (Dublin printed; London reprinted for A. Dodd, 1728), ESTC T5538.

19. Alexander Pope, *The Dunciad. An Heroic Poem. In Three Books* (Dublin printed; London reprinted for A. Dodd, 1728), ESTC T5538, 34, 6.

20. Pope, 'The Publisher to the Reader', *The Dunciad. An Heroic Poem. In Three Books.* (Dublin printed; London reprinted for A. Dodd, 1728), ESTC T5538, v.

21. Pope, 'The Publisher to the Reader', *The Dunciad. An Heroic Poem. In Three Books.* (Dublin printed; London reprinted for A. Dodd, 1728), ESTC T5538, vi–vii.

22. Jonathan Swift to Alexander Pope, 16 July 1728, *Correspondence of Alexander Pope*, vol. 2, ed. Sherburn, 504–5.

23. Jonathan Swift to Charles Wogan, July to 2 August 1732, *Correspondence of Jonathan Swift*, ed. Woolley, vol. 3, 516.

24. Alexander Pope to Samuel Wesley [the younger], 6 January 1729, *Correspondence of Alexander Pope*, vol. 5, 7.

25. Edward Harley to Alexander Pope, 27 May 1728, *Correspondence of Alexander Pope*, vol. 2, ed. Sherburn, 496.

26. Edmund Curll, *A Compleat Key to the Dunciad*, 1st ed. (London, 1728), 13.

27. Curll, *A Compleat Key*, 1st ed., 13.

28. The three editions are *A Compleat Key to the Dunciad* (London: printed for A. Dodd, 1728), ESTC T84887; *A Compleat Key to the Dunciad. With a Character of Mr Pope's Profane Writings. By Sir Richard Blackmore Kt. M.D. The Second Edition* (London: printed for E. Curll, 1728), ESTC T480; *A Compleat Key to the Dunciad. With A Character of Mr Pope's Profane Writings. By Sir Richard Blackmore Kt. M.D. The Third Edition* (London: printed for E. Curll, 1728), ESTC T101143.

29. Curll, *A Compleat Key*, 3rd ed., 11; Curll, *A Compleat Key*, 1st ed., 16; Curll, *A Compleat Key*, 2nd ed., 16; Curll, *A Compleat Key*, 3rd ed., 16.

30. For detail of the changes, see Rumbold, *Dunciad in Four Books*, 28.

31. Alexander Pope, *The Dunciad. An Heroick Poem. In Three Books. Written by Mr Pope* (Dublin, 1728), ESTC T5543.

32. Pope, *The Dunciad. An Heroic Poem. In Three Books.* (Dublin printed; London reprinted for A. Dodd, 1728), ESTC T5538, 6.

33. Pope, *The Dunciad. An Heroick Poem. In Three Books. Written by Mr Pope* (Dublin: G. Faulkner et al., 1728), ESTC T5543, 11.

34. Alexander Pope, *The Dunciad, Variorum* ([Dublin] London: printed for A. Dod, 1729), ESTC T5551, 9.

35. Alexander Pope, *The Dunciad. An Heroic Poem. In Three Books. The Second Edition* (Dublin printed; London reprinted for A. Dodd, 1728), ESTC T5538, Hertford College Library,

University of Oxford, XXX.2.20(2). Edmund Curll, *A Compleat Key to the Dunciad*, 1st ed. (London, 1728), ESTC T84887, Hertford College Library, University of Oxford, XXX.4.24(2).

36. Pope, *The Dunciad. An Heroic Poem. In Three Books. The Second Edition* (Dublin printed; London reprinted for A. Dodd, 1728), ESTC T5538, Hertford College Library, University of Oxford, XXX.2.20(2), 7.

37. Curll, *A Compleat Key to The Dunciad*, ESTC T84887, 1st ed., 9.

38. Critics have been puzzled over the relationship between the notes and the main text. Ronald Paulson describes the relationship in terms of contrast between Pope's 'beautiful, clear, balanced, well-leaded' verse on the top half of the page and the 'cramped, double-columned, dense, greyish pedantry', collected 'at the bottom of the page, like a kind of sediment'. Ronald Paulson, 'Satire, and Poetry, and Pope', *English Satire, Papers Read at a Clark Library Seminar*, 15 January 1972 (Los Angeles: William Andrews Clark Memorial Library, 1972), 80.

39. 'Testimonies of Authors', *The Dunciad, Variorum* (London, 1729), ESTC T5551, 44–45.

40. 'Testimonies of Authors', *The Dunciad Variorum* (London 1729), ESTC T5548, 34.

41. John Oldmixon, *An Essay on Criticism: As it regards Design, Thought, and Expression, in Prose and Verse.* (London, 1728), 72.

42. Aaron Hill to Alexander Pope, 18 January 1731, *Correspondence of Alexander Pope*, vol. 3, ed. Sherburn, 164–65.

43. Alexander Pope to Aaron Hill, 26 January 1731, *Correspondence of Alexander Pope*, vol. 3, ed. Sherburn, 165–66; Aaron Hill to Alexander Pope, 28 January 1731, *Correspondence of Alexander Pope*, vol. 3, ed. Sherburn, 166–68.

44. See Harold Weinbrot, *Eighteenth-Century Satire: Essays on Text and Context from Dryden to Peter Pindar* (Cambridge: Cambridge University Press, 1988), 236, note 7.

45. Aaron Hill to Alexander Pope, 28 January 1731, *Correspondence of Alexander Pope*, ed. Sherburn, vol. 3, 167.

46. Sutherland, Introduction to *The Dunciad*, TE, vol. 5, xxxii.

47. Pope, *The Dunciad Variorum*, ESTC T5551, 97.

48. Pope, *The Dunciad, Variorum*, ESTC T5551, 98

49. Pope, *The Dunciad, Variorum*, ESTC T5551, 97.

50. Pope, *The Dunciad, Variorum*, ESTC T5551, front matter, advertisement, 4.

51. Pope, *The Dunciad, Variorum*, ESTC T5551, 59.

52. Sutherland, introduction to *The Dunciad, TE*, vol. 5, xxxviii.

53. Emrys Jones, 'Pope and Dulness', *Pope: Recent Essays by Several Hands*, ed. Maynard Mack and James A. Winn (Hamden, CT: Archon Books, 1980): 612–51.

54. Samuel Richardson to Aaron Hill, 7 November 1748, *The Cambridge Edition of the Correspondence of Samuel Richardson: Correspondence with Aaron Hill and the Hill Family*, ed. Christine Gerrard (Cambridge: Cambridge University Press, 2013), 273.

55. Thomas Green, diary entry for 11 February 1798, *Extracts from the Diary of a Lover of Literature* (Ipswich: John Raw, 1810), 63.

56. Frances Evelyn Boscawen to Elizabeth (Robinson) Montagu, [September?] 1753, Elizabeth Robinson Montagu Papers, Huntington Library, mssMO 495, 5–6.

57. Emrys Jones: 'The Twickenham edition is by no means obsolete, but many Pope scholars have acknowledged that its textual apparatus (especially in James Sutherland's *Dunciad* volume)

is unfriendly and that scholars and general readers alike require editions updated to reflect more recent research'. Jones, 'An Appetite for Ambivalence', 3.

## Afterword

1. On the social function of collective Wordle-playing, see C. Thi Nguyen, 'The Word on Wordle: It Is Bringing People Together by Letting us See into Each Other's Minds', *Los Angeles Times*, 21 January 2022, https://www.latimes.com/opinion/story/2022-01-21/op-ed-wordle -game-minds-play#:~:text=eNewspaper-,Op%2DEd%3A%20The%20word%20on%20 Wordle%3A%20It%20is%20bringing,see%20into%20each%20other's%20minds.

2. See Eden Litt and Eszter Hargittai, 'The Imagined Audience on Social Network Sites', *Social Media + Society* 2 (2016): 1–12.

3. For a good discussion of memes and their reappropriation, see Ryan Milner, *The World Made Meme: Public Conversations and Participatory Media* (Cambridge, MA: MIT Press, 2016), esp. chapter 2.

4. On the phenomenon of true crime case solving in the online community, see Theodora Sutton, 'Digital Sleuths', *The Digital Romantic*, 25 November 2021, https://thedigitalromantic .tumblr.com/post/668828325886722048/digitalsleuths.

# INDEX